THE POLITICS OF EMPOWERMENT?

The Politics of Empowerment?

PETER MCLAVERTY
Department of Politics and Public Policy
University of Luton

Dartmouth

Aldershot • Brookfield USA • Singapore • Sydney

Published by
Dartmouth Publishing Company Limited
Gower House
Croft Road
Aldershot
Hants GU11 3HR
England

Dartmouth Publishing Company
Old Post Road
Brookfield
Vermont 05036
USA

British Library Cataloguing in Publication Data
McLaverty, Peter
   The politics of empowerment?
   1.Local government - Great Britain 2.Right and left
   (Political science)
   I.Title
   352'.041

Library of Congress Cataloging-in-Publication Data
Library of Congress Catalog Card Number: 96-83686

ISBN 1 85521 803 8

Printed and bound in Great Britain by
Ipswich Book Co. Ltd., Ipswich, Suffolk

Contents

Acknowledgements

There are a number of people I want to thank: Geoff Brown, ex-lecturer in the Adult Education Department, University of Nottingham without whose encouragement and practical help I would never have re-entered full-time education; my brother Jim for his unstinting support over the years; all those who took part in the research, some of whom I fear will not like what I have written; my Ph D supervisors, Par Seyd and Bill Hampton; my fellow Ph D students Mary Marston and Fiona Brooks for their support; everyone concerned at Dartmouth for their forbearance; and the ESRC for awarding a grant which enabled me to complete the Ph D on which this book is based. But, above all, I want to thank Usman Khan, for without his friendship and intellectual stimulation, not only would my Ph D thesis not have been completed but this work itself would never have seen the light of day.

1 Introduction

From about 1980 in a number of urban local authorities a new type of leadership gained control of the council Labour Group and, where Labour controlled the authority, the leadership of the council itself. This happened with the Labour victory in the Greater London Council (GLC) elections in 1981 and the subsequent change in the leadership of the Labour Group when a more radical group of councillors around Ken Livingstone, who became Council Leader, took control. Before that, in 1980, a new leadership was elected to Sheffield City Council Labour Group. The new leader of the council, David Blunkett, was far to the left of his predecessor and his accession to the council leadership marked, and was a result of, a shift to the left in the council Labour Group (cf. Child and Paddon, 1984 and interviews with Blunkett and Betts). Later in the 1980s, left leaderships were elected to head Labour councils in a number of geographical areas. In Liverpool, for example, in 1983, a Militant Tendency dominated leadership was elected when Labour gained control of the council. In Manchester, in 1984, the old right wing leadership of the Labour controlled council was replaced by a new left wing group around the leadership of Graham Stringer. In other areas, including many of the Labour run London Boroughs, as well as places like Edinburgh in Scotland, Basildon, Walsall and Harlow, the left gained control of councils even if only, as in the case of Basildon and Walsall, temporarily.

Socialist theory

This book is concerned with examining the nature of the new left leaderships in local councils in the 1980s. Consideration will be given to the question of whether there was something unique that linked the disparate leaderships and united them. I will consider the extent to which the left leaderships in local government after 1980 represented a coherent group, with a distinct, new, socialist theory and practice. I will argue that while there were certain policy commitments and a certain style which was common to many of the new left leaderships, there was also much that divided them. It would be wrong, I will contend, to suggest that the left leaderships and the forces behind them, who together made up the 'new urban left', had in any real sense, a clearly defined and distinct socialist theory which informed and helps to explain their political practice. Some of the leaderships, for example Liverpool and Lambeth, were avowedly Marxist. Others, like Sheffield under the leadership of David Blunkett, were much more in an ethical socialist tradition. Still others, like the GLC under Ken Livingstone, were heavily infused with the ideas and practices of 'new social movements', such as feminism and black organizations. What seems to have united the new urban left was a belief that local government offered a means of putting forward an example of socialist government in practice. This socialist government would differ, both in the methods it employed and in the outcomes it hoped to achieve, from traditional British national Labour governments and the governments of the 'state socialist' societies which then existed in Eastern Europe.

The emphasis of much new urban left thinking aimed at avoiding the 'bureaucratic paternalism' of British Fabianism and traditional British 'labourism'. A main concern was to produce a new democratic form of socialist government in which government would help groups of workers, and other oppressed groups, to do things for themselves. In that way, much of the new urban left thinking suggested, it would be possible to offer a clear, distinct and attractive alternative to the Thatcher government. That alternative would provide an example of what socialist government might mean and prepare the ground so that a popular mobilization against the Thatcher government and in favour of socialism might be achieved. Crucial to this new urban left project was a commitment to change the way the council operated so that the users and providers of council services and activities, as well as the local community, would be able to exercise much more influence over the workings of the council and specific departments and services.

New urban left council failures

Trade union worries and councillor power

I will argue that the efforts, by new urban left councils, to fundamentally change the way in which local councils operated largely failed, or at best had only limited success. A number of reasons explaining the failure will be advanced. Examples from some of the councils who have tried to decentralize council structures and involve users of services and the local community in service delivery and development, will be examined. The examination will show that only limited progress towards greater user and local community involvement was achieved. The lack of progress resulted in part because new left councillors did not succeed in linking that objective with trade union and worker apprehension about 'outsiders', that is service users and representatives of the local community, having an influence over the working arrangements of council staff. Council trade unions, and the workers they represented, did not really accept user and local community involvement in internal council workings, as they saw such involvement as 'blurring the lines' of management control, confusing negotiating structures and possibly resulting in worse pay and working conditions. New left councils, it will be shown, largely failed to ally such fears. Additionally, as will be shown in detail later, council efforts to increase user and local community involvement in council service development were not more successful because of the unwillingness of councillors to relinquish or reduce their formal control over policy development and the level and type of service provision. This is also a main reason why new urban left councils largely failed to develop new forms of industrial democracy in their councils.

The nature of the state

I will argue that the new urban left failed in its aim of developing a distinctive form of socialist government and to mobilize popular opposition to the Thatcher governments and for socialist government in the 1980s, because new left councillors did not fully recognize the nature of the state in modern Britain. While the new urban left in local government opposed 'old fashioned' labourism and Fabianism and recognized to some extent the class nature of the British state, and while the new urban left in principle supported, and recognized the need for, mass popular mobilization in support of its programmes, I will argue that in many respects the new urban left failed to appreciate the power of the central state and central government and the problems this represented for the implementation of its programmes.

The history of central-local government relations (cf. Duncan and Goodwin, 1988 and Chandler, 1988) and the outlook and approach of the Thatcher government from 1979, suggest strongly that the Conservative central government, with the backing of the central state more broadly, would deal strongly with any opposition from local government in carrying out its programme of restructuring the British economy and society in the interests of private capital (cf. Gough, 1983; Duncan and Goodwin, 1988; Cochrane, 1993). The whole history of the Thatcher governments from 1979, in relation to local government, was one of trying to increase central control over local government and to remove the ability of local authorities to offer an alternative to the government's strategy. This was true from the passing of the *Local Government Planning and Land Act* in 1980 (cf. Duncan and Goodwin, 1988). Of course, such centralization has continued under John Major's premiership (cf. Stoker, 1991 and Cochrane, 1993). In these circumstances, the actions of the central government could only be defeated in three ways. One was if real mass support for local government and the programmes of the new urban left Labour councils had been activated or mobilized and manifested in a form which would have forced the government to change tack or to leave office. The second way was if, as occurred in respect of the Community Charge or Poll Tax, public opposition to a particularly unpopular government policy forced a change of policy. The third way was if action outside local government, for example militant trade union industrial action, had defeated the government's general intentions.

A central argument of this work is that the new urban left councils were either unwilling or unable to mobilize the necessary support and the Labour movement was unable to bring sufficient pressure to bear on the government to force it to change course or to remove it from office. In addition, of course, active public opposition to specific Thatcher government policies was limited, although the opposition shown to the Poll Tax played a big part in Margaret Thatcher's downfall. The new urban left failed to develop a clear strategy for mobilizing popular support and harnessing it in effective action. Over rate capping in 1984-85, when a number of new left councils tried to mobilize effective action against the government, this proved, in the end, impossible. This, it will be shown, was partly due to the defensive nature of the campaign. Despite the commitment of new left councils to promote a new form of socialist government, the campaign over rate capping in 1984-85 was largely about defending local government and the traditional independence of local councils. The campaign was not about the merits of one type of government, stressing democratic participation and involvement and the meeting of social needs, and striving to reduce social inequality, over another, stressing the role of the free market, individual responsibility and the profit motive, and striving to increase social inequality.

Efforts were made by the Labour councils involved in the anti-rate capping campaign to mobilize the users of local services, the local community and council workers in support of the actions of Labour councillors. Such efforts, however, had limited success. The lack of success can be explained in part by the nature of the anti-rate capping campaign which, at least at the crucial stage, revolved, not around efforts to win positive, active support for the defence of a participatory form of socialist government but for the defiance being conducted by the Labour councillors. The media focused on the action of councillors and splits within Labour Council Groups and many of the broader issues underlining the campaign were lost in the concentration on internal Labour Group politics.

The field work

In order to examine in detail how successful, at least one, new urban
left Labour council was in changing the internal running of the council
so that council workers could gain more control over the running of
council departments and services, I will set out the results of a
comparative study into industrial relations in Sheffield City Council
and Doncaster Metropolitan Borough Council carried out in 1987 and
1988. The case study involved interviewing union representatives,
leading Labour councillors and senior council officers in three
departments, as well as consulting various council records, Labour
Party and trade union documents. The aim of the case study was to
compare industrial relations in two different Labour councils - one a
new urban left council, the other a 'traditional' Labour council - and to
see how far the Sheffield City Council Labour Group had succeeded in
changing the internal workings of the council in line with various
policy commitments. In so far as the experience in Sheffield is
comparable with that in other new urban left councils, the case study
has relevance for an understanding of the situation in this area in new
urban left councils more generally.

The field work provides material which contributes to the debate
about whether different council trade unions, especially when 'facing'
new urban left councils, acted differently because of conflicting union
outlooks and approaches produced by the opposing interests of groups
of workers. Light is shed on the question of whether the biggest white
collar union in local government in the 1980s the National and Local
Government Officers Association (NALGO) was less sympathetic and
supportive of councils trying to introduce radical and imaginative
policies in comparison with blue collar council trade unions like the
National Union of Public Employees (NUPE) (which has since merged
with NALGO and the health union COHSE to form Unison) and the
General, Municipal, Boilermakers and Allied Trade Union (GMB).
The argument advanced will be that NALGO was generally more
sceptical of initiatives introduced by new urban left councils but,
unlike the beliefs of certain leading Labour councillors in the two
councils studied, was not in any sense a 'class enemy', intrinsically
opposed to radical policies or an essentially and irredeemably
reactionary organization. Probably the majority of the radical changes
introduced by new left councils, or changes attempted by those
councils, affected white collar workers to a greater extent than other
council workers. In a number of cases, what Labour councillors, and in
some instances blue collar trade unionists, regarded as NALGO
obstructiveness and bloody-mindedness was, from NALGO's point of
view, just the union trying to protect the legitimate interests of its

members, without harming the interests of other workers. The case study findings on NALGO's attitude is supplemented by a theoretical consideration of the nature of professional workers in advanced capitalist society.

Socialist management

Of course, it could be that the interests of NALGO's members, or some of them, especially in senior positions in the council, were opposed to the efforts of the new left councils to improve council services and to democratize the running of those services and the related council departments. But, while such opposition is perhaps potentially present, as is opposition between the interests of blue collar workers and increased user involvement in the running of council activities, the solution to this problem lies mainly at the political level. For, as will be argued in detail in the body of the book, new left Labour councils failed to develop a new, distinctively socialist method of management and organization. Such a socialist management method would harness the experience, energy, knowledge and enthusiasm of council workers within structures which would involve council workers, service users and the local community, along with Labour councillors, determining the development of council services and activities. The purpose of such a socialist management method would be to ensure both that people's human capacities are developed and that council services more nearly meet the needs of the users of those services and the local community. As will be argued in detail later, the failure to develop new council structures and management practices which would have involved reducing the power, redefining the role, of senior council officers, was crucial in limiting the success of the new urban left in local government.

Benefits of case studies

The case study provides important insights into the nature of British trade unionism and the relationship between trade unions and the introduction of radical, socialist change. I will argue that trade unions are basically reactive organizations, aiming to attain the best they can for their members and for working people generally within the capitalist system. While the trade unions, along with the Independent Labour Party, the Fabian Society and the Social Democratic Federation, were responsible for the formation of the Labour Representation Committee in 1900, which became the Labour Party in

1906, there has been a fairly strong demarcation line between political action, which is carried out through, and by, the Labour Party, on the one hand, and industrial action, which is the preserve of trade unions, on the other. This split has helped to produce a limited economistic trade union consciousness among British workers. If the basic economistic and reactive practices of British trade unionism are to be broken down, and trade unions are to adopt a more proactive and wide ranging position, it is suggested, a political lead will be necessary. This was something that the leadership of many new urban left councils sought to do in their early days. However, as I will attempt to show, in the case of Sheffield Council, the promise was not fulfilled.

Structure of the work

After this introductory chapter there follows a chapter on the Roots of the New Urban Left. In Chapter 3, the development and nature of the new urban left in local government in the 1980s is considered. Chapter 4 looks at the relationship between trade unionism and socialism in Britain. After a chapter introducing the case study, there follows three chapters (6, 7 and 8) where the findings of the case study into industrial relations in Sheffield City Council and Doncaster Borough Council are described and discussed. In the final chapter, I will draw conclusions from the case study material and consider some of the major issues arising out of the whole new urban left experience in local government.

2 The Roots of the New Urban Left

The roots of the new urban left, as it developed in local government in the early 1980s, were heterogeneous and people from different backgrounds, political and social, made up the new urban left. The term new urban left was first developed by John Gyford (1983a and 1983b). For Gyford the new urban left 'includes councillors, party activists, community workers and local government officers (some of them councillors after working hours)' (Gyford, 1983a, p. 91). The new urban left also developed in response to specific economic and social factors. The main elements which fed into the new urban left and gave it a unique character can perhaps be identified in summary form, as follows: a response to the failures of the 1964-1970 and 1974-1979 Labour governments; the legacy of 'labourism'; activity in, and the influence of, community, peace, environment and student politics; feminism; the radicalization of welfare professions; the influx of new elements in the Labour Party; economic and industrial decline; the defeat of the Labour government in 1979 and the actions of the ensuing Thatcher administration towards local government. The impact each specific element had in particular new urban left councils differed considerably. In some new urban left councils, for example, feminism and new forces in the Labour Party had a major impact, while in others the impact of those factors was limited. The relative force of the different elements in specific councils also affected the weight given to particular policies within councils. The type of policies, and politics, adopted by new urban left councils will be considered in detail in the next chapter. First, however, it is necessary to examine why the new urban left in local government developed and from where it sprang, in much greater detail. For, without an understanding of its roots, a comprehension of the praxis of the new urban left is unlikely to be achieved. This will be done by examining each of the elements, including some more minor ones not mentioned above, which fed into the new urban left.

The failures of the Labour governments of the 1960s and 1970s

The development of the new urban left was in large part a response to the failures of the 1964-1970 and 1974-1979 Labour governments to implement radical policies and to fulfil the high hopes on which they had been elected. Both in the 1960s and again in the 1970s, the Labour governments ended up cutting public expenditure on social programmes which were of great importance for Labour Party members, including local government funding on a large scale in the 1970s (cf. Townsend and Bosenquet, 1972 and Coates, 1979a). The radical economic and industrial policies on which the Labour governments of the 1960s and 1970s were elected were also abandoned, if not always explicitly, then none the less in reality. In the 1960s, the attempt at national planning soon came to grief, partly as a result of Treasury opposition to the newly formed Department of Economic Affairs, the indicative rather than imperative nature of the proposed planning and the failure of the government to bring the 'commanding heights of the economy' under public control and to curb the obstructive power of the city (cf. Coates, 1975, pp. 97-129 and Howell, 1980, pp. 251-256). In the 1970s, the economic strategy on which the government was elected was never really implemented in anything other than a half-hearted manner. True, a National Enterprise Board (NEB) was established and the aircraft and shipbuilding industries were nationalized. But the NEB's powers were much more limited than had been envisaged in the Labour Party's *1973 Programme* and, in addition, only one planning agreement was signed with a private company, Chrysler, thus nullifying one of the main elements of the industrial strategy. Moreover, the commitment to introduce industrial democracy was completely ignored in the private sector due, in part, to a lack of trade union interest, and apart from very limited 'experiments' in the Post Office and British Steel Corporation, nothing was done in the public sector either (cf. Forester, 1979; Coates, 1979b; Kelly, 1987). Under Labour governments of the 1960s and 1970s, as with the governments of 1945-1951, the nationalized industries and publicly owned enterprises pursued traditional commercial criteria in their operations.

The periods of Labour government in the 1960s and 1970s both included efforts by the government to control workers' wage increases which, along with efforts to control trade union activities through legal restraints in the *In Place of Strife* proposals in 1969, produced damaging splits and conflicts with the trade unions and/or groups of workers (cf. Barnes and Reid, 1980, pp. 49-128; Hall, 1983; Howell, 1980, pp. 256-267; Jenkins, 1970; Taylor, 1987). At the same time, great efforts were made to increase the international competitiveness and profitability of British industry, to gain the support of leading industrialists and to placate the financial markets (cf. Coates, 1975, pp. 97-129 and 1981 and Coventry, Liverpool, Newcastle and North Tyneside Trades Councils, 1980). In both periods, and particularly in

1974-1979, unemployment rose significantly while Labour was in office (cf. Cripps and Morrell, 1979 and Minkin, 1974).

The experience of the 1964-1970 Labour government created, among some sections of the Labour Party and among some on the periphery of the party, from the late 1960s, a feeling that the Labour Party, or at least the Labour government, had 'lost its way'. This feeling was given an added boost by the record of the 1974-1979 Labour governments. This led some people to question why Labour governments elected on seemingly radical programmes ended up pursuing very different policies from those on which they were elected. One possible explanation was that the problem lay in the Labour Party's ideology: labourism.

Labourism and its legacy

From the publication of Ralph Miliband's *Parliamentary Socialism* (Miliband, 1961) there had developed a strong 'academic' body of thought which saw the failure of the Labour Party to further the socialist cause, either inside or outside government, as due to the ideology and practice of labourism. For this tradition, the Labour Party from its inception has been a trade union party and has adopted a very passive relationship with its trade union and working-class base. Labourism, it is argued, has always been at best ambivalent or lukewarm in its support for extra-parliamentary forms of politics and has always promoted an elitist and essentially passive relationship between the Labour Party and its supporters. This point is strongly advanced, for example, by Stuart Hall (1987).

In Hall's view the Labour Party has always worked from the premise that Labour politicians would be elected, at national and local levels, and would then, in combination with neutral experts, do beneficial things for the working-class or 'the people'. This basic elitism, Hall argues, has its roots in Fabianism but is also prevalent on the left of the party. It represents a political ideology and practice which is far removed from the argument, or position, advanced by Marxists, such as William Morris (1962), Guild Socialists, like G. D. H. Cole (1918), and those in the Ethical Socialist tradition of Robert Blatchford (1894) and others, that socialism was predominantly about working-class and general human liberation which would be achieved through working-class self activity. In place of the commitment to working-class self liberation which stressed the crucial importance of empowering the working-class, that is enabling workers to gain control over the decisions which determine their futures, and believed political activity should be directed to this end, 'labourism', in this definition, became a commitment to rule by the expert and planner. Hall (1987, p. 14) puts it as follows:

> What I mean by Fabianism is not so much the idea of the people who have associated themselves with the Fabian current. I mean the version that the working class cannot do anything for themselves. The left raises the agitation, and then they vote - for somebody else. And what they vote for is somebody inside the machine, mainly middle class and mainly intellectuals, who then take power in the name of the working class and do it for them. That I think has been the major factor in Labourism, which has depoliticised and de-democratised the working class over long periods of time. Now if you think about it, the old left is as much into that as the right wing.

While Hall's contention that the 'old left' supports, and has always supported, an elitist form of politics in which, 'experts' do things for the working-class is an over simplification (Bevan, 1961, pp. 128-130 for one, was strongly committed to the introduction of industrial democracy) there is much evidence to support this point of view.

In the 1920s and 1930s, in the wake of the Soviet experience, the left, inside as well as outside the Labour Party, became committed to a centralized form of economic and industrial planning from the top downwards, a commitment which has maintained strength among a section of the left ever since (cf. Samuel, 1986). For Foote (1986, pp. 183-186), while the Socialist League, the most prominent left wing pressure group in or around the Labour Party, remained committed to a form of industrial democracy - the representation of union leaderships on the boards of nationalized industries - which in itself was top heavy, it also, and crucially, supported the development of centralized economic and industrial planning. As Pimlott (1977, p. 59) puts it: 'Though the Socialist League increasingly adopted the rhetoric of Marxism, its heritage included a body of ideas whose source was closer to Keynes than Marx and which it shared with politicians of the centre and right'. The authors of the book *State Intervention in Industry* (Coventry, Liverpool, Newcastle and North Tyneside Trades Councils, 1980, pp. 141-158) criticized the policies of the Labour Party in the 1970s, as well as the actions of the 1974-1979 Labour governments, for failing to give sufficient emphasis to the need to empower the working-class in the workplace. For those authors, the whole strategy devised by the Labour left in the 1970s, while it included commitments to industrial democracy and giving workers a greater say in decision making, was elitist and misguided in conception, with its commitment to the setting up of a National Enterprise Board and the placing of state nominees on the Board of Directors of private firms in return for state financial help.

Moreover, in support of Hall's argument, the whole Leninist tradition, based on the concept of dedicated revolutionaries leading the working-class to socialism, is extremely elitist. The Leninist tradition, while in theory it regards working-class struggles as the basis on which socialism will be constructed, nonetheless, believes that, left to themselves, working-class people will be unable to develop beyond a trade union form of consciousness which is very limited in its aims and essentially entails an accommodation with the capitalist system. A party of dedicated, trained revolutionaries is needed to educate and lead the working-class and inculcate a socialist consciousness among the working-class. The democratic centralist organization of Leninist groups, by concentrating decision making and control at the top of these organizations, further accentuates the elitism of Leninist groups (cf., for example, Hodgson, 1984, pp. 8-18 and 46-64 and Miliband and Liebman, 1986, p. 485).

Labourism is also depicted as a perspective in which the state is seen as neutral. In this Labourist perspective, the top civil service and the judiciary, for example, are seen as helping ministers to implement their policies and as providing disinterested, technical advice. Whereas the reality, it is argued, is that top civil servants and the judiciary, along with members of the armed forces and the police, work to uphold the existing capitalist social order and cannot be relied upon to help a Labour government, elected on a radical programme, implement that programme. (Miliband, 1969 outlines this case clearly and Meacher, 1979 chronicles how the top civil servants in the Department of Industry plotted to discredit Tony Benn and the policies for which he stood in the period 1974-1976). The whole experience of the Labour governments of the 1960s and 1970s, as Wainwright (1987, p. 13) argues, led some Labour Party activists to take up those types of argument and to question whether the state was really a neutral instrument which could simply be taken over, as it was, and used for socialist ends.

As will be shown later, the foregoing analysis of the nature of labourism undoubtedly had a big, if sometimes unconscious, influence on many of those who formed the new urban left in local government in the early 1980s. That was so whether or not they had read the relevant texts. The arguments of the authors of *In and Against the State* (London Edinburgh Weekend Return Group, 1980) and Cynthia Cockburn (1977) who applied a similar analysis to local government also had a big impact. For the London Edinburgh Weekend Return Group and Cockburn, state organs in modern Britain are oppressive and repressive at the local level, just as they are at the national level, and just as tied into the imperatives of private capital accumulation. The local state is no more neutral in class terms than the national. However, in the respective analyses, the local state is not seen as simply the instrument of the capitalist class and is, in a real sense, an arena, and result, of class struggle. In particular, for the London Edinburgh Weekend Return Group, who see the capitalist state as part of the capital-labour relation, it is possible for Labour councillors to use their positions to aid the self activity of the working-class and other oppressed groups. In that way, Labour councillors can help to prepare the ground for the long term victory of the working-class in the class struggle under capitalism and the victory of socialism over capitalism (cf. also Poulantzas, 1978). Those arguments about the state were important for the new urban left for, as Green (1987, p. 207) argues, 'Though few councillors had read the theoretical reformulations of the state by marxist intellectuals, these ideas filtered down in pamphlets and conversational second-hand'.

The campaign to democratize the Labour Party

Another development which helped to produce elements of the new urban left were the efforts to change the Labour Party's constitution and the relationship between MPs and their local constituency parties, and the Party Leader and the wider party which took place from the mid 1970s. The interest in accountability in the Labour Party was a response to the perceived failures of the Labour governments of the 1960s and 1970s. It was an effort by party activists to prevent a gap developing between the policy of the party as agreed at party conference and the actions of Labour MPs and particularly the party leadership in parliament. The aim was to provide a counterweight to the institutional and class forces pulling Labour MPs and the party leadership away from the party's radical commitments. The 'Bennite left', as the groups behind those efforts became known, accepted the need for the Labour Party to engage in a major task of political campaigning and questioned the neutrality of the state. 'The Bennites' saw that extra-parliamentary activity was often legitimate and a necessary support for activity at the parliamentary level (cf. Wainwright, 1987, pp. 53-56; Tariq Ali and Hoare, 1982 and Kogan and Kogan, 1983). Many of those who were later to take leading parts in new urban left councils (such as Ken Livingstone) were very active in the Bennite campaigns of the 1970s and early 1980s and this activity helped to forge their thinking. Moreover, the interest in accountability in the Labour Party fed through to the local level and affected attitudes within the Labour Party to local government. In

Sheffield, for example, a group of party activists in the Brightside Constituency (including David Blunkett and Clive Betts, both of whom were to subsequently lead the council) took up the issue of accountability in the local council and fought for a change in the relationship between the District Labour Party and Labour councillors. This group formed the early nucleus for the new left in local government in Sheffield (cf. Wainwright, 1987, p. 109 and Seyd, 1987, pp. 144-149).

That the new urban left was a response to the types of theoretical arguments and political developments outlined above is strongly suggested by Gyford's analysis (Gyford, 1985). The new urban left consisted for Gyford, 'perhaps most fundamentally, [of] a commitment to notions of mass politics based upon strategies of decentralization and/or political mobilization at the local level (Gyford, 1985, p. 18). In trying to offer a picture of socialism in action and to mobilize popular support at the local level, the new urban left, in Gyford's view, was trying to find a new road to socialism freed from the centralizing practices of the parliamentary and insurrectionary roads. Gyford (1985, pp. 17-18) defined the new urban left as the local government wing of the extra-parliamentary new left.

Moreover, John McDonnell (1984), who was Deputy Leader of the GLC in the 1980s, has seen the policies pursued by the GLC, at that time, as the result of three interconnected factors: a shift in the ideology of socialists; a shift in demands made by council workforces; and a shift in the theory of public administration and economics. For him, in the early 1980s, there was a move away from the traditional Labour Party view of local government. The Labour Party traditionally viewed involvement in local government in 'statist terms - that is that socialism can be achieved or advanced by capturing positions of power, and then delivering socialist policies on behalf of the repressed class which we seek to represent'. The move away from this position was due, in McDonnell's view, to certain Marxist insights, including principally the understanding that the capitalist state is not a set of institutions which can be captured, it is not simply a vehicle which can be hijacked and re-routed.

> The new ideology said, on the contrary, that capitalism is a social relation of production and domination that pervades all aspects of our lives, including that of local government. So now we sought not merely to lay hands on positions of power within local government but also to recognise that we were both in the state and against it. We sought to undermine the capitalist form of social relation by replacing it with a relation

which we defined as socialist: to replace domination with co-operation and democratic control (McDonnell, 1984).

Local government defeats

Gyford (1985, pp. 24-27) has also argued that the major defeats suffered by the Labour Party in the 1967 and 1968 local government elections in urban areas played a very important role in the long term development of the new urban left. For Gyford the 1968 defeats removed many long standing Labour councillors, including leaders of many Labour groups, and by 'opening up' Labour local government in this manner, cleared the way for the future ascent of the new urban left in local government. After 1968, it was no longer taken for granted that Labour councillors would necessarily retain their positions, often without challenge, for many years or that the leadership of Labour groups would remain unaltered for long periods. However, while there is much to commend this argument, it must be stressed that the new Labour leaders in local government who emerged after 1968 were not, on the whole, the radical politicians who made up the new urban left in the 1980s.

Community action

Beyond those type of internal Labour Party developments, however, the roots of the new urban left are to be found in the community action of the 1960s and the central government appointed Community Development Projects (Boddy and Fudge, 1984, p. 7). The importance of community action in the development of the new urban left is a feature explaining the urban nature of this phenomenon. For the type of community politics which fed into the new urban left is a basically urban development which took shape in response to the economic decline of the inner cities and the accompanying social and environmental problems. Community action in the 1960s was at first conceived in opposition to the Labour Party and squatting and housing campaigns, for example, often occurred in opposition to the housing policies of Labour councils (Cockburn, 1977, pp. 67-93 shows the experience in Lambeth in the 1960s). With the establishment of the Community Development Projects from 1969, however, community action came more and more to be associated with the Labour Party (Gyford, 1985, pp. 33-36) and drew community activists into the Labour Party.

Anti-war, peace and student politics

Involvement in the Campaign for Nuclear Disarmament and campaigns against the Vietnam war also provided a root which fed into the new urban left. Like community and radical student politics, particularly in the late 1960s, involvement in black organizations and feminist groups, which also fed into new urban left politics (cf. Boddy and Fudge, 1984, p. 7 and Gyford, 1985, pp. 38-40), the politics associated with CND, or at least a strong element within the organization, and action against the Vietnam war, was very different from traditional labourist politics. Labourist politics, as defined above, was, and is, essentially about working within the existing constitutional framework to achieve reforms. The politics of the anti-war movement, radical student groups and community action groups, however, was very much an oppositional force, standing outside the constitutional framework and working against the state. Those who came into Labour Party politics from those routes came with a very different political background from those who had been 'brought up' within Labour Party and trade union activity. Community action, radical student politics, involvement in peace and ecology issues, as well as feminist and black politics, gave those, often in professional or supervisory jobs, a different outlook on politics which, as will be discussed fully in another chapter, helped to create tensions with local government trade unions, as Weinstein (1986, cf. also Hoggett, Lawrence and Fudge, 1984, pp. 70-71) argues.

New element in the Labour Party

While in the 1960s there had been an exodus of radical elements from the Labour Party, in the late 1970s there was a movement of radical socialists back into the Labour Party (Wainwright, 1987). The influx of radical new members, often from a non-manual worker background and with degrees and professional jobs, had a major effect on the workings and activities of many local Labour Parties. The influx was crucially motivated by the 'Bennite' struggles in the Labour Party. The people joining the party had often been active in community, feminist, peace and environmental politics and adopted a fairly theoretical attitude to political and social issues. For writers like Whitely (1983), the recruitment of 'middle class' members of the Labour Party allowed, accompanied or even perhaps encouraged the drift of manual working-class people out of the Labour Party. But, as Gyford (1985, pp. 22-23) argues, the resulting change in the social composition of many Labour Parties may be, in part, a reflection of the growth of white collar and professional jobs, as well as the result of manual working-class disillusionment with the Labour Party. This may mean that many of the so-called 'middle class' elements in the Labour Party came from a working-class background and had parents who were active in the Labour Party and/or the trade union movement. They had moved onto the 'middle class' when, after an extended formal education, they entered professional or supervisory jobs. A number of such people would have grown up in a working-class family and 'Labour movement' environment and conceivably, may have retained their links with their working-class roots.

Moreover, in the wake of the 1964-1970 Labour government and the early years of the Heath government, there was some recognition among manual working-class people that their interests could best be furthered by joining the Labour Party (cf. Seyd, 1987, pp. 37-75 and Green, 1987, p. 205). The importance of this greater working-class involvement in the Labour Party should not be ignored. However, certain of the new 'middle class' members found their way into local government as Labour councillors (the surveys of Gordon and Whitely, 1987 and Lipsy, 1982 suggest that increasingly Labour councillors were from non-manual positions) and others became active within District Labour Parties, County Labour Parties or Local Government Committees and played a part in the development of the new urban left by working for the adoption of more radical policies and a new way of working within Labour Council Groups.

The radicalization of welfare professions

The growth of a body of criticism of the actions of professionals in general, and professionals within the welfare state in particular, had a radicalizing effect on certain local government professional workers. The work of academic authors like Patrick Dunleavy (1979 and 1981), Terrance Johnson (1972), M.S. Larson (1977) and Paul Wilding (1982), as well as the arguments in work like *In and Against the State* and their contact with community activists and others, led certain professional workers, particularly social workers, but town planners and others as well, to question their positions and their relationships with their 'clients'. The activities of the Community Development Projects also influenced the thinking and climate in local government professions, along with the growth of corporate management techniques and increasing bureaucratic control of professions in local government, as Bolger et al. (1981, pp. 60-78) argue, in respect of social workers. This radicalization of local government professionals linked into the radical new elements among Labour councillors and was an important strand in the new urban left (cf. Boddy and Fudge, 1984, p. 7 and Gyford, 1983a, p. 91).

Economic and industrial decline

The new urban left developed in local government in response to economic decline in certain major cities, and one of the main aims of the new urban left was to use local government, in novel and radical ways, as an instrument of economic regeneration. In Sheffield, for example, the growth of the new urban left was bound up with the decline and destruction of the steel industry since the late 1970s (cf. Goodwin, 1985). In London, the left led GLC was concerned about, and committed to reversing, the decline of the capital's traditional industrial and economic base (cf. Mackintosh and Wainwright, 1987, pp. 1-19). New urban left thinking, in this area, was greatly influenced by the radical, imaginative plans against redundancy and for socially useful production formulated by groups like the Lucas Aerospace Shop Stewards in the 1970s and the report of the Coventry, Liverpool, Newcastle and North Tyneside Trades Councils (cf. Gyford, 1985, pp. 38-39 and 80-81).

The new urban left in local government, then, developed in response to the failure of the 1964-1970 and 1974-1979 Labour governments; the theoretical analysis and legacy of labourism; activity in, and the influence of, community, peace, ecological, student and black politics; feminism; the radicalization of welfare professions; economic decline and the influx of new elements in the Labour Party. But it was given a real spur by the impact of the defeat of the Labour government in 1979 and the actions of the ensuing Thatcher administration towards local government.

The impact of Thatcherism

In response to the Thatcher government's attack on local government, it became clear to certain elements among Labour councillors that a purely defensive approach would not succeed in protecting local government services or jobs. People were unlikely to be mobilized in support of existing local government services and the way they were provided and popular mobilization in support of local government was seen as essential if the Thatcher offensive were to be defeated. As Blunkett and Green have argued, in order to protect local government 'an administration which might prefigure a wider socialist society' was needed (Blunkett and Green, 1983, p. 2). In other words, the feeling developed that traditional 'labourist' ways of operating in government, both local and national, would not be adequate, either to defeat the Thatcher offensive or provide the basis for a movement towards socialism. For the new urban left, as Gyford (1985, p. 18) has argued, local government activity was seen as a way of fighting the Thatcher government and showing socialism in action.

In some councils, Manchester being perhaps the best example, but in other councils such as Islington as well, the new urban left developed as a coherent group in opposition to the failure, as they saw it, of the 'old guard' on the council to fight the demands for cuts in council services made by central government (cf. Wainwright, 1987, pp. 114-126). The willingness of the dominant elements in Labour groups to accede to central government demands for cuts created a strong opposition force within certain Labour groups and within District Labour Parties and Local Government Committees. Such pressure eventually led in Manchester to a change in the personnel and nature of the local council leadership and the strategy pursued by the council. In Islington, the bulk of Labour councillors defected, or joined, the Social Democratic Party in 1981 with the new urban left Labour councillors sweeping the board at the subsequent May 1982 local elections (cf. *London Evening Standard*, 1982).

Hypotheses

The roots of the new urban left were, therefore, heterogeneous. As suggested in the introduction, the different elements feeding into the new urban left had varying impacts in different new left councils. It was probable that, in new urban left councils where feminism and 'alternative politics' had a major impact, the policy and political emphasis would be different, in important respects, from that in other new urban left councils where the Labour group's links with trade unions and the traditional Labour movement were very strong. In councils where feminism and 'alternative politics' were strong it was likely that a great emphasis would be given to helping social movements of oppressed people, such as women's groups, black organizations and organizations of gays and lesbians, improve their positions. While in councils with strong Labour movement links such issues would probably be given only minor prominence, taking second place to a more 'traditional' class based politics.

However, one would expect, from their disillusionment with the 1960s and 1970s Labour governments, the impact of the critique of labourism and the importance of community politics on their thinking, new urban left councils would have been more concerned about developing a novel, more participatory form of politics as compared with other Labour councils. One would also expect new urban left councils to have been concerned about creating a relationship with workers which enabled workers to do things for themselves, rather than the council doing things for them, on their behalf. A concern about changing the way the council operated internally could also reasonably be expected.

Whether those tentative suggestions are borne out by the evidence will be considered in the next chapter, where an examination of the distinctive policies and politics of the new urban left will be considered.

3 The Politics of the New Urban Left

The new urban left, as defined in the preceding chapter, was only dominant in a small number of urban councils. In a number of big city councils under Labour Party control like Birmingham, Newcastle, Leeds and Bristol, the new urban left made little impact and in small cities and towns like Hull and Salford the impact of the new urban left was again marginal. Writers differ about which councils were under new urban left control at various times in the 1980s. Gyford (1985, pp. 16-17), for example, questions whether Liverpool City Council from 1983 to 1987 should be on a list of new urban left councils, while Seyd (1987, p. 140) unequivocally includes the Merseyside council. Most of those writing on the subject recognize that councils under new urban left control had a certain style and certain basic commitments but did not form a homogeneous, clearly definable and united whole (cf., for example, Gyford; 1985, Boddy and Fudge; 1984, Wainwright, 1987). Taking a very broad view one could say the following councils at various stages during the 1980s were part of the new urban left: the GLC; the Inner London Education Authority; Sheffield City Council; Manchester City Council; North Tyneside District Council; Harlow District Council; Basildon District Council; Edinburgh City Council; Walsall District Council; South Yorkshire County Council; Merseyside County Council; Lothian Regional Council; Tamesdown District Council; Stirling District Council; and the London Boroughs of Islington; Camden; Lambeth; Hackney; Haringey; Brent; Greenwich; Ealing; Hammersmith and Fulham; Lewisham; Wandsworth and Southwark. What, therefore, distinguished the new urban left led councils from other Labour controlled councils and is it true that the people who led these councils lacked a clear, common, united theoretical position and political practice?

Drawing together the evidence from a number of disparate sources it can be tentatively suggested that councils under new urban left control had twelve distinctive policy and political commitments and practices. Not all new urban left councils necessarily subscribed to, or supported, all these commitments but together the commitments define the 'ideal type' new urban left position. The twelve points, and the connections between them, are perhaps most clearly represented in diagrammatic terms.

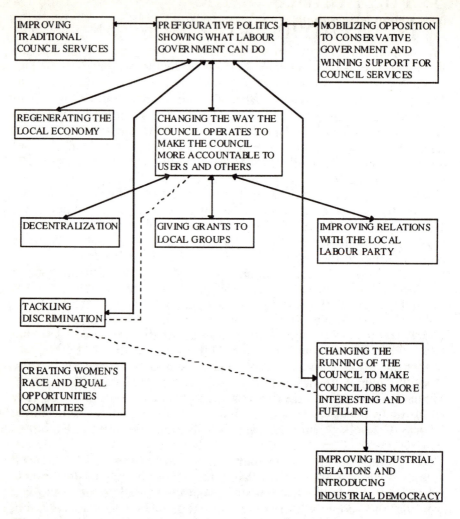

Figure One: The Commitments of the New Urban Left

Note: Single line with arrows at both ends denotes a relationship between two commitments and a direct two-way connection between the commitments. Single line with an arrow at one end only denotes one commitment directly coming out of another. A dotted line denotes a weak or possible relationship between commitments.

New urban left councils

The new urban left council which probably came nearest to meeting the 'ideal type' was the Greater London Council from 1981-1986. This council supported, or adopted, all the new urban left policy positions except the physical decentralization of council services, which was never a key element of GLC practice in this period. However, Hambleton and Hoggett (1987), regard the making of grants to community groups by councils, which was something the GLC did on a large scale, as part of the decentralization process. Sheffield City Council also adopted the vast majority of the policies but its commitment to giving grants to local groups on a large scale was not that strong and tackling discrimination, in terms of sex, race and equal opportunities was subordinated to the need to pursue a more traditional class based politics. Liverpool from 1983-1986 supported some of the 'new urban left' positions such as mobilizing opposition to the Conservative government and trying to show what a Labour government could do, as well as trying to improve traditional council services, changing relations with the local party and between the Labour group and the trade unions. However, the autobiography of Derek Hatton (1988) ex-Deputy Leader of Liverpool City Council from 1984 to 1986 and the book by Peter Taaffe and Tony Mulhearn (1988), as well as the views of David Blunkett (interview, 1988), strongly suggest that the leaders of Liverpool Council did not regard themselves as part of the new urban left nor was the council they controlled considered to be a new left council by at least some of the leaders of other new left councils. However, as Liverpool City Council was such a focal point in the life of the local government left between 1983-1987, in this chapter, the Liverpool experience will be drawn upon and where appropriate contrasted with that of other left councils.

Certain of the policies associated with new urban left councils were also supported by councils other than those of the new urban left. For example, certain Conservative councils, such as East Sussex County Council, can be seen as trying to make local services more accountable through the decentralization of the Social Services Department. Some Liberal Democrat councils, as they would now be known, Tower Hamlets being the prime example, were also committed to decentralizing council services and hence, presumably, making council services more accountable (cf. Community Care, 1985, p. 19, and Marphet, 1987). Moreover, nearly all councils, if not all of them, would have claimed in the 1980s they were trying to improve traditional council services and a very large number of councils by the end of the decade regarded themselves as equal opportunities employers. However, it was the way in which the different policies were adopted and combined and the aims behind them which distinguished new urban left councils. Before the reasons why different new urban left councils adopted different of the twelve policy positions is considered in detail, it is important to set out more clearly the implications and nature of the policies and commitments.

Prefigurative politics

The commitment to prefigurative politics and the mobilization of popular support for Labour local government as part of the task of winning support for the Labour Party nationally and providing an example for a future Labour government was central to the action of new left councils. Gyford (1985) makes this point clearly. Blunkett and Green (1983) stressed that local government should be used by socialist councillors to prefigure a wider socialist society. Blunkett (interview, 1988) saw the role of new left councils in the following terms, 'We could innovate in such a way that provided a genuine alternative which could have been picked up by a Labour government and other authorities'. Livingstone (1984) argues that the activities of the Greater London Enterprise Board (GLEB) showed what a Labour government could do at national level. The Liverpool City Council from 1983 to 1986 also believed that its staunch support for better services and socialist policies provided a model for a future Labour government (cf. Parkinson, 1985, and Taaffe and Mulhearn, 1988). By changing the way in which local government operated, improving the standard of services and showing practically that policies met people's needs, something new left councils have attempted to do, in Livingstone's view support for the Labour Party would be secured (Livingstone, 1984). This commitment to creating a prefigurative socialist politics was distinctive and new. In the past, most Labour councils had seen their task as providing the services that circumstances allowed and this was still probably how most Labour councils saw their task throughout the 1980s.

User and community politics

An element running through the statements of leaders of new urban left councils up to mid 1985 was that the way local councils operated must be changed if support for local government in a difficult financial and political climate was to be achieved and a prefigurative socialist politics instituted. This thesis was particularly prevalent in the comments and written work of David Blunkett. For example, it ran through *Building from the Bottom* (Blunkett and Green, 1983). In an interview in *Marxism Today* in 1985 Blunkett (1985) saw Labour local councils playing a major part in fulfilling the task facing the Labour Party, which he sets out as follows:

> We have to win people for a vision of the future, not just against Thatcher. Therefore people's participation in democracy, in their own lives, is a key question now being raised.... We need to... develop a socialist response, to win them to what we want in a world where people work and pull together and share their talents and resources.

The new left wanted to see people doing things for themselves, to raise a socialist consciousness and see socialist ideas implemented in a community setting (cf. Blunkett, 1981, p. 102, and Blunkett and Green, 1983, p. 28).

Decentralization

The commitment to changing the way local councils operate, so that users of council services and the local community have greater control over council activities, was one of the central aims behind the decentralization of council services which was pursued by new left councils (cf. Hodge, 1987). The commitment to decentralization in turn tied into the commitments to provide an example of a prefigurative socialist administration and of opposing central government spending cuts as they applied to local government (cf. Fudge, 1984). The commitment to decentralization was important because it was one of the ways in which new urban left Labour councils hoped to avoid one of the main pitfalls of Labourism: politicians and 'experts' doing things for the workers' and local community's own good. John McDonnell (1984) related the commitment to decentralization to the adoption of the Marxist insights described in the last chapter and the efforts to create a socialist form of social relation. 'To ensure this we aim to break down the councillor-officer relation which did not allow either the recipients of our services, or the providers of them, that is our workforce, to have any real democratic control'.

However, not all Labour councils committed to decentralization pursued the issue in the same way. After 1980 in Sheffield, for example, moves towards decentralization were largely restricted to the establishment of area management schemes in housing and the formation of a small number of neighbourhood forums, despite David

Blunkett's comment: 'and at the same time we are trying to delegate, to decentralize services to the community, to bring the community into the process with tenants, works department shop stewards and councillors, for example, meeting together and forming working groups, trying to get people involved in the running of social services at local level' (Blunkett, 1984, p. 249). By the end of the 1980s, the council had abandoned commitments to physical decentralization and the devolution of power (Sheffield City Council Working Party on (Policy) 7 October 1988b). Liverpool City Council up to 1986 gave decentralization no priority at all (Gyford 1985, p. 16).

In other councils, for example Islington and Manchester, decentralization was adopted as a major, if not the major, plank of the council's policy. In Islington, a number of neighbourhood offices were established with neighbourhood forums relating to them. The neighbourhood offices covered the whole of the Borough (cf. Heery, 1987, and Hambleton and Hoggett, 1987, pp. 77-79). In Manchester, a similar priority was given, in principle, to decentralized organisational structures (cf. Wainwright, 1987, p. 125). Other Labour councils started off with a strong commitment to decentralization but ended up taking a much more cautious approach. Hackney was the main example of such a council (cf. Hoggett, Lawrence and Fudge 1984; Tomlinson, 1986b; Davis et al., 1984; Puddephatt, 1987). Moreover, in Manchester the progress made on decentralization was limited (cf. Jensen, 1989). Jensen argued, in respect of Manchester, 'these progressive policies were not accompanied by fundamental structural changes in the Town Hall. With the same old management structure the users of Council services and the Council trade unions had little influence on the implementation of decisions'. It was not only left Labour councils which embraced the decentralization of local services - Conservative East Sussex, Liberal (Democrat) Tower Hamlets, and right-wing Labour Birmingham and Newcastle councils all, for example, at one time or another in the 1980s, pursued some form of decentralization (cf., for example, *Community Care*, 1985, p. 19; Marphet, 1987; Baker, Hambleton and Hoggett, 1987; Hambleton and Hoggett, 1987, pp. 57-59).

It is contended by certain writers (cf. Deakin, 1984a, 1984b; Hambleton and Hoggett, 1987, pp. 53-83; Tomlinson, 1986a and 1986b) that decentralization is not intrinsically socialist and is as likely to be used by Conservative and other councils as by socialist ones. Moreover, writers like Beresford and Croft (1983, pp. 26-27, and 1984, p. 34) and Wainwright (1984) see decentralization, as practised by Labour councils, as about tinkering with council structures rather than changing social relations and coming from, and expressing the interests of, councillors rather than resulting from community demands. The argument that decentralization may conflict with traditional socialist principles of equality, which require central control, is put forward by Stewart (1984). There may be other, and possibly better, ways of making council services and activities responsive to the needs of users and the local community than physical decentralization - for example giving grants to community and oppressed groups to do things for themselves.

The different political and theoretical aspects of decentralization were perhaps expressed best by Hambleton and Hoggett (1987). They argue there are basically two broad concepts of democracy: representative democracy and direct democracy. Representative democracy is concerned with the behaviour and activities of political parties and with people's activities as voters within the traditional representative political system. Direct democracy is concerned with activities relating to people's direct involvement in organizations outside the traditional representative political system, such as tenants' associations, women's groups, leisure and sports clubs. For Hambleton and Hoggett, different strategies towards decentralization reflect different basic attitudes towards democracy. A way of distinguishing between different decentralization strategies adopted by councils is to ask if the council sees decentralization as a means to extend or improve representative as opposed to direct democracy or as a means of combining the two. Those councils who introduce decentralization because they are concerned with extending representative democracy see the policy as helping to make existing council structures and ways of working more efficient. Whereas those councils who use decentralization as a means of extending direct democracy see the policy as creating new structures for involving people in the workings of the council.

Hambleton and Hoggett (1987, pp. 56-65 and 76-79) conclude from this that councils like Birmingham and Newcastle were concerned to use decentralization as a means of improving representative democracy, whereas Islington was using decentralization as a means of infusing representative with direct democracy. From the Hambleton and Hoggett position, Manchester City Council would be seen as having had the aim of moving towards a more direct kind of democracy through its commitment to devolve power to the local level through neighbourhood committees (cf. Wainwright, 1987, p. 125). The question mark over the actual progress that was made in Manchester, and the strength of the initial commitment to devolve power, must be noted, however. The Liberal (Democrat) Tower Hamlets council would be seen, on this analysis, as trying to change the nature of representative democracy by making ward councillors more responsible for what happens in their wards (cf. Marphet, 1987).

Councils, like East Sussex, would be seen as using decentralization as a means of improving the administrative structures of the council.

Decentralization can also be used, according to Hambleton and Hoggett, to increase the influence of people as consumers of council services - the consumerist approach - which involves the use of market research techniques aimed at ascertaining the attitudes of council service users to council services. The consumerist approach can be extended, Hambleton and Hoggett argue, to help secure greater use of a council's services. Nottinghamshire County Council Leisure Department, for example, set up special panels to try to find out why ethnic minorities were not making more use of the council's countryside recreation facilities (Hambleton and Hoggett, 1987, pp. 79-80).

From this analysis it would be difficult to classify the position of Sheffield City Council. The council made efforts to involve tenants in the development of housing services (this may be due to the number of councillors who had been active in tenants' groups and to the experience of the 1967 council house rent increase which cost Labour control of the city in 1968) and pursued a novel system of school governing boards where control over individual schools was devolved to school governors, to a large extent. At the same time, as the issues of removing corporal punishment from schools and ending the compulsory wearing of school uniform illustrates (cf. Blunkett, 1984), the council Labour group believed it should retain strong control over policy decisions. On the issue of the removal of corporal punishment in schools and the compulsory wearing of school uniform, Sheffield District Labour Party made a firm commitment to abolish corporal punishment and the compulsory wearing of school uniforms in its 1980 manifesto. In subsequent discussions with parents, strong support for the retention of corporal punishment and the wearing of school uniform was expressed. However, when it received those views, the Labour Group made it clear that the consultation should not have been around whether corporal punishment in schools and the compulsory wearing of school uniform should be abolished but about how those aims were to be achieved.

There may also be differences between the aims of councillors, senior officers and the trade unions in their attitudes to decentralization. It may well be that senior officers and some trade unions, those representing higher grade staff, will want to integrate any moves towards decentralization into existing council structures, while councillors want to promote new forms of 'popular democracy'. Whether that is the position in Sheffield will be considered in a later chapter when the findings of my case study into Sheffield City Council are reproduced.

Improving relations with the local Labour Party

For writers such as Deakin (1984a, and 1984b) and Wainwright (1987, p. 109) Sheffield City Council was more concerned with maintaining and improving the accountability of the Labour group to the District Labour Party than it was with making services and council activities more responsive and accountable to the users of those services and the local community. For example Wainwright (1987, p. 110) has argued 'The proposed aim was "socialism from below" but the process in Sheffield did not quite have the degree of independence and unpredictability that it had in sharing power in the same way as the GLC Women's Committee did, or Manchester's Neighbourhood Forums are trying to do'. While many of the writings of David Blunkett (cf. 1984, 1985) would dispute this point, the Labour group on Sheffield Council after 1980 clearly did put a high priority on maintaining accountability to the District Labour Party.

Similarly, other new urban left councils tried to improve or change relations with their local District Labour Party, County Party or, in London, the Local Government Committee. In Liverpool, for example, Tony Byrne has argued: 'Working class organization in this city lies in the Labour Party and the trade unions and not in housing associations' (cf. Parkinson, 1985, p. 131). As Parkinson's study shows, the Labour group on Liverpool Council saw itself, between 1983 and 1986, as accountable almost solely to the District Labour Party, even though the membership of the latter body was clearly, at times, manipulated. Manchester City Council, under new urban left control, also tried to improve working arrangements with, and accountability to, the District Labour Party, while maintaining the autonomy of the DLP as a campaigning organization, in order to avoid the problems which beset the previous right wing Labour leadership of the council (cf. Wainwright, 1987, pp. 118-120, 122-124). New urban left councils generally supported the development of a strong District Labour Party or Local Government Committee which, in many ways, distinguished such councils from most other Labour authorities. Tensions between some 'left' council Labour Groups and their local Labour Parties may have grown, however, in the late 1980s, especially over spending cuts. Some redefining of the role of the two bodies may have taken place in some areas, as a result (cf., for example, the debates in *Labour Briefing* in the late 1980s). Certainly, that seems to have been the case in Sheffield (cf. my interviews with the Leader of the Council, the Secretary of the District Labour Party and other DLP members).

New industrial relations

Another main way in which new urban left councils hoped to avoid the pitfalls of labourism and offer a new type of socialist administration was by changing the way in which councils operated internally. This aim tied in to the commitment to increase users' and community control over council activities. For Sheffield, Blunkett and Green (1983, p. 6) have written, 'We intend with the commitment and co-operation of those who work for us and those who receive services to change the way in which services are delivered to make them more sensitive and responsive. We intend to extend democracy within the workforce to generate ideas and the power to implement changes'. Or again, Blunkett (1981, p. 102) has stated that local authority workers

> should be able to see that they are part of community action, that they are part of the political education, with a small 'p'. Then the whole of our services can be thrown behind working people, the local state used as an example of what we could do as a Socialist government at national level, not paternalistically doing things for people but throwing our weight as a community behind them, both at local and national level, to do what they want to do in their own way in their community.

Ken Livingstone (1982) saw trade unions as playing a key role in uniting disparate consumers and providers of local government services in a coherent class strategy for radical social change. The Labour manifesto for the 1981 GLC elections called for a new system of industrial democracy (cf. Soto, 1987, p. 82). Manchester Council also intended to change the internal working practices of the council through the involvement of council workers at all levels in the neighbourhood initiatives (cf. Wainwright, 1987, p. 125). Seex (1987, p. 25) argues that the new leadership of Manchester Council in 1984 recognized the need to involve workers at all levels as an important means of developing a wide range of policy initiatives, while the council retained the right to decide policy after drawing upon senior officer expertise. On decentralization, Manchester council established a Trade Union Forum Neighbourhood Service Working Party in 1986 which gave all trade unions the right to receive reports on proposals to vary existing service delivery, working practices, collective agreements and conditions of employment before they were brought before the employing committee or the local departmental representatives (Seex, 1987, p. 25). Similar overall commitments were made by Islington council whose decentralization proposals involved moving towards generic working in neighbourhood offices (cf. Heery, 1987).

Hackney council also wanted to use decentralization to introduce greater worker involvement, until the defeat of the first *Redprint.* (cf. Davis et al., 1984). In a document (*Hackney Labour Parties 1982 Manifesto - why we want it, how it will work - proposals for discussion*), Hackney Labour Parties (1982) professed the following commitment:

> We must challenge the hierarchical structure within the council and break down the concentration of power at the top. Responsibility and power must be shared more widely among Council workers. We must provide a framework to tap their enthusiasm and desire to work for the community. We must break down the boundaries between those who carry out decisions and those who make them, between those who meet the public face to face and those who have little contact, and between those who do manual work and those who do mental work.

Moreover, big commitments were made by new left councils to tackle low pay and promote equal opportunities. The GLC had major commitments in those areas (cf. Soto, 1987), as did Islington council, for example. The 1982 and 1986 Labour manifestos in Islington both included strong proposals to fight low pay in the council and to promote equal opportunities employment practices, as well as promoting greater worker involvement (Islington Labour Party Local Government Committee, 1982, and 1986). Camden, Greenwich and Lambeth all launched minimum earnings guarantees and Sheffield and Hackney had commitments to the development of low pay supplements. Hackney, Greenwich and Sheffield were also committed to promoting 'single status' employment practices for all their employees (cf. Stoker, 1988, pp. 198-199).

Geoff Green (1987, p. 212) set out the aims of new urban left councils in the area of industrial relations, as follows:

> Industrial relations thus became a top priority: no-redundancy policies, the elimination of low pay and bonus systems which failed to guarantee basic wages above the poverty line, equal opportunities for women and ethnic minorities, equal status for manual and white-collar workers.

Once again, the aim of changing the relations between the council and its workforce, developing forms of industrial democracy and positively trying to fight discrimination in the council is novel for Labour as well as Conservative and Liberal Democrat councils, except for rare examples like the Poplar Council in the 1930s which pursued an active strategy to increase the pay of its low paid workers (cf. Branson, 1979). The traditional position has been that Labour councils should provide good wages and conditions of service, within nationally negotiated guidelines. However, action by individual councils, outside the national guidelines, to try to remove low pay and tackle discrimination in the council, have generally been unusual. Moreover, the traditional position has been that policy making and policy implementation will be carried out by Labour councillors and senior officers with minimal worker involvement.

Many of the efforts to promote industrial democracy and to tackle discrimination in employment practices proved disappointing or unsuccessful. In many cases the new urban left councillors failed to bring about major changes in the internal working of their councils. There are those who argue that this was largely due to the negative attitude of trade unions and particularly the white collar union, NALGO (The National and Local Government Officers Association which merged with the National Union of Public Employees and the Confederation of Health Service Employees in the early 1990s to form the new union Unison). Hoggett and Hambleton (1984, p. 103) argue:

> It seems a great pity that in most boroughs the trade unions have declined the initiative to step outside their normal traditional role. They and their membership have preferred instead to assume the more passive role of responding to others' proposals in order to maintain the usual employee/employer relationship. The ultimate and most radical form of decentralisation would involve a partnership between worker self-management and community control. Public sector unions seem to be lagging behind some of their private sector counterparts when it comes to asserting control over the labour process.

More specifically, in Hackney, for example, the decentralization proposals of the council were defeated in large part, it is argued, because of the opposition of NALGO and the National Union of Public Employees (NUPE) staff branch (cf. Hoggett, Lawrence and Fudge, 1984). However, it must be borne in mind that the then Leader of the council, Anthony Kendall (1984), accepted the unions were not properly involved in the development of the decentralization proposals through the formal negotiating machinery. In Islington, Heery (1987, pp. 202-210) contends that NALGO took a very negative attitude to the council's decentralization proposals, which aimed, in part, at improving the jobs and working conditions of council workers. Leading Labour councillors in Walsall in 1980 organized to overcome and defeat what they foresaw as likely opposition from the NALGO branch to the council's decentralization proposals (cf. Seabrook, 1984). In more general terms, Hoggett (1987, pp. 33-35) has argued that NALGO acts to preserve the privileges of highly paid professional workers and is thus a negative influence on council policy and an opponent of radical policies. Similar conclusions were reached by Sharron (1985) after an examination of the disputes in 1984 in Sheffield and St. Helens Councils with NALGO. Against those views, however, Tomlinson (1986a) argues that in Hackney the Labour councillors rushed into decentralization without considering the consequences for the workforce and without a clear understanding of the limited amount decentralization could achieve. That the real and legitimate fears of workers about safety and work loads were not taken into account when they formulated and pressed ahead with their plans, is a criticism levied by Islington NALGO Branch (various, 1986) at the council, which was also criticized for trying to introduce decentralization at a time of acute financial stringency.

A further criticism of new urban left councils is made by Weinstein (1986). He argues that, in Southwark at least, the left councillors had little understanding of, or commitment to, trade unionism. Moreover, having adopted radical stances in the manifesto and on issues like rate capping, Southwark council created disillusionment with many, including those in the NALGO Branch, who supported the policies, when the Labour councillors failed to put their radical rhetoric into practice. The failure of many new left councillors to understand trade unionism was also pointed out by Hoggett, Lawrence and Fudge (1984, pp. 70-71). Ken Livingstone (1984, pp. 21-22) has argued:

> Many of the radical left councils are often locked in disputes with their own trade unions. It often starts because they've made a miscalculation and some faction or group seeks to try and exploit that. But then there's an immediate intolerance, the idea that somehow they know best and how can anybody challenge them particularly as they're radical left wingers. And so there's still a lot to learn and that sort of arrogance is still there even in parts of the Labour Party currently being renewed by people who've come into politics post-1968.

Moreover, Hoggett (1987a), while critical of NALGO attitudes and practices, accepted that Labour councillors have almost universally failed to develop a socialist style or method of management which has created major problems. A similar view was also put forward by Wolmar (1984) in his discussion of developments in Hackney and the 1984 Sheffield NALGO dispute. In that article, Wolmar called on Labour councillors to develop an active and distinctively socialist approach to management, something which in Wolmar's view they had singularly failed to do, and for council unions, especially those like NALGO, to move away from their automatic opposition to any proposed changes in the internal organization of councils which affect their members. While a full analysis of the 1984 dispute in Sheffield will be set out in a later chapter, it is pertinent here to note the comments of two ex-Sheffield City Council NALGO members who were involved in the strike. Darke and Goulay (1985) maintain that the many workers who were attracted to work for Sheffield Council because of its radical reputation were disillusioned by the authoritarian attitudes and working practices of many managers. This factor, they maintain, was crucial in the 1984 dispute between the council and NALGO.

On the general question of the attitude of senior council officers in new urban left councils, Livingstone (1987 cf., also, Carvel, 1984, p. 126) and Murray (1987), from their experience with the GLC, stressed the power of senior management to block radical change. They argued that senior officers deliberately tried to block radical policies, such as the setting up of the Greater London Enterprise Board and the Fares Fair policy.

The question of who was to blame for the lack of progress on internal restructuring of new left councils and changing new urban left council relations with users of services and the local community is an issue which will be discussed in more detail in a later chapter, after the results of my case study of Sheffield and Doncaster Councils and a consideration of the experience within the GLC have been set out. But it can be suggested here that the issue is not simply one of Labour councillors in left Labour councils lacking trade union experience themselves and hence not understanding the nature of trade unionism. That may be part of the problem, but even in councils, like Sheffield City Council, where links between councillors and trade unions were quite strong, as has been seen, disputes between the council and groups of workers occurred. The subject seems to get to the heart of the relationship between the attitudes of trade unions, the nature of trade unionism, the power of senior council officers, the attitudes of Labour councillors to, and the relationship between, representative and direct democracy and the consequential problem of introducing or achieving socialist change. Those issues will be considered in detail later in the work.

Disadvantaged and oppressed groups

While new urban left councils were committed to policies to help disadvantaged groups in the community, they approached this matter in different ways. The GLC, as has been already mentioned, gave a high priority to making grant payments to groups so that they could do things for themselves (cf. Mackintosh and Wainwright, 1987, p. 421). This was one of the ways in which the GLC hoped to avoid the pitfalls of bureaucratic paternalism. The policy was applauded by socialists like Hall (1984, pp. 28-29). There were, however, dangers with this policy in that groups could lose their independence and become dependent on a council for legitimation of their activities. The council could also refuse a grant to a group whose policy or make up it disliked (cf. Mackintosh and Wainwright, 1987, p. 401, and pp. 421-426). Moreover, it was possible for the GLC to pursue the policy because it was responsible for few statutory council services unlike other councils which had many more calls on their finances from service departments. Other councils did, however, give grants to groups but generally not on the same scale as the GLC (cf., for example, Gyford, 1985, pp. 54-56 and Sheffield City Council, 1986a).

Another way of trying to improve the position of disadvantaged and oppressed groups is to create council committees, or sub-committees, to deal with specific problems. For example women's committees, race committees, equal opportunities committees and so on can be established. The GLC once again gave a priority to the establishment of a women's committee and an equal opportunities programme (cf. Goss, 1984, and, on race issues Ouseley, 1984). Manchester Council also gave a high priority to its equal opportunities programme (cf. Wainwright, 1987, pp. 121-122). A number of London Boroughs established race and other committees (cf., for example, Prashar and Nicholas, 1986). On the other hand, Sheffield Council was slow to make any move on the issue of women's oppression and disadvantage, at least in terms of setting up council departments or committees to deal with this issue. Blunkett (1984, p. 255) has summed up the attitude in Sheffield Council by arguing that the women's issue should not detract from the main issue, that of class struggle. Even at the end of the 1980s, the council gave the women's issue only limited importance (cf. Seyd, 1987, pp. 150-151). The dangers associated with policies like those adopted by the GLC, as Boddy and Fudge (1984, pp. 10-14) argue, are that women's groups, blacks and others can become part of the local government structure and lose their ability to articulate popular grievances as a result. The argument is that activists will be 'incorporated' by the council on the council's terms and lose their critical independence. Moreover, by setting up single issue committees, women's, black, and gay and lesbian issues will be marginalized and not become a part of the council's main concerns.

The differences of approach between new urban left councils on this issue may have been due, in part at least, to the different social compositions of the councils. In the GLC, for example, feminism had a big impact. Ken Livingstone, the council leader, was, and is, deeply influenced by a feminist analysis which has coloured his whole political outlook. Similarly, Valerie Wise, a leading member of the council, came from a tradition of feminist politics. The early 1980s saw a number of efforts in London to have commitments to set up women's committees inserted in the 1982 Borough council election manifestos (cf. Livingstone, 1987, pp. 238-240). In addition, many of the senior officers appointed to the GLC, like Hilary Wainwright, Sheila Rowbotham and Irene Breughel, were active feminists. Those factors led the council to give a high priority to women's issues. In Sheffield City Council the influence of feminism was slight with the council giving its greatest priority to a traditional class based politics because of its very close links, stretching back a long way, with the local labour movement (cf. Wainwright, 1987, pp. 107-111). For the Liverpool Labour Group a concern with issues such as gender, race and sexual politics, were all secondary to, and subsumed by, the traditional class struggle (cf. Wainwright 1987, pp. 126-136). It should also perhaps be noted that Labour councils who are not part of the new urban left tried to pursue equal opportunity or anti-discriminatory policies. For example, Derby City Council, under Labour control, had an Equal Opportunities Committee and Leicester City Council tried hard to improve the council's responsiveness to the needs of the local Asian population.

Economic and industrial regeneration

As argued in the last chapter, the new urban left developed, in part at least, in response to growing economic decline in certain urban areas and it saw as one of its prime aims the regeneration of the local economy through council employment and economic initiatives. This was one of the main concerns of the GLC (cf. Mackintosh and Wainwright, 1987a) and of Sheffield City Council (cf. Blunkett and Green, 1983). It does not seem to have been a prime concern of all London Boroughs however or of Manchester City Council. In the case of the London Boroughs this may have been due, in part, to the activity of the GLC up to 1986. Both Sheffield and the GLC saw their activity in this area as providing an example of what a Labour administration could achieve and acting as an example for a future Labour government. Both councils saw their economic initiatives as part of their effort to involve people more fully in the council's activities. The Popular Planning Unit at the GLC tried to further this aim (cf., for example, Phillips, 1987) and the terms of reference of Sheffield's Employment Department involved it 'not simply in providing services itself but also in acting as resource for groups and organizations outside the town hall' (cf. Bye and Beatie, 1982, p. 2). The councils aimed to expand the public sector locally and to provide socially useful employment for the unemployed and those threatened with the loss of their job (cf. Mackintosh and Wainwright, 1987a; Blunkett and Green, 1983; Boddy, 1984). The councils were attempting to move away from a position where Labour councils simply tried to attract private capital by offering bigger grants and inducements than other councils. The aim of trying to provide an example for a future Labour government on economic restructuring was not confined to new urban left councils, however. The West Midlands County Council with its Enterprise Board and planning policies believed it was pioneering a new type of socialist industrial policy (cf. Edge, 1981).

The policies of the GLC and Sheffield Council proved only marginally successful. Unemployment in both cities grew remorselessly in the 1980s and while both councils helped to set up worker co-operatives and developed good employment practices it is hard to see any economic restructuring which occurred in Sheffield and London as in the interests of labour rather than capital. In addition the public sector far from expanding was pushed back (cf. Mackintosh and Wainwright, 1987, pp. 12-16; Seyd, 1987, pp. 149-152; Green, 1987, pp. 212-213).

Improving council services and political mobilization

As part of their efforts to present examples of prefigurative socialist administrations, new urban left councils believed it was imperative to improve the standard of council services. The GLC, for example, tried to improve London's transport services until prevented from doing so by the Law Lords and the government (cf. Forrester, Lansley, Pauley, 1985); Merseyside County Council also attempted to provide a better public transport service and South Yorkshire County Council ran a cheap fares policy (cf. Stoker, 1988, p. 198). Liverpool City Council built thousands of new council houses between 1983 and 1987 (cf. Taaffe and Mulhearn, 1988, pp. 19-162); Sheffield developed an imaginative leisure and recreation policy (Sheffield City Council, 1986a) and other new urban left councils, such as Manchester City

Council, also tried, despite stringent financial constraints, to improve their services (cf. Stoker, 1988, pp. 198-199 and Goss, Hillier and Rule, 1988, p. 5). In part improving council services was one of the objectives of decentralization and tied into another aim, that of political mobilization (cf. Gyford, 1985, pp. 81-94).

As Gyford stresses this commitment to political mobilization was one of the main factors distinguishing the new urban left from traditional Labour councils. The aim of popular mobilization was to defeat the Conservative central government attack on local government and to win support for the Labour Party. The aim was to show the importance of council services and to mobilize people so that they would fight to protect those services (cf. Blunkett, 1985). Nevertheless, within that broad aim, there were big differences within new urban left councils about the best way of mobilizing popular support. As Gyford (1985, pp. 81-91) has argued, many new urban left councils, particularly in London, were concerned about forging alliances between minority groups. The GLC, for example, was very concerned, as Livingstone (1984, pp. 269-271) argues, that the Labour Party could no longer rely on the support alone of white male skilled manual workers if it was to be electorally successful. Livingstone (1981) has also stated that:

> The organised working class, industrial, skilled, trade unions have left London... and that means a considerable weakening of the base here. Now, it is not a question of recreating the base because there's no prospect of skilled crafts moving back into London at all. It's a question of building on this new sort of alliance... we have to start to articulate the needs of the minorities and the dispossessed, in a way that Labour governments and the Labour Party never have in the past.

Many efforts were thus made to win the support of blacks, women and oppressed gays and lesbians. On the Islington Neighbourhood Forums, for example, the council was concerned to ensure that women, blacks and other disadvantaged groups gained adequate representation (Hambleton and Hoggett, 1987, pp. 77-79, and Hodge, 1987). Other councils, once again Sheffield was a prime example, on the new urban left were much less concerned about building rainbow coalitions and much more concerned with maintaining the support of manual workers (cf. Seyd, 1987, pp. 143-158).

Once again, the differences between new urban left councils may have been due to the influence of different social elements in the councils. But it may also have been due, as Livingstone's quote suggests, to differences in the social composition of the areas covered by the various councils. The councils, in other words, may have been responding to influences internal to the council, such as feminism, the experience of black and Asian councillors, and to the needs of the external social environment. In London, for example, the case to develop a 'rainbow coalition' which, in Livingstone's view, would take account of the nature of the modern working-class in London (Livingstone, 1987, p. 243) may not have been so strong in a city like Sheffield with its more homogeneous, largely white, working-class.

Rate capping

If new urban left councils were only loosely united in the early 1980s, the experience of rate capping forced the latent differences between, and within, councils into the open. In 1984 the central government acquired powers to prevent certain so called 'high spending' local authorities in England and Wales from raising their rates above a certain level. 'Rate capping' as this process became known applied, and has applied since, in its various guises (poll tax capping, council tax capping) almost exclusively to Labour councils. The Labour councils included in the list of rate capped authorities in 1985 determined to fight the government and its rate capping policies by refusing to set a rate. In retrospect, Blunkett and Jackson, (1987, pp. 166-198) have argued that the campaign against rate capping was not properly thought out. The different councils, many, though not all, of which can be regarded as new urban left led, were not all as firmly committed to the agreed strategy and within councils opposition to the strategy was often quite strong within Labour groups. While the date by which district councils had to produce a rate was unclear in law, for county councils, or the equivalent, the position was crystal clear: such councils had to produce a rate by the 10 March. That meant that councillors in different types of council faced different problems. Moreover, in order to maintain unity the serious problems associated with, and the aims of, opposition were not thought through. It was always likely that when it came to the crunch a number of councillors would not be prepared to take opposition all the way and risk personal financial surcharge. In any case, on most of the councils a number of councillors did not support illegal opposition to the government's actions. Lansley (1985) has argued that only two or three rate capped councils were likely to take opposition to the government's action and defiance of the law to its ultimate conclusion. That view was endorsed by David Blunkett (interview 1988) who argued, 'What we did realise is that we weren't going to be able to overturn the government. I mean, that was the difference between Sheffield and Lambeth, for instance, in rate capping'. Clive Betts (interview, 1987) and Councillor Mike Bower (interview, 1988) both confirm that there were major differences in Sheffield Council towards the rate capping campaign.

Moreover, while great efforts were made by some councils to mobilize the support of council workers, the local labour movement and the local community to take action in support of the Labour councillors opposing rate capping this was, at best, only partly successful. In many councils trade unions adopted different and conflicting attitudes and strategies to rate capping (cf. Parkinson, 1985, and Blunkett and Jackson, 1987, pp. 176-194). Moreover, Laffin (1989, pp. 111-118) shows the tensions that existed between the unions and the council leadership in the new urban left council he called Labton. In the end, despite all the rhetoric of mounting an effective campaign against the government, the opposition crumbled as one council after another set a legal rate. In the end only two councils defied the government almost to the end: Lambeth and Liverpool whose Labour members, or those supporting the 'unlawful' action, were subsequently surcharged by the District Auditor.

Why did the Labour councils, one after another, relinquish the fight against rate capping and why did Liverpool and Lambeth keep the fight going longest? Why did the local community and council workers 'fail' to actively support the anti-rate capping campaign? Are there any answers in the compositions and thinking of different councils? Nearly all the councils involved in the anti-rate capping action saw themselves as involved in a campaign to mobilize support for the maintenance of council services and against the Conservative government. But there were differences about how this should be done. Most of the councils saw the campaign against rate capping and defiance of the law as a tactic to force the government to change track (cf. Blunkett, 1985). Some, however, saw it in much greater terms as an effort, along with the miners on strike and others, to defeat the government and force it out of office, as Blunkett argued (interview, 1988). For those people, taking the campaign against rate capping to the end was a way of mobilizing the working-class in a class war against the government. That view was particularly strong in Liverpool and Lambeth because of the influence of a particular form of Trotskyite Marxism.

Whether the strategy of mobilizing the working-class against the government through the campaign against rate capping could have succeeded is a debatable point. But in Liverpool the failure of the council to win all the council trade unions in support of their position, and the problems in winning support among the wider trade union movement in Liverpool, suggests the strategy would have faced immense difficulties, even if all the rate capped authorities had pursued the same course in a totally united way. A major factor which probably held back the mobilization of working-class support was the way in which the anti-rate capping campaign, at the crucial stage, became absorbed with the actions of councillors and splits, or potential splits, in Labour groups. People were encouraged to support the action of the 'heroic' councillors. In that concern, almost obsession, with the actions of councillors many of the broader issues of the campaign became submerged. Instead of people being involved in the development of the campaign in an active way, they were always entreated to support councillor led and councillor based action. Moreover, Clarke and Cochrane (1989, p. 53) argue that by making the campaign revolve around the issue of immediate budgetary constraints and spending cuts 'the councils effectively moved away from the broader issues of the campaign, which was not about whether a budget could be made in one particular year, but about the longer term impact of the new legislation on the local welfare state and the scope to mobilize resistance to the centre'. They make the telling point that 'despite the rhetoric, the political alliance developed in 1985 was not between local communities and Labour councils, but between councillors and chief officers trapped in the traditional languages of local government'.

Perhaps the most significant long-term factor to come out of the anti-rate capping campaign was the lack of enthusiasm shown by local communities, local Labour movements and council workforces for strong, determined action to protect the councils involved in the campaign. Whether that was because the campaign was essentially defensive and failed to concentrate on the threat to local services and jobs of the government's action, as Hatton (1988, pp. 90-91) argues, or due above all to other factors, for example the failure of the campaign to pit one form of autocratic government against a popular democratic socialist form of government, is debatable. What the episode shows, however, is that all the new left councils concerned did not succeed during their periods in office in so winning active popular support for what they were trying to do that local people were anxious to take action in support of the councils and the councillors and what they stood for. On this criterion the new urban left project can be judged a failure.

The rate capping campaign suggests that, while the new urban left developed as a reaction to the failures of traditional labourism, both its theory and its practice, there was still probably a vestigial belief that if the action of the central government and central state could be shown to be unjust, or improper, the central government would stop. There seems to have been at least some failure to recognise the determination of the Conservative governments to push through their policies and to use to the full the organs of the state to do so. The leaders of the new urban left may have recognised the class nature of the Thatcher governments and of the state which stood behind them, but they probably underestimated the determination and tactical skill of the Conservative central governments. The Conservative governments had 'chipped away' at local government autonomy and power in the years since 1979 and prepared the ground for the major confrontation over rate capping (cf. Duncan and Goodwin, 1988). The government had been prepared to make tactical retreats, as over forcing local councils to hold a referendum if they wanted to levy a supplementary rate (cf. Duncan and Goodwin, 1988, pp. 115-118) and to prepare the ground for the introduction of rate capping in England and Wales by conducting a 'dummy run' in Scotland (cf. Duncan and Goodwin, 1988, pp. 171-179). Moreover, the ability of local councils to circumvent many of the Conservative governments' earlier measures may have prevented some people, council workers and service users, recognizing the importance of the rate capping proposals.

The results of the rate capping opposition were that the unity achieved between councils nationally in the early period of the campaign was destroyed and within individual councils splits within the left developed. In the GLC the leader, Ken Livingstone, who supported setting a rate in the end, and the deputy leader, John McDonnell, who opposed setting a rate to the end, split, as did the whole left on the Labour group, and in Sheffield many left councillors became demoralized and even left the local council (cf. Seyd, 1987, pp. 157-158).

Post 1985

After that, and particularly in the wake of the Conservative general election victory in June 1987, the left in local government adopted a far less optimistic, some might argue more realistic, stance. No longer were there great claims about what Labour councils could achieve in a hostile economic and political climate. As Wolmar (1987) has shown, in the London Boroughs, such as Camden and Islington, there was a belief that London Labour councils should put their primary effort into improving council services, a view endorsed by John McDonnell (1987) as secretary of the Association of London Authorities. In Sheffield as well, according to Geoff Green, (1987) the Labour group adopted a much more low key approach, no longer trying to mould the political agenda in such a positive, campaigning way. A mixture of central government spending cuts and restrictions on local government activity, along with the rise of 'new realism' in the Labour Party and past defeats meant that after 1987 the new urban left ceased to exist (cf. Lansley, Goss and Wolmar, 1989). It is important, however, to understand in greater detail what progress was made within new urban left councils. I will attempt to do this in respect of one area, by setting out the results of a case study into industrial relations in two Labour councils, one, Sheffield, a new urban left authority, the other, Doncaster, a more 'traditional', or right wing Labour council. First, as a background to the case study, consideration will be given to the relationship between trade unionism and socialism.

4 Trade Unions and Socialism

The aim of this chapter is to provide a framework for understanding the actions and attitudes of the trade unions in the two councils I have studied and of industrial relations in Labour controlled local authorities. A number of themes will therefore be discussed. The nature and consequences of the links between the Labour Party and the trade unions will be examined in detail. This will be done, initially, by looking at the links different unions have with the Labour Party. From there the relations between the trade unions and national Labour governments will be considered. This will enable the issue of whether the Labour Party, in office, has better relations with affiliated, than with non-affiliated, trade unions to be examined. The implications of the findings from this analysis for an understanding of industrial relations in Labour controlled councils will then be considered. The different nature and practice of manual and non-manual trade unionism will be another theme considered. This will lead into an analysis of the relationship between professionalism and trade unionism. An understanding of this relationship is essential in considering industrial relations in Labour local authorities and in analyzing the case studies. Only if these issues are accurately analyzed will it be possible to understand why the strike between Sheffield City Council and NALGO occurred in 1984, or to shed light on the attitudes and practices of different unions in Sheffield and Doncaster councils. Understanding such issues is also important if the attitudes and actions of Labour councillors and senior council officers in the councils studied are to be comprehended. Theoretical insights are essential if light is to be shed on the themes to be considered in this chapter. Empirical observation alone will not produce an accurate understanding of the issues under examination. Therefore, theoretical material will be introduced to help an understanding of the case study material and of industrial relations in Labour councils.

The Labour Party/trade union links

The Labour Party was partly formed out of the trade unions. In 1900 a number of trade unions and socialist organizations, the Independent Labour Party, the Social Democratic Federation and the Fabian Society, joined together to form the Labour Representation Committee. Since then, there have been close institutional links between the Labour Party and the trade unions. However, just as some trade unions stayed out of the Labour Representation Committee when it was formed, so in the 1980s there were a number of major unions which were not affiliated to the Labour Party. As far as local government trade unions were concerned all the main manual unions and their white collar sections - the General, Municipal, Boilermakers and Allied Trade Union, the National Union of Public Employees, the Union of Construction and Allied Trades and Technicians, the Transport and General Workers Union - were affiliated to the Labour Party in the 1980s; most of the non-manual trade unions, the National and Local Government Officers Association, the teachers' unions, were not. (The pattern of trade unionism in local government has changed in the 1990s, largely as a result of the formation of Unison. The 'old NALGO' part of Unison is not affiliated to the Labour Party but the 'old NUPE and COHSE' parts are.) However, even those trade unions which were not affiliated to the Labour Party but were members of the Trades Union Congress had links of one sort or another with the Labour Party, through their membership of the TUC.

An important aspect in trying to understand the relations between Labour councils and council trade unions in the 1980s is to consider whether, as one might expect, Labour councils had better relations with trade unions which were affiliated to the Labour Party. If this was so, it is important to examine if this can be explained by the institutional links between the party and those trade unions. Related to this is the issue of whether trade unions which were affiliated to the Labour Party had an outlook and perspective which was much closer to that of the party than non-affiliated unions. If so, it is important to ask what effect this had on relations between different unions and Labour local authorities.

Explanations of the Labour Party/trade union links

The nature of the links between the Labour Party and the trade unions can be viewed from a number of standpoints. The formal internal links between the Labour Party and the trade unions can be seen as holding back the advancement of socialism in Britain. The Labour Party leadership and the Constituency Parties, it is argued, are constrained in what they can do by their dependent relationship with the non-socialist leaders of the trade unions. At its crudest this view sees trade unions as basically a negative force concerned with gaining improvements for their members within the existing capitalist system and preventing the Labour Party developing in a socialist direction (cf. Anderson, 1965; Nairn, 1965). However, others argue that the presence of the trade unions in the Labour Party provides it with a unique possibility of furthering the socialist cause. Writers like Michael Barratt Brown (1972) and Ken Coates (1973) see the Labour Party's links with the trade unions as providing a connection with the organized working-class which any socialist party will need if it is to be effective in bringing about socialist change. For writers in this tradition, trade unions are not intrinsically and necessarily defensive organizations, concerned with simply winning improvements within the capitalist system (cf. Coates and Topham, 1988).

These two arguments are at diametrically opposed ends of the spectrum and there are many positions in between. But in order to evaluate which end of the spectrum has the greater explanatory power, it is necessary to look in some detail at how the relationship between the trade unions and Labour Party has worked in practice. To do this consideration will be given to the relationship between the last Labour government (of 1974 to 1979) and the trade unions.

Union Labour government links

Lewis Minkin in various works (1974, 1977, 1978) has studied the relations between the Labour Party and the trade unions in the 1970s. For Minkin (1978, p. 463), a major imperative of social democratic parties, like the British Labour Party, rests on the need to win electoral support. For the trade unions, however, a major imperative is to protect their members' industrial interests whichever party is in government. Conflicts between these bodies is, therefore, to be expected, especially if one believes the industrial interests of the trade unions are electorally unpopular. Minkin's (1977) work shows that the trade unions in the 1974-1977 period were loath to impose their interests and power on the Labour government. The trade unions were committed to helping to maintain the Labour Party in government and did not push issues of a sensitive nature with great vigour. The important point for Minkin (1978, pp. 460-461) is that the relationship between the trade unions and the Labour Party is based on the trade union leaders giving priority to industrial rather than political issues. For Minkin, the trade union leaders during the 1974-1979 Labour government had a fundamental concern with maintaining their own organizational integrity and freedom of action. The union leaders did not want to be in a position where it would be possible to say they were controlling the Labour Party. For the trade unions, agreement with the Labour Party rested on the acceptance that the Labour government was there to protect the industrial and political freedom of organized labour (Minkin, 1978, p. 462).

Minkin's analysis suggests strongly that the influence of the trade unions on the Labour governments of the 1970s was fairly slight. Certainly the trade unions, including left wing union leaders, did not push hard for increased public ownership, unilateral nuclear disarmament or increased public spending (Minkin, 1977, 1978, p. 479). The unions were only militant on issues affecting their direct industrial standing (Minkin, 1977). In putting their emphasis on issues of direct practical concern, the trade union leaders of the 1970s were carrying on where their predecessors had left off. The conclusion from Minkin's analysis is that the unions did not prevent the Labour government of 1974-1979 pursuing radical socialist policies nor did they push the government to do so. Moreover, non-Labour Party affiliated trade unions, like NALGO, played a part in developing trade union relations with the Labour government which were not very dissimilar from other affiliated unions. Through their positions in the TUC, the leaders of unions like NALGO had an input into the Labour Party/TUC Liaison Committee and there seems little evidence that non-affiliated unions were more hostile or supportive of the Labour government than affiliated unions (cf. Taylor, 1987).

The work of Martin Harrison (1960) supports many of Minkin's arguments. Writing of the 1945-1950 Labour government, Harrison (1960, p. 24) shows that the unions were very loyal to the government but that most of the votes at party conference against government policies came from the unions. The government was also very concerned about the unions' failure to maintain a wage freeze and their hostility to the *Control of Engagements Order* - both matters directly affecting basic trade union industrial activity. Arguing that the unions do not form a coherent, single-minded force in the party, Harrison (1960, pp. 209-261) says 'the stereotyped image of the unions as a sort of orthodox lump of suet pudding clogging the Party's progress is a potentially disastrous over-simplification' (Harrison, 1960, p. 238). The unions, for Harrison, are normally prepared to let the political leadership initiate policies which do not directly effect the unions' interests. However, Harrison (1960, p. 239) also argues that the trade unions are not a revolutionary force in the Labour Party.

> If the only possible line of advance for Labour were towards traditional red-blooded Socialism, then the balance of union power has undoubtedly been a brake. A movement with the immense entrenched interests of the unions will never be the revolutionary force the extreme Left looks for. But are the unions the only break?

Another study supporting many of Minkin's positions is that of Andrew Taylor. Once again, the trade unions are seen as being primarily concerned with protecting their basic negotiating and industrial strength. For Taylor (1987, pp. 3-4) the trade unions' involvement in Labour Party politics is based on a hesitancy, an unwillingness to be seen as imposing solutions. He also sees the relationship between the trade unions and the Labour Party in the early 1970s as essentially an accommodation between the leaders of the party and the trade unions and that the spirit of co-operation did not seep down to lower levels (Taylor, 1987, p. 28). Taylor reinforces this part of his work by arguing that while Labour's policies often appear sound and attractive from the perspective of the National Executive Committee and Party conference, shop floor and office floor workers just do not accept that the policies will work as suggested (Taylor, 1987, p. 123).

For Taylor, the trade unions exist to protect the interests of their members and dislike legal action which limits, or interferes with, their independent ability to further their members' interests. The unions are committed to free collective bargaining and only support state intervention in their affairs when this enhances their role in collective bargaining, wins freedom from external constraints and secures goals collective bargaining is incapable of achieving (Taylor, 1987, p. 85). This commitment to what Taylor calls 'voluntarism' necessarily has an impact on the relations between the party and the trade unions, and particularly when there is a Labour government. On this analysis even when there is a Labour government, conflicts are inevitable. For while unions will try to protect the sectional interests of their members, the government will try to promote the national or public interest (Taylor, 1987, p. 86).

Trade union sectionalism

If trade unions are sectional organizations, often operating against the public interest, as Taylor argues, this clearly has implications for the relationship between trade unions and the Labour Party. The issue of whether trade unions are sectional organizations and if so what effect that has on the 'socialist project' has been well debated in the socialist literature. The issue of sectionalism can be viewed from two broad aspects. It can be seen either in terms of the trade unions, en bloc, protecting their collective interests, or the interests of their collective members, at the expense of the rest of society. Or it can be viewed as individual unions or sections of workers pursuing their specific interests at the expense of the wider working-class.

Among Marxists, trade union sectionalism has been seen as a major problem. This is because of the damage it does to working-class unity. For Marxists, trade union sectionalism is not a problem because it means trade unions operating against the interests of society. On the contrary, Marxists see sectionalism as a problem only in as much as it prevents workers securing their collective interests (cf., for example, Kelly, 1988). Taylor sees trade union sectionalism as a problem for the Labour Party because it conflicts with the public interest. If Taylor's position is correct, then a Labour government is justified in opposing trade union interests in pursuing policies which are in the national interest. If, however, the Marxist analysis is correct and the general interest of workers represents the general interest, then the job of a Labour government is to try to unite the divided workers by helping them to recognize their common interests as opposed to the interests of the minority owners and controllers of the means of production.

The crucial point is where the general interest rests in society and how it is to be secured. The debate around this issue has crucial implications for how one believes a Labour government should approach its relations with the trade unions and the workers they represent. If individual unions are simply sectional organizations, out to get all they can for their particular members, then the trade union links with the Labour Party are unlikely to mean much if a union feels the interests of its particular members are being threatened by the actions of a Labour government, even if the government's actions serve the interests of workers as a whole. Good relations between a Labour government and the trade unions, or a Labour council and the council trade unions, are unlikely to be sustained in such circumstances. However, if there is an over-riding class interest among workers which represents the general interest, then there is no intrinsic reason why good relations between a Labour government and the trade unions and a Labour council and the council trade unions should not be achieved.

Workers' interests

A crucial point, therefore, is the extent to which groups of workers share a common class interest and the nature of that class interest. Also important is the closely related issue of whether, if workers do share a common interest, different groups of workers can become aware of this unity of interest. To examine this issue it is necessary to look at the factors underpinning this problem in more detail.

It has long been contended that while manual workers share a common position in capitalist society this position differs from that of white collar workers (cf., for example, Banks, 1970, pp. 195-196). Manual workers generally have to 'clock on' and 'clock off' at work, their holiday entitlements are smaller, they work longer hours and, in very many cases, their basic rates of pay are lower. As Taylor shows, this view has implications for an analysis of white collar trade unionism. Very often analysts contrast the attitude of white collar unions with those of manual trade unions, arguing that the latter have a very different set of priorities and a greater socialist inclination. For Taylor (1987, p. 169) such arguments are wrong. White collar unions aim to protect and advance their members' employment conditions, as do manual workers' unions. The commitment to advance their members' employment conditions is, for Taylor, the main trade union commitment. He rejects the idea of unionateness advanced by R. M. Blackburn and K. Prandy (1966). Blackburn and Prandy's argument is that unions can be placed on a continuum according to their degree of unionateness. By unionateness Blackburn and Prandy mean the willingness of a union's membership to take industrial action, to affiliate to a trade union centre and a political party and to engage in solidarity action. For Blackburn and Prandy, unionateness is more developed in manual than white collar unions. For Taylor (1987, p. 169), however, the term is of little use in distinguishing white collar from manual trade unions, for white collar unions are as willing to strike and most non-manual unions are affiliated to the TUC.

Taylor (1987, p. 169) argues that many white collar unions do not affiliate to the Labour Party because for them it is not seen as necessary for the exercise of effective trade unionism. Affiliation to the Labour Party and political action are not seen as relevant to the immediate work situation (Taylor, 1987, p. 191). While Taylor denies the explanatory use of the term unionateness his work does suggest that there may be reasons behind the refusal of many white collar unions to affiliate to the Labour Party that reflect differences in the outlook of manual trade unionists and white collar trade unionists. Taylor lists the following factors as helping to explain why white collar unions have not affiliated to the Labour Party: status, dislike of Labour's policies, political affiliations formed before people joined a union, affiliation to the Labour Party seen as infringing individual liberties and running counter to the ethos of the unions and their members.

Support for Taylor's contention that the use of the term unionateness has only very limited effectiveness comes from the work of Bain, Coates and Ellis (1973) and from the survey carried out by Cook, Clarke, Roberts and Semeonoff (Cook et al., 1975/1976). However, the research of Cook et al. casts doubts on Taylor's assumptions about the different ways manual trade unionists and white collar workers view political action. Cook et al. claim that research in the mid 1980s strongly suggested that traditional sociological views which equate white collar workers with the middle class and blue collar workers with the working-class are wrong. For there may be big differences between and within the attitudes and behaviour of manual workers on the one hand and the attitudes and behaviour of white collar workers may not be uniform, on the other hand. In fact, rather than one set of views being uniformly held by manual workers and another set uniformly held by white collar workers, the views and behaviour of manual workers and white collar workers have much in common. Of course, the view of class associated with this position suggests that class is as much about attitudes as it is about position.

From a questionnaire survey of 474 active males, randomly selected in two adjacent wards in Liverpool, Cook et al. (1975/1976, pp. 49-51) found that while there were differences between white collar and blue collar workers in their views of class structure and their position in it, there was also a high degree of overlap. They found little support for the argument that white collar trade unionists have a fundamentally different view of trade unionism from blue collar workers. Both blue collar and white collar workers were found to take a largely instrumental attitude towards trade unionism. White collar workers did not generally see trade unionism as concerned with protecting their privileged positions, although there were differences about tactics between the groups, with more white collar trade unionists believing unions should work with management to raise productivity. Many more white collar workers believed trade unions have too much power (Cook et al., 1975/1976, pp. 56-57).

The above evidence is very interesting and informative. However, one must be wary of reading too much into a fairly limited survey in a politically rather unusual part of Britain. Moreover, there is a theoretical problem with the position advanced, as with the argument of Taylor. Both works look at white collar workers as a block. As a result the potential, if not actual, differences in the positions and interests of various white collar workers are ignored. A much more plausible starting point is to assume that white collar workers are a heterogeneous group and that while the majority of white collar workers have a position in capitalist society and interests which are fundamentally similar to those of manual workers, there are a minority of white collar workers for whom this is not the case. If this assumption is correct it clearly has consequences for the nature of white collar trade unionism. However, before those consequences are fully discussed, it is important to test the plausibility of the assumption being made about white collar workers in advanced capitalist society. To do this a brief examination of the internal structure of local government will be carried out. This will both aid an understanding of the general point under discussion and provide important material for a consideration of the actions of the trade unions in the two councils studied. The examination of the internal structure of local government will lead into an examination of another related and crucial issue: the relationship between white collar trade unionism and professionalism.

Local government

In local government there is a hierarchy of control and power. Traditionally, as Stewart (1986) has argued, local authorities are internally organized on a hierarchical and bureaucratic basis. In local government there are clear layers of responsibility and control. The vast majority of workers are concentrated in the lower, more routine grades. Only a tiny proportion of local government employees occupy the higher professional and senior officer grades, and especially the positions of chief officer and deputy and assistant director, where the sole 'right' exists, in most councils, to offer policy advice and make policy recommendations to councillors. Most council staff, non-manual as well as manual, are denied those formal rights. It is fair to say, I think, that the majority of local authority workers are in 'powerless' positions at their workplaces, experiencing real subordination. This is true of clerical and other low grade office workers and manual workers and may also apply to some professional workers, although this is problematic and an issue which will be discussed in detail later.

If one accepts that most council workers are in a subordinate and powerless position at work, assuming one rejects arguments that they are in those positions for pathological reasons, then it would seem reasonable to argue that those workers have an interest in changing, ending their subordinate positions. It would also seem not unreasonable to suppose that those small number of senior council employees who are in an, at least relatively, powerful and dominant position have an interest in maintaining their powerful and dominant positions. In that case, there would seem to be at least a potential conflict of interests between senior council staff and the majority of council workers. This is so because the majority of subordinate and powerless council workers can only improve, or fundamentally change their position at the expense, to some degree at least, of those in senior positions. Thus the Marxist argument of class struggle at the workplace, while it does not take the same form as in profit making organizations, where the conflict revolves around the nature of the ownership of the means of production and the extraction and realization of surplus value, would seem to apply to local government as it is normally organized.

Professionals and lower managers

However, while routine, low grade office workers may share a common class position in capitalist society with manual workers and top managers may have a very different class position and set of interests, what is the position of professional and lower management and supervisory workers? To consider that issue a number of theoretical works will be outlined and critically assessed, as simple empirical observations will not provide an adequate answer.

Erik Olin Wright, from a reformulated Marxist position, argues that professional and managerial workers in capitalist society have interests which are fundamentally different from those of workers (Wright, 1985, p. 285). For Wright, class is based on relations of exploitation. Exploitation occurs whenever one group, class, in society gains material privileges at the expense of another group, or class. For exploitation to occur the economic privileges of one class must rest upon, and result from, the labour of another class (Wright, 1985, pp. 65-75). Wright argues some groups of workers are in a contradictory class location in that they are both exploiters and exploited (Wright, 1985, pp. 86-89).

Wright sees three basic forms of economic exploitation under capitalism - those based on ownership of physical production assets, those based on the control of organization assets and those based on the ownership of skill assets. Those owning physical production assets have a direct material interest in preventing those physical assets being taken off them, for those owning such assets are able to employ wage-labour and extract surplus value from those they employ. People owning skill assets have an interest in preventing those without such assets acquiring them. If skill assets are scarce then those owning them are able to gain a higher income and to exploit those without skill assets in the sense that their higher income is won at the expense of those lacking skill assets. People controlling organization assets are able to co-ordinate and control the complex division of labour in organizations and, sometimes, between them. Control of organization assets, for Wright, is a basis of exploitation because non-managers and non-bureaucrats would be better off and managers and bureaucrats worse off if the control of the organization were taken away from the managers or bureaucrats and made democratic. Moreover, through their control of organization assets managers and bureaucrats are able to control part or all of the economic surplus which is socially produced (Wright, 1985, pp. 64-82).

The argument of Wright fits into many of the other analyses of professionalism, especially as it relates to British local government, which are advanced. Writers like Paul Hoggett (1984) have argued that professional workers have immense power because of their usurpation and exercise of knowledge. The professional exercise of knowledge, for Hoggett, gives professional workers the ability to control and appropriate resources and to limit what is considered to be possible. The exercise of professional knowledge creates a relationship of dependency between the professional workers and the client users of the services provided by the professionals. (Similar arguments are advanced by Esland, 1980, pp. 213-214.)

Alan Fox (1974) has distinguished between jobs with low discretion, those with middle level discretion and those with high discretion. Taking up Fox's conception, Salaman (1979, pp. 73-76) has argued that professionals and academics, along with managers, are in jobs with high level discretion; that is, they have jobs where the worker has a high degree of 'trustworthiness'. Such jobs involve the political application of professional knowledge, which is not neutral, but is applied and developed in the interests of the existing social order. For Salaman (1979, p. 151), professional workers aim to maximize their autonomy and resist the imposition of bureaucratic control and work patterns. They try to secure their own interests. He accepts that this can sometimes lead professional workers into conflict with the bureaucratic control of their work practices.

Martin Laffin (1986, p. 23) distinguishes between public service professionals, such as teachers, social workers, housing managers and town planners who are involved in welfare or the regulation of 'external' activities and practices in the public interest and technocratic professionals, those who manage and administer public services. Public service professionals he sees as having an orientation in favour of their clients because they are in the 'front line' of service provision. Managers and administrators have an orientation which puts the interests of the organization before that of the client. The claim of managers and administrators to professional status, he argues, helps to underpin their position in the hierarchy. This suggests that professionals at different levels in the public service hierarchy may have different interests and aspirations. However, like Hoggett and

Salaman, Laffin (1986, p. 27) too sees professionals exercising knowledge to increase their power by, among other things, providing unnecessarily complicated and technical advice. He sees professionals as exercising autonomy in three areas: the immediate work situation, in self-regulation and self-government at the level of the profession and in being autonomous sources of influence in the formation and implementation of government policy.

All these analyses suggest that a union like NALGO in local government which represents all levels of white collar workers from the lowest grade clerical assistant to the Director of Services will face contradictory demands because its members have very different interests. However, the analysis of Hoggett suggests that in such unions the interests of the professional and managerial workers will 'win out'. Thus Hoggett (1987) argues NALGO fought to maintain the 'professional privileges' of its members in left wing Labour councils during the 1980s and this accounts for the conflicts between new left Labour councils and NALGO over a host of issues (cf. also Sharron, 1985). However, like Wolmar (1983), who advances a very similar argument to Hoggett, Hoggett accepts that Labour controlled councils, and the councillors in them, failed to develop a distinctively socialist management practice and this may account in part for the actions of NALGO.

In addition, there are those like Peter Dickens (1988) who saw the fight to protect local government in Britain in the 1980s as overwhelmingly an effort by professional and technical workers and managers in local government to protect their interests and positions. It is members of what Dickens calls the 'service class' who, on this argument, have largely defined the terms and nature of the campaigns to defend local government autonomy and democracy. For Dickens (1988, pp. 180-181), it is members of the 'service class' in local government who have managed to protect their positions.

But perhaps of even greater importance has been the influence of the public sector workers themselves. These, in 1980s Britain, were amongst the most powerful sectors of the organized workforce. There are, however, big differences within the public sector. The 'service class' elements of this group (such as teachers, social services workers and upper level white collar managers) remained largely well organized, well unionized and highly influential as regards local government strategy. Others, especially the blue collar manual workers, were in a considerably weaker position and were much less able to defend themselves from attacks.

For Dickens, it was manual and low grade, low paid council workers and users of council services who suffered from the cut backs in local government spending in the 1980s and the restrictions on local government activity. Dickens (1988, p. 145) argues,

> White-collar public sector workers (arguably one of the most powerful groupings in terms of influence on contemporary government policy) have strengthened their position in the process: on occasion at the expense of those groups of people for whom the original demands were made.

However, there are major problems in lumping all professional, technical and top managerial workers together in one 'service class' as Dickens does. For, as I will argue in detail later, there are differences of interests between and within professional and technical workers and managers (as Laffin's analysis strongly suggests). Professionals, technicians and managers in local government in the 1980s were affected by changes in local government in different ways, with many social workers' and teachers' jobs coming under increasing management control (cf. Bolger, Corrigan, Docking and Frost, 1981 and Joyce, Corrigan and Hayes, 1988 in respect of social workers and the provisions of *The Education Reform Act* 1988 and Simon, 1989 in respect of teachers).

Critique of the analysis of professionalism

Many of the arguments advanced about professionalism have, on the surface, much validity. While Laffin's distinction between 'public service professionals' and 'technocratic professionals' has great force and the position of Wright seems useful in trying to understand the bases of class cleavages in advanced capitalist society, nevertheless, it seems hard to see how professional workers in non-managerial positions have interests which differ fundamentally from those of routine office workers and manual workers. If, as Wright argues, those without organization resources will benefit from the democratization of the work process, why should this not benefit professionals like social workers whose control over their work activity is limited as they do not control how resources are distributed and are under external pressure to produce satisfactory results on criteria often not decided by them? Moreover, if one accepts the de-skilling thesis of Harry Braverman (1974) it has to be questioned how far the ownership of skill resources can be taken as a basis of exploitation in advanced capitalist society. Braverman's thesis is that since the end of the nineteenth century, with the advent of scientific management, there has been a particularly strong trend, an overriding imperative, within capitalism for management to systematically strive to reduce the control workers have over their work so as to increase the rate of surplus value (the unpaid labour of workers) and with it profits. At first this strategy was applied to skilled manual workers but it then advanced to encompass office and other workers. The strategy of management, spurred on by the imperatives of capital accumulation, has led to the wholesale de-skilling of jobs, Braverman argues.

Braverman's thesis has been heavily criticized (cf., for example, Wood, 1982). There clearly are problems with the thesis in its most extreme form, for empirical evidence shows employers adopting a number of control strategies and in some cases workers have proved very successful in retaining job controls and even avoiding de-skilling (cf. Wood, 1982 and Thompson, 1983). Moreover, it is argued that skill is not a purely objective entity, the sum of a number of positive, distinct factors, but socially constructed, the result of the ability or inability of groups of workers to win recognition from employers and the state that their jobs are skilled (cf. for example, Beechey, 1982, pp. 62-67). However, many of the measures introduced by Kenneth Baker when he was Secretary of State for Education in the 1980s, for example, (the introduction of the national curriculum, and the loss of teachers' control over what is taught in schools, the greater assessment of teachers' performance, the direct imposition of pay awards, the extension of merit pay and so on) can be seen as an effort to de-skill and 'proletarianize' teachers in Britain (cf. Simon, 1989). If there is a strong de-skilling tendency in capitalist society, because of the need to increase labour productivity and to reduce costs, and applies to public services as much as profit making businesses, then the position of public service professionals generally, and not just teachers, may not be very secure. As a result, the interests of such workers may not be as different from those of routine office and manual workers as at first sight they appear to be. Conclusions on the applicability of Braverman's de-skilling thesis to the position of professional workers are, however, highly provisional.

The changing face of NALGO

Having considered some of the theoretical analyses of the position of professional workers, it is now possible to apply the insights gained to the question of whether NALGO was likely, because it works to uphold the interests of its professional members, to be a blocking force on the introduction of radical change in local government. To aid that analysis, NALGO's development as a trade union since the 1960s will be briefly outlined.

It seems that the nature of NALGO changed in the late 1960s, as the result of growing central government interference in local government pay bargaining and the growth of organizations like the National Economic Development Council which had TUC representation along with representation from the government and the employers and discussed a range of economic questions. Non-TUC affiliated unions were debarred from membership of the NEDC. NALGO's joining the TUC can be seen very much as a reaction to those developments. The union wanted to both protect the pay of its members and be involved in the national level negotiations with government more generally. Both considerations led logically to TUC affiliation, something the union had vigorously avoided up till then (cf. Undy, Ellis, McCarthy, Halmos, 1981; Newman, 1982; Fryer, 1989). The changing nature of local government management, such as the introduction of corporate planning and corporate management, which led to a more 'authoritarian' management style in local government, also contributed to the growing radicalization of NALGO and its members, it is argued (cf. Joyce, Corrigan and Hayes, 1988). From the early 1970s NALGO nationally became increasingly prepared to support industrial action by sections of its membership (cf. Newman, 1982; Joyce, Corrigan and Hayes, 1988).

NALGO members in local government, as well as being more prepared to take industrial action since the early 1970s and the national leadership being more prepared to support such action, also played a leading part in campaigns against public spending cuts in the late 1970s and early 1980s (cf. Fryer, 1979 and Joyce, Corrigan and Hayes, 1988). The public spending cuts of the 1970s contributed strongly to the more radical stance adopted by NALGO and its becoming what might be seen as a 'real' trade union. Up to the late 1960s, NALGO was very much a union for professional council officers who saw their positions at work as very non-political (cf., for example, Newman, 1982). Such people did not regard NALGO as part of the labour movement. The growing radicalization of NALGO was associated from the mid 1970s with the development of a strong shop stewards organization in many local government branches (cf. Newman, 1982). The radicalization of local government professions, mentioned in chapter 2, also helped to produce a more radical stance in NALGO. It is also interesting that while NALGO consistently voted not to affiliate to the Labour Party, there was overwhelming support for the setting up of a political fund among NALGO members in 1988.

Of course, NALGO's growing militancy could be seen, on the one hand, as an effort to protect the interests of its privileged professional members which were threatened by the financial and other restrictions and controls introduced in the 1980s in local government, as well as by the actions of new urban left councils. On the other hand, NALGO's growing militancy in the 1980s could be seen as a recognition that its members interests', including those of professional workers, lay in forging links with other workers and the users of council services. Certainly, if the above discussion of professionalism provokes any conclusions, even if they are only tentative, one of them would be that there seems little theoretical reason why NALGO's actions in trying to protect the interests of its members, professional and non-professional alike, should make the union any more opposed to the introduction of radical policies in local government than the manual local government unions. For most NALGO members do not exercise control over the workings of local services in the way Hoggett and others argue. Moreover, in a hostile political climate the union's members will need all the allies they can get if their interests are not to be greatly undermined.

That argument is supported by NALGO joining with the manual unions NUPE and COHSE to form Unison. The link perhaps shows the acceptance by NALGO's members that the union was part of the labour movement and the acceptance by other unions of NALGO's place in the labour movement. Certainly the formation of Unison even thirty years ago would have been impossible given the views of NALGO members and the place of NALGO in the trade union movement.

Trade union defensiveness

The issue of whether NALGO, in trying to protect the privileges of professionals, acted as a negative force in left wing Labour councils in the 1980s has an echo in arguments about the essentially defensive nature of trade unions. A consideration of some of the theoretical arguments on that issue may well aid an understanding of the actions of trade unions in new urban left councils. For many writers put forward the view that trade unions are essentially concerned with protecting their hard won gains. There are commentators, writing from a Marxist and from non-Marxist positions, who have argued that trade unions are essentially defensive and reactive organizations.

Among Marxist writers, Lenin (1902) viewed trade unions as essentially concerned with making gains within the confines of the capitalist system. For Lenin, workers, on their own, would only be able to achieve 'trade union consciousness', which involved striving for higher wages and welfare benefits. For a socialist consciousness to be achieved by workers a socialist party, manned by committed revolutionaries and 'intellectuals' was required. It should perhaps be noted that in other works Lenin took a more charitable view of trade union activity and saw it as helping to raise the consciousness of workers (cf. Lenin, 1899, 1905 and 1917). Among modern Marxists, Perry Anderson (1967) argues that trade unions can never become a vehicle for socialist advance because their aim is to bargain concessions within the capitalist system. Trade unions have only very limited aims. For him, strikes are negative, a withdrawal, whereas socialism requires an over-participation in the capitalist system which will abolish it and produce a new social order.

From a non-Marxist position, writers like Colin Crouch (1982) also see the trade unions as essentially defensive organizations. For Crouch (1982, pp. 122-123), even many supposedly radical trade union initiatives like the Clyde Workers Committee in the First World War, which supported demands for workers' control are basically a defensive response to outside events. For, Crouch argues, the Clyde Workers Committee was as much concerned with preventing the dilution of skilled jobs as about promoting workers' control. The 1973-1974 miners' strike he also sees as basically defensive because it was concerned about improving the position of miners in the wages league. The action was not concerned with achieving radical social change (Crouch, 1982, p. 124). For him, new goals will be adopted in place of old ones only when their relative attractiveness is very high because unions will set a high price on the risk of novelty. 'Workers' actions will usually be incremental, concerned with short-term advantage within known parameters' (Crouch, 1982, p. 131). Trade union action is very unlikely to be revolutionary and the more successful the trade unions are the more their practices encourage acceptance of the capitalist system (Crouch, 1982, pp. 127-138).

These and similar arguments have much to commend them. Yet if trade unions are simply defensive organizations how can one account for the gains that unions are allegedly fighting to maintain for their members? Unless one believes, that is, that workers gains are due to the beneficence of employers or the state! In any case the defence of working-class gains by trade unions can often require the making of new gains. The argument that democratic gains can only be maintained if new ones are added to the list can be applied in respect of trade union gains, if it has any validity at all. Moreover, trade unions can take a more 'proactive' stance, as the example of the Lucas Aerospace Shop Stewards Corporate Plan showed (cf. Wainwright and Elliott, 1982). The workers there came forward with proposals and detailed plans to produce 'socially useful' goods. The employers, however, refused to negotiate with the shop stewards on their plan and management exercised their right to manage in the interests of the private owners of the company. Similarly, plans were adopted by workers at Vickers and in the school meals service in Haringey (cf. Beynon and Wainwright, 1979 and Blunkett and Jackson, 1987, p. 125). Moreover, in the early 1970s the workers at Upper Clyde Shipbuilders threatened with redundancy through the closure of the shipyards occupied the yards and started a 'work-in' to maintain their jobs and prevent closure of the yards. Similar action subsequently occurred in a number of other works in the 1970s (cf. Coates, 1981).

These actions, while a reaction to management decisions, can be seen as a direct threat to management's right to manage and to the logic of the capitalist market with its insistence that enterprises close if they cannot be operated at a profit. But the actions, in a sense, were highly defensive with the workers involved trying to defend their jobs. It is perhaps unfair, therefore, to view trade unions as defensive organizations *per se* or to regard all defensive trade union action as necessarily supporting the capitalist system. Trade unions do, however, basically tend to react to initiatives from elsewhere, employers or the state, for instance, and the reactions are often defensive and very limited in terms of extending workers' control, as the case study material will confirm.

Conclusion

From the evidence advanced it would seem that the majority of wage labourers do have an interest in seeing social change so that their subordinate positions can be ended. It also seems that those who have gained power and privileges at the expense of those in subordinate positions have an interest in maintaining existing social inequalities and the mode of production from which these social inequalities derive. Whether workers have the ability to bring about the changes which would end their subordination at work and in the wider society is more problematical. It would seem that most workers do have interests which are, at the very least, not incompatible with the general interest. This means that there is no intrinsic reason why a Labour government trying to promote the general interest should not have good relations with the trade unions. Nor is there any reason in principle why a left wing Labour council should have poor relations with any of the council trade unions. There would seem to be little evidence to suggest that non-Labour Party affiliated trade unions are more likely, simply because they are not affiliated to the Labour Party, to oppose the radical policies of a Labour government or a Labour council.

However, while trade unions can play a proactive and 'aggressive' role at the workplace, unions are often defensive organizations which react to measures introduced or proposed by employers and the state. Unions are wary of changes which attack in any way their industrial or bargaining freedom. It may also be that whatever their 'objective' position, groups of workers may feel they have an interest in fighting to maintain the status quo. If a group of workers feel that their interests are threatened in a negative way they will fight to prevent this. This may be one way of analyzing the disputes between new left Labour councils and NALGO members. The disputes may not be due so much to NALGO trying to protect professional privileges as to the union's members seeing changes being introduced at their expense, without any compensating benefits and their union, in traditional trade union style, fighting to protect its members' interests. If the interests of manual workers had been threatened in the same way, disputes between Labour councils and the manual unions may have ensued. Moreover, if one accepts, as argued in chapter 2, that the radicalization of local government professions was one of the factors feeding into the new urban left, then this radicalization is likely to have affected a union like NALGO too. If that is true, the union is unlikely to oppose radical policies proposed by left councils on principle. If NALGO has opposed radical policies, this may tell us as much about the failures of new left Labour councillors as employers as it does about NALGO.

The insights into the nature of trade unionism outlined above and the speculations about left Labour councils and the council trade unions will now be applied to the case studies I have conducted into industrial relations in Sheffield and Doncaster councils which will be set out later in the work. A dialectical process will be used in analyzing the case study. The case study will be used to test some of the insights set out in this chapter and those insights in turn will be used to explain the case studies.

5 Outline of Doncaster and Sheffield Councils

Doncaster and Sheffield are located in the county of South Yorkshire. Doncaster Borough Council and Sheffield City Council, as presently organized, were created by the 1972 Local Government Act. As a result of that Act a number of smaller councils were brought together to form the much larger Metropolitan Borough Councils of Doncaster and Sheffield. Like all other metropolitan borough councils, Doncaster Borough Council and Sheffield City Council have control over the following main services: council housing; personal social services; recreation and leisure; libraries and museums; environmental health; planning; education and some responsibility for highway and road maintenance.

Different community profiles

Both councils are, and have been since 1974, controlled by Labour councillors. In Doncaster, of the 63 councillors on the council in 1988, no less than 54 were Labour - the remaining nine seats were held by Conservatives. In Sheffield in 1988 of the 87 council seats, 66 were held by Labour, 12 by Conservatives and nine by Liberal Democrats. However, despite the broad similarity in party political make up, the two councils cover very different areas and populations. While Doncaster Council covered a population of 290,100, Sheffield Council covered a population nearly twice as large at 532,000. Sheffield is the fourth largest city in England. It has been defined both as the largest village in England and the first and most complete proletarian city in the country. Doncaster is an ancient market town surrounded by traditionally coal mining dominated villages. Sheffield's rateable value in 1988 was over twice that of Doncaster at £66,689,687 compared to £29,671,639. The rate in Sheffield was also higher at 347.27p, compared with 301.74p in Doncaster. While Doncaster Council had a debt of £208,000,000, the debt associated with Sheffield Council stood at £225,856,977 (cf. *Municipal Yearbook 1989*, vol. 2, pp. 971-972 and 998-999).

The Sheffield Labour Movement

The new leadership in Sheffield Council after 1980 was in many ways the product of, and linked into, changes which occurred in the Sheffield Labour movement. In the 1980s the prominence of the steel unions in Sheffield labour movement politics declined in parallel with the decline in steel industry employment - down from 39,000 in 1979 to 13,000 in 1987 on the estimate of Sheffield City Council (Sheffield City Council Department of Employment, 1987). The largest affiliated branches to the Trades Union Council in Sheffield in 1985 were the NALGO Sheffield council branch, NUPE branches and branches from the white collar union ASTMS (cf. Goodwin, 1985, Table 1, p. 32). In the past that body and its predecessor the Trades and Labour Council, was dominated by manual worker unions from steel and engineering. Unions like NUPE and NALGO, with large memberships in the council were concerned about, put a great emphasis on and wanted an input into, developments in the council. Moreover, the city council in the 1980s became the biggest employer in the city, which helped to move council politics to the centre of labour movement politics.

In the late 1970s and 1980s, there was an influx of new younger and more radical elements into the Sheffield Labour Party, as Goodwin (1985, p. 30) argues. Seyd's research into Hallam and Attercliffe CLPs largely supported Goodwin's argument although he found the 'activists' in Attercliffe were considerably older than those in Hallam (Seyd, 1987, pp. 65-75). These new elements were very concerned about issues of accountability in the Labour Party and the relationship between the City Council Labour Group and the District Labour Party. It was in part as a result of an effort to change the relationship between the DLP and the Labour Group and to increase rank and file Labour Party involvement in council activities that the new leadership came to power in Sheffield Council in 1980, as argued in an earlier chapter.

From the mid 1960s, in addition, it appears that a more open and 'democratic' form of leadership within Sheffield City Council Labour Group developed. The change was associated with the election of Ron Ironmonger as leader of the Labour Group in 1966, as he inaugurated a more open style on the council (cf. Hampton, 1978). The defeat of the Labour Party in the 1968 council elections, and the splits between the Labour Group and council tenants which preceded the electoral set back, may also have helped to 'open up' local government in the city (cf. Blunkett cited in Seyd, 1987, p. 144 and also Hampton, 1970, pp. 246-277 for details of the split).

South Yorkshire radicalism questioned

Alcock and Lee (1981) in their article on South Yorkshire questioned the nature of the radicalism in the county. While accepting that Sheffield council moved to the left from the late 1960s, they still saw traditional 'labourist' practices influencing labour movement politics. For example, they defined the cheap fares policy pursued by South Yorkshire County Council, in the following terms, 'a combination of a basic desire to continue to administer services in the interests of the working-class (as perceived by the Labour politicians!) combined with a fierce political and regional independence' (Alcock and Lee, 1981, p. 81). A similar point was made by Child and Paddon (1984). They stressed the parochialism and insularity of Sheffield labour movement politics and saw that as both a strength and a weakness. One of the weaknesses was the difficulty in responding to changes in the local economy and the local workforce. It was against that specific background of what might be called 'paternalistic radicalism' that the leadership of Sheffield City Council after 1980 attempted to achieve its aims. Many of the comments of David Blunkett, set out elsewhere in this work, can be seen as a recognition of the need to move away from the paternalism or 'bossism' associated with South Yorkshire Labour politics, even in its more radical guise.

The position in Doncaster

It appears that the type of changes which occurred in Sheffield labour movement politics did not happen in Doncaster. (Incidentally, the information on Doncaster labour movement has come mainly from interviews with councillors, council officers, trade union representatives and informed academics.) While the two immediate past leaders of Doncaster Council were graduates and the chair of the Education committee at the time of the research was a teacher, the culture and style of operation of Doncaster Council did not seem to have changed greatly. The type of changes inaugurated by the leadership of Ron Ironmonger in Sheffield and accentuated and given a much more radical content by the leadership after 1980, did not seem to have occurred in Doncaster Council. Doncaster Council over the years was dominated by a closed style of council leadership and an 'economistic' outlook. The traditional 'coal mining culture' associated with Doncaster Council was not basically affected either by changes in the council leadership, changes in the local trade union movement (associated with the decline of coal mining in the area) or by changes in the Labour Party. The 'coal mining culture' is one of deep loyalty to the labour movement, a strong sense of community inclusiveness and exclusiveness, 'macho' hardness and discipline (cf., for example, Dennis, Henriques and Slaughter, 1969).

The paternalism or 'bossism', which Alcock and Lee associated with South Yorkshire politics, appeared to have survived in Doncaster in its less radical form. That may help to explain why, as will be shown in subsequent chapters, Doncaster Council did not 'take up' in a big way many of the issues associated with the new urban left, such as equal opportunities policies and try to increase user and producer democracy.

The 'frame of reference' of the Sheffield and Doncaster councils also appeared to be very different. My strong impression, acquired during my fieldwork, was that while Sheffield Council compared itself with councils and areas the size of Manchester, Birmingham, Newcastle and Bristol, Doncaster Council compared itself with surrounding areas in South Yorkshire, such as Rotherham and Barnsley. Those differences in conception seem to be a cause for conflict and contention, certainly within Doncaster Council. For the impression I gained from interviewing councillors and officers in Doncaster Council, was that they regarded Sheffield as having 'pretensions' and 'aspirations above its station'. The 'frame of reference' of the two councils may be important in explaining their overall different approaches.

Formal industrial relations structures

Having summarized the most relevant differences between the two areas and sketched the changes in the local labour movements, it is now necessary to consider the formal industrial relations procedures in the councils. In Doncaster Borough Council there was a union-management agreement covering the manual and craft workers but not Administrative, Professional, Technical and Clerical (APT and C) staff. In Sheffield City Council there were union-management agreements covering manual and craft workers and APT and C staff. There were many similarities in the industrial relations procedures of the two councils. Both had formally laid out disciplinary procedures which involved a series of stages. In both councils there were bodies for consulting with groups of workers. For workers who were dissatisfied, there were grievance procedures in both councils. However, within these structures which were common to both councils, there were big differences in the formal industrial relations procedures in the two councils. On the face of it, the variations reflected different emphases placed by the two councils on different aspects of industrial relations. Setting out the formal procedures of the two councils will provide an essential backdrop to an understanding of the attitudes expressed by, and the experience of, different people in the case study of industrial relations in Sheffield City Council and Doncaster Borough Council.

Grievance procedures

Doncaster Borough Council had a grievance procedure which aimed at resolving issues quickly at the lowest possible level in the council hierarchy. A worker aggrieved about an employment issue took the issue up first with his or her foreman or supervisor. If dissatisfied about the result, the employee should approach his or her trade union who would then re-approach the foreman or supervisor. If the response was still unsatisfactory, a meeting would be arranged with the Director, or a nominee, of the department concerned. If there was still a feeling of grievance, the worker could take the matter to the Grievance Sub-Committee of the council. From then on further procedure would be within the appropriate conciliation machinery. There were short time limits governing all the stages outlined. Those could be extended provided both sides agreed.

Once an appeal reached the Appeals and Grievance Sub-Committee a further number of stages could ensue, if agreement was not reached. Both sides could prepare a written statement for the committee and call witnesses. The appellant could be represented by a trade union official or someone else of his or her choosing. Witnesses for one side could be questioned by the other and by members of the committee. The sub-committee, consisting of councillors and its secretary, would discuss the appeal in private, after both sides had produced their evidence, and convey the decision to the appellant.

The grievance procedure for individual workers was similar in Sheffield City Council to that set out above for Doncaster Borough Council. In the case of Sheffield Council there were four internal stages of the grievance procedure. The first stage was where a matter was taken up with a supervisor or manager. The second stage was implemented if the first one failed to produce a satisfactory conclusion. Here the chief officer or head of department became involved. If this stage brought no resolution, the matter then proceeded, if the worker wished, to elected member level. At stage three, matters were referred to the chair or vice-chair of the relevant programme committee. From there an appeal could travel to the Appeals Panel of the Personnel Services Sub-Committee. If no resolution was agreed at this level then a dispute could be referred to the Provincial Council of the Local Government Whitley Council or even to the National Committee.

Similar rights of external appeal applied in Doncaster Council. There were time limits in the procedures in Sheffield, as in Doncaster, within which appeals were meant to be processed. In both councils, councillors become involved only at a fairly late stage and were supposed to act as 'independent umpires'. Whether this is a role councillors can really play will be discussed later.

Disciplinary procedures

In Sheffield Council, the aim was for matters to be discussed on an informal basis to avoid formal warnings. Once again, there were a number of stages of the disciplinary procedures, unless an employee was dismissed for gross misconduct. At the first stage, a supervisor or manager should issue a formal oral warning. If the misconduct were repeated, or other misconduct ensued, a further warning should be issued in writing. At this level the worker would be interviewed and given a chance to answer the charges. A statement would be issued saying that any further misconduct would lead to a final warning. If misconduct continued, the worker would be given another written warning which, in appropriate circumstances, would be a final warning. Once again, the worker would be interviewed and given the chance to explain the misconduct. If misconduct continued the worker would be dismissed by an authorised manager. At any stage a worker could appeal against a disciplinary decision. If the worker wanted to appeal further he or she could take the matter to the council's Appeals Panel where the matter would be dealt with by councillors. Once again, there were time limits attached to the procedure.

In Doncaster Council, a similar system operated, although a final warning was normally given after a second case of misconduct and not after three examples. Again there were time limits to the procedure, as to the appeals procedure. Workers had the right to appeal at any stage against a disciplinary decision to the council's Appeals and Grievance Sub-Committee where councillors would be present and hear the appeal. The decision of the Appeals and Grievance Sub-Committee was final. There were very strict time limits on appeals to the Appeals and Grievance Sub-Committee. Councillors were expected to act as neutral umpires.

Negotiating machinery

In Doncaster Borough Council, there existed Departmental Employees' Joint Committees for manual workers. Similar structures existed for white collar workers. The equivalent bodies in Sheffield City Council were Local Joint Committees which covered all workers, although there were committees for different groups of workers (manual and craft, APT and C and teachers all had their own committees). In Doncaster, the Departmental Employees' Joint Committees for manual employees consisted of three employers' side representatives, including the chair or vice-chair of the appropriate service committee. The employees side varied according to the trade union representation in different departments. The chair and vice-chairs of each committee alternated annually between the employers' side and the employees' side. At any one time the chair would be from one side while the vice-chair would be from the other. The terms of reference of the committees were to provide a forum for discussion between members of the directorate's service committee and trade union representatives of manual workers in the directorate on matters of mutual interest, including prevention and reconciliation of differences. In addition, the DEJCs considered the terms and conditions of service of employees covered by the committee. A committee also considered any relevant matters referred to it by the council, a committee of the council, the council's Manual Employees' Joint Committee or a trade union representative on the committee. If the sides could not agree to adjourn, matters of dispute would be sent to the main Manual Employees' Joint Committee.

The Manual Employees' Joint Committee in Doncaster Council had nine members appointed by the trade unions and nine by the council. The chair and vice-chair alternated annually between the two sides. At any one time the chair would come from one side and the vice-chair from the other. The committee provided a forum for discussion between members of the council and representatives of manual employees on matters of mutual interest, including the prevention of differences and recommendations to the council on the terms and conditions of service and other matters relating to the employment of manual workers. The Minutes of the Departmental Employees' Joint Committees went to the MEJC, where they were either approved, referred back or recommendations were made arising out of the minutes. This committee also dealt with any matters referred to it by the council, a department, a Departmental Employees' Joint Committee, or a trade union represented on the committee. If the two sides could not reach agreement on any issue the differences were recorded and the matter sent to the Disputes Procedure of the Appropriate National Agreement, unless they agreed to adjourn the meeting. For white collar workers the equivalent body was the Joint Staff Consultative Committee.

In Sheffield City Council, there was no equivalent of the MEJC. The Local Joint Committees (LJCs) in Sheffield acted as a forum for communication, consultation and negotiation between the council and the trade unions on all matters relevant to the employment group, including the ratification of any negotiating arrangements delegated to the Programme Liaison Committee and any other Joint Committee. The council had six members on each LJC and the trade union members were drawn from the relevant trade unions. The chair and vice-chair alternated annually between the two sides. When the chair was from one side, the vice-chair was from the other.

At other levels in the formal procedure in Sheffield City Council, there was provision for the existence of Programme Liaison Committees (PLCs). The aim was that those committees should reflect the Programme Committee structure on the council and bring together the political leadership and all trade unions relating to each programme area. In those committees the aim was for there to be consultation and communication on all relevant matters. Negotiation would only take place in areas specifically delegated by the relevant LJCs, however. The aim was for there to be six councillors and trade union representatives from the departmental Shop Stewards Committee on the PLCs. However, the PLCs made a very cautious start and did not develop as envisaged, according to those I interviewed. In the document *Industrial Relations, A New Procedural Framework* it was envisaged that a Corporate Joint Committee would be set up. This would include the political leadership and all trade unions in a single forum to communicate and consult on issues such as implementing the manifesto, budget strategy, issues raised by central government policy and so on which were important to the council and its workforce. My field work findings show that this body was not a great success in bringing about the community of interests between the council and its workforce and the trade unions which was the aim. It never worked as envisaged by the Chief Personnel Officer who proposed it. However, the Programme Liaison Committees and the Corporate Joint Committee represented a novel advance and, on the face of it, should have given the workers, through their trade unions, a real involvement and influence in major policy decisions. Why the reality was different, or why many of those interviewed believed the reality was very different, is something that will be discussed in detail later.

Other procedural differences

In Sheffield Council, the Personnel Department had overall control of the personnel issues effecting all employees. In Doncaster, the

Personnel Section had ultimate control of personnel matters for all groups of workers except teachers. Personnel matters affecting teachers were dealt with by the Education Department and the Chief Education Officer. Also, in Sheffield, there were representatives of the Chief Personnel Officer in all departments. Those representatives were called Principal Industrial Relations Officers and there were Personnel Officers in each department below this level. The personnel and industrial relations system within departments existed to aid good industrial relations and was a sign of the overt commitment given to the promotion of good industrial relations by Sheffield City Council. There was no equivalent system in Doncaster Council. While the Chief Executive had ultimate responsibility for industrial relations matters in Doncaster, in Sheffield, this responsibility rested with the Chief Personnel Officer.

Importance of industrial relations for Sheffield Council

The aims behind the new industrial relations procedure introduced in Sheffield in the mid 1980s show the importance given to industrial relations by the council, in principle at least. One key objective was set out in Point 2.3 of the document, *Industrial Relations, A New Procedural Framework*, as follows :

> Establish procedures which emphasise the partnership of the Council and all its workers through the trades unions at a time of unprecedented crisis and change, breaking down class divisions between workers and ensuring single status for all employees (Sheffield City Council, 1986b, p. 51).

The document showed a commitment to 'introduce trade union representation on council committees' (Sheffield City Council, 1986b, p. 51). The council also gave a commitment to 'Support the establishment of a Joint Shop Stewards Committee within the Council as an integral part of the corporate industrial relations framework' (Sheffield City Council, 1986b, p. 51). Similar commitments were not to be found in Doncaster's formal industrial relations documents.

Having placed the two councils in their social, economic and political contexts, and outlined the formal industrial relations procedures in the two councils, I will, in the next three chapters, set out the findings of my case study. The views of those interviewed will be described and analyzed in respect of a number of themes.

6 The General Industrial Relations Position

The findings of the field work will be set out in this and the following chapters. The results will be presented under a series of themes. In most cases the responses of councillors in Sheffield and Doncaster will be considered before the attitudes of trade union representatives and then council officers are examined. In this way it will be possible to compare and contrast the responses from members of the different groups within the two councils and across the councils. It will be possible to compare attitudes of say councillors in Sheffield and Doncaster with those of trade union representatives in the two councils to see if there are common views within the same groups and differences between groups. It will also be possible to compare the approaches of councillors in Sheffield with those of councillors in Doncaster, for example. Where responses relating to just one department in one council are concerned they will be handled in a slightly different way as will issues concerning the way in which union representatives view their relationship with other unions.

Council as good employer

Councillors

All the councillors whom I interviewed, in both councils, believed their council tried to be a good employer. However, many of them accepted the aim was not always fulfilled. Councillors in Sheffield, after claiming the council tried to be a good employer, added caveats, such as 'but I'm not sure it always succeeds'. Some implicitly accepted there had probably been more rhetoric than achievement in many areas. The development of good service delivery was seen as the council's main job by a number of Sheffield councillors and being a good employer was a means to that end. As one councillor put it 'The aim is to provide good services but that doesn't mean the need to be a good employer is ignored'. Another councillor believed the council had to be a good employer to provide good services, but as the priority was good service delivery, workers' demands sometimes had to be refused. While accepting Sheffield Council tried to promote good industrial relations practices, a leading councillor said he was not sure if such a thing as a model employer existed. He saw the biggest problem socialists face in local or national government as coming to terms with being an employer, 'There's nothing harder than being an employer, especially if you've a background in the unions'. This councillor stressed the importance not just for councils to be model employers but for employees of Labour councils to be model employees, 'It cuts both ways. They need to show some commitment to the council'.

Among councillors in Doncaster there was unanimity that the council tried to be a good employer. Terms and conditions provided by the council were often better than those laid down in national and provincial agreements. There was an acceptance, however, that financial constraints limited what the council could achieve. The then Leader of the Council saw industrial relations as good in all departments, with very little variation between them. This view was backed up by the other Doncaster councillors interviewed.

There was a fairly common view, therefore, among councillors that their council tried to be a good employer. One or two views were expressed, however, which raise bigger issues, relating to the compatibility of being a good employer and providing good services, whether formal objectives were put into practice, the responsibilities of council workers and financial constraints. It is interesting that these issues were raised by councillors independently of any prompting from me, for they open up major issues about the purposes of local government and the way those purposes should be achieved. These issues, and respondents' views on them, will be considered later. For now, it is important to see if council officers and trade union representatives had views about whether their council was a good employer which differ from those of the councillors.

Trade Unionists

There was more variety of view expressed by trade unionists on this issue than by councillors. To some degree the differences cut across the divide between manual and non-manual trade union representatives, as well as reflecting differences between these two broad groups.

A Sheffield shop steward for a manual workers trade union was very critical of the attitude and practice of councillors. 'Councillors still treat workers as dirt', was the comment made. It was felt that councillors were too cut off from what was happening in day to day council affairs. Some manual worker trade union representatives argued that budget constraints were used by the council to avoid doing things on the industrial relations front. However, other manual worker shop stewards were more complimentary and enthusiastic. For one shop steward, the council set out to be a good employer and to produce good industrial relations. 'I'm not sure that has been the result of these [industrial relations] changes', was the conclusion reached, however. Another shop steward argued that *Working for Sheffield, The Industrial Relations Framework* and other measures introduced in the mid 1980s showed the council's efforts to create an overall corporate approach. For this person, those developments showed the council had definitely tried to be a model employer, 'there's no question about that'.

With regard to NALGO shop stewards in Sheffield, reactions on this issue were mixed. A branch officer accepted that the council tried to be a good employer on paper. The commitment went no further than that, however: 'It's all talk but very little action to back it up'. Another, while accepting the paper commitment, believed there were problems due to the size and nature of the organization. 'Leading Labour councillors have certainly had it in mind theoretically to be a good employer. But not much thinking has been done about what socialist management would mean', was a comment from that Sheffield NALGO shop steward. A very sceptical view was adopted by a NALGO steward in the Family and Community Service Department who believed the council tried to be a good employer provided this requirement did not conflict with its financial commitments: 'They'll say they're committed to doing things but if it costs them any money, that's a different matter'. A more positive view, however, was expressed by a NALGO steward in the Recreation Department. For that person the council's intention to be a good employer was expressed in developments like *Take Ten* (an educational initiative, which will be considered later), the Low Pay Scheme and Single Status.

In Doncaster the manual worker union representatives, full-time and lay, all regarded the council at councillor level as trying to promote good industrial relations and to make the council a good employer. There was an agreement with councillors on this, as there was on the way financial constraints often prevented aims in this area being fulfilled. A NUPE representative argued that problems sometimes arose because councillors' aims did not always filter down to, or were not always accurately reflected by, senior council officers. As he said: 'The councillors may want to do something in a certain way but when it gets to the officers things don't always turn out as the councillors wanted'.

On the NALGO side in Doncaster, views were uniformly hostile or at least sceptical on this issue. For one steward, the council tried to be a good employer in theory. It liked to create jobs for the unemployed. In practice, however, the council disregarded its workforce and did just what it wanted, irrespective of union views. As an example of council heavy-handedness, this steward cited the council's determination to implement the Job Training Scheme in the council (a central government scheme in the 1980s for unemployed school leavers to gain some form of work training), despite the opposition of the council trade unions. Another steward argued that the failure of the council to take anybody else's views into account made the council a bad employer in practice. Hence the council's subconscious efforts to be a good employer were worthless in practice. 'They [councillors] don't want to know what the workers think. Once they've made their mind up that's it. They think they know it all'. This steward argued that NALGO activists were victimized by the Doncaster Council in an unprincipled way. For a third NALGO steward, the attitude and practice of the council had changed in recent years. Until the late 1980s the council tried to be a good employer but now the only concern was survival. Budget cuts and financial constraints had made the council less concerned about winning over workers. 'Things have changed a lot recently. They just want to save their skins. They say there's no money to do anything these days. It's very much a top down approach they're using'. One representative commented: 'The Labour councillors have become set in their ways. It would do them good if some of them lost their seats. It might wake them up a bit'.

Hence, one can see some similarities between the position of the councillors and those of the trade unionists, especially manual trade union representatives. However, there was a fair amount of scepticism especially among NALGO representatives about council intentions. On the whole, however, NALGO stewards in Sheffield, while critical, were more convinced of their council's formal commitments to being a good employer than were their counterparts in Doncaster.

Council Officers

The attitudes of those senior council officers interviewed, in both councils, on this issue, were strongly that the council tried to be a good employer. In Sheffield, officers believed the council tried to be a good employer, without exception. However, some chief officers saw the council as often trying to go too far in promoting industrial relations so that service delivery suffered, raising once again the relationship between being a good employer and providing good services. One chief officer argued: 'The council tries to be a good employer but there are problems between what the council wants to do with its Labour Party hat on and what it has to do as an employer'. In recent years the council had adopted a more 'hard line' attitude to excessive union demands and the officer believed 'the balance is about right' now. This raises issues about whether the practicalities of being an employer imposes necessary constraints on what councillors can do. For another chief officer, Sheffield Council put its role as employer before service delivery, all too often. 'I think in the recent past perhaps there's been too much concern with how the workers, or rather the unions, might react if the council did certain things. That's sometimes harmed service delivery'. For other officers, the councillor commitment to being a good employer was expressed in the council industrial relations codes which went further than those of other organizations. The low pay initiative and single status were also efforts, on the council's part, to be a good employer. As one senior officer put it: 'Yes, the industrial relations procedures are better than you'd find in most other councils, then there's the Low Pay Supplement, Single Status and so on. So, yes, they do try to be a good employer'.

For the Principal Industrial Relations Officer in the Housing Department, the council clearly tried to be a good employer but failed to take into account practices in other councils or outside bodies in the private sector and so on. That limited the council's outlook. The council was very good, this officer argued, at setting up procedures but not nearly so good at seeing people as individuals or in dealing with people's problems. 'The approach is a bit limited. If you set up a good procedure it's expected that that will solve all the problems. The council's a bit too inward looking'.

In Doncaster, officers also saw the council as trying to be a good employer. For one officer, this expressed itself in the willingness of the council to provide pay and conditions above those agreed by the national and the provincial councils. This officer also stressed that the council had a no compulsory redundancy agreement. Other officers stressed the implementation of national agreements. For one officer, industrial relations came very high up the council's list of priorities. 'It's very important. The staff are the council's greatest asset'. The question of financial constraints on what the council could achieve was raised by another Director of Service who strongly believed an important aim of the council was to be a good employer. For him, the actions of central government and other outside bodies did not always make that easy, by imposing financial and other restrictions on the council. 'The council does aim to be a good employer but it's hard when central government's holding the purse strings and not giving the money the council needs'.

Thus one can see that on the question of whether the councils are good employers there are a variety of views. There was wide agreement that both councils in theory try to be. There were differences, however, about what the term 'good employer' means. There was more doubt about its actual achievement among councillors in Sheffield than in Doncaster. In both councils, with one or two exceptions, the manual union representatives were more positive in their estimation than NALGO representatives. The findings would seem to complement those of Marchington and Armstrong (1982, p. 40) who from their study, and interviews with shop stewards in two local authorities and two private firms, found the NALGO members in large urban local authorities as most critical of their employers. Officers in Sheffield were generally more critical of the council's priorities and successes than those in Doncaster. The view expressed by officers in Sheffield that the council was often too concerned about being a good employer implies that officers may not give the same priority to the council's industrial relations aims as the councillors.

Formal industrial relations procedures

Councillors

The various 'actors' were questioned about the working of the formal industrial relations procedures in the councils. They were asked how far they thought the procedures aided the development of good industrial relations and helped the provision of good service delivery. For councillors in Sheffield, there was an acceptance that the procedures were not faultless. One councillor argued that *The Industrial Relations Framework* was forced, the result of the 1984 NALGO strike, and there were problems with its procedures, as a result. He foresaw negotiations with the unions in the near future over the amendment of the *Framework*. For him, as for others, the procedures encouraged people to keep issues in the system rather than solving them as quickly as possible. The then Chair of the Personnel Sub-Committee argued the formal procedures 'have slowed down and obstructed change'. Many cases had become 'lost' in the procedures. He, therefore, regarded his most immediate priority as dealing with outstanding cases quickly.

Among councillors in Doncaster, there was little feeling that the procedures represented a blockage to the introduction of changes or were unwieldy and restrictive. On the whole, councillors were of the opinion that the procedures worked well and were necessary. Once again, however, the view was expressed that Doncaster Council wanted to reach decisions and did not support endless negotiations with the council trade unions. As the Leader of the Council put it: 'We want to give people a fair chance but, at the end of the day, we want to reach a decision. Endless negotiations don't help that'.

Trade Unionists

The trade union representatives interviewed had opinions closer to those of the Sheffield than the Doncaster councillors. For many of those interviewed, in this group, issues were allowed by management to 'drag out' in the procedures. This problem, as one NALGO steward in Sheffield saw it, was compounded by management taking a very long time to set out their proposals and then expecting the trade unions to come up with answers quickly. For him, unless decisions were made at local level no real negotiations took place. 'Once issues get into the council-wide machinery management wants a decision from us yesterday sort of thing. If not, it imposes its position. And that does happen, more often than it should'. For another NALGO steward, the procedures did not work well from the trade union point of view. The problem, it was contended, was to stop the council by-passing procedures. However, the issue was more about management wanting changes quickly and seeing the agreed procedures as preventing this, than management using procedures to stop issues being settled. 'Management try and make decisions on the quick and then when we tell them it has to go through procedure they accuse us of blocking change. All we're doing is stopping management imposing its will'. For two trade union representatives, on the manual side, the procedures in Sheffield worked quite well. The procedures were only long winded if the parties wanted them to be. But, in the opinion of a NALGO steward, the procedures worked appallingly. Timetables were never met, with councillors often the worst offenders. Councillors often failed to turn up for meetings and could take a very 'high handed' attitude. This steward gave an example of a stage four hearing which was delayed for six months, due to councillor indifference: 'Senior councillors never turned up and a decision couldn't be reached without them. To be honest, they showed contempt, because someone's future was on the line'. This view, that agreed procedures could be long winded, was endorsed by a manual union full-time officer who saw cases lasting for years sometimes when they entered the machinery and had to go through the Provincial Council and even the National Whitley Council.

In Doncaster, the view that the formal industrial relations procedures were not there for the benefit of workers was frequently, either explicitly or implicitly, endorsed. The procedures, for one NALGO steward, were loaded strongly in favour of management. The grievance procedure was seen as very, very slow. Another steward clearly believed NALGO was willing to use the formal procedures for constructive purposes but was prevented from doing so by council, councillor and management, unwillingness to treat NALGO as a potential ally. As he put it, 'NALGO is willing to enter into much more seriously the problems that face the council. But this opportunity has been missed, despite the formal machinery'. As a result 'staff are mistrustful of their employers'. There is 'no sense of will on the employers' side to deal with issues quickly'. Hence, while the formal industrial relations procedures were clearly set out they did not work very well in practice.

A NUPE representative argued that in theory the formal procedures were adequate. However, the problem in Doncaster, was that the then Chief Personnel Officer prevented them working. If the Chief Personnel Officer did his job properly there would be few problems. He also believed there were too many councillors on appeals committees. The unions were pressing for this situation to be reviewed but the councillors involved were not happy to give up their involvement in this area. He accepted, when asked, that the regrading system was really very slow. However, the reason for this was NALGO putting in regrading claims as a matter of course. NUPE, on the other hand, was much more circumspect in the regrading claims it made.

There was, therefore, a high degree of agreement among union representatives, that the formal procedures in practice did not work that well. That may be due to the parties, unions and management, not using the procedures properly, management deliberately trying either to by-pass procedures or to drag them out, or management incompetence. On the whole, the manual representatives were more willing to accept the basic soundness of the procedures than NALGO representatives. This may, in part, be due to the greater use NALGO made of grievance and regrading procedures and other procedures as compared with the manual unions. It may also reflect the lower expectations of manual workers, a conclusion supported by some of the field work findings. The criticisms of councillors on this issue are interesting, for Marchington and Armstrong (1982, p. 41) in their study found the non-manual shop stewards regarded consultations with councillors and departmental consultation as the only useful types of consultation because of the attitude of chief officers.

Officers

Among officers, while some strongly supported the need for formal procedures, some also felt they were weighted in favour of the trade unions and encouraged unions to take any case into the formal machinery. For one chief officer in Sheffield, the procedures provided absolutely no disincentive to the unions taking any case right through the system. Only sensible cases should be taken up and the procedures should ensure this. In his view, at one time the concern to be ultra fair to individual workers was given priority over service delivery. Now service delivery was being given a much higher priority. 'Councillors traditionally have been too concerned about acting as a court of appeal at every stage', was his comment. The new Leader of the Council was now tackling that problem, he said. For another chief officer, the procedures were over bureaucratic. Local government, he argued, was not renowned for generating managers or boards of directors. The procedures ensured everything was brought up to chief officer level with lower managers prevented from taking decisions. 'That stifles what can be done quickly and avoids decisions being taken sensibly. It really shouldn't be like it is - far too top heavy'.

The PIRO (Principal Industrial Relations Officer) in housing said that four years ago, when he started with the council, he would have said the procedures were cumbersome, over lengthy and encouraged the unions and management to keep issues going through the system. Now he was not so sure. *Responding to Change* and *The Industrial Relations Framework* both came out of the 1984 NALGO strike, they were a direct result of that dispute. They, therefore, reflected a fear, on NALGO's part, that the management would not let them know fully what they intended to do and management's fear that NALGO would stall on issues and avoid making agreements. For him, the changes probably represented an improvement on what existed before but he believed there was a limit to what could be achieved by tampering with procedures. The PIRO in F and C S argued strongly that the unions used the procedures to delay issues, management to bring them to a conclusion. For him, important elements of the procedures, such as joint shop steward committees, had not been introduced fully and problems had resulted from that.

One can see that there are differences of quite a pronounced nature over this issue. While councillors in Doncaster believed the formal industrial relations procedures worked very well, neither trade union representatives or council officers, in either council, were so sure. Indeed many trade union representatives believed the procedures worked badly as did many council officers. The reasons advanced to explain the poor working of the procedures differed, however, both within groups and across groups. Sheffield councillors also, in some cases, agreed that the procedures did not work as well as could be hoped. An interesting finding is that, while many trade union representatives believed the formal procedures worked against their interests, many officers were of the view the procedures were too concerned with being fair to workers. This later view was particularly strongly expressed by some chief officers in Sheffield. It suggests, once again, that officers in Sheffield may have given a lower priority to developing good employment practices than leading Labour councillors although, as has been shown, some union representatives doubted the commitment of councillors on the industrial relations front.

Council relations with manual and non-manual trade unions

As has been shown in earlier chapters, much published work suggested that new urban left councils generally had better relations with manual than with non-manual council trade unions. To see if key actors in Sheffield and Doncaster Councils agreed with this view was one of the aims of my field work. If the respondents did support that view, it is important to ask why relations should be better with manual than non-manual trade unions. These directly related issues will be discussed in the following section.

Councillors

There was a general agreement among councillors in Sheffield and Doncaster that the councils have better relations with the manual trade unions than with non-manual unions and especially NALGO. The then Leader of Sheffield City Council argued that the manual unions were far better at seeing the need to improve council services. For him, the problem area had been NALGO. That union in Sheffield City Council acted, he argued, like a 1960s private sector union, dealing with a profitable company. It engaged in demarcation disputes and tried to gain financial rewards for its members in all changes proposed by the council. He complained that while NALGO nationally said much about the need to improve council services, little of this commitment was shown at local level. The Deputy Leader of the Council saw relations as better with the manual unions because, 'They call a spade a spade, whereas white collar go round the houses'. For him NALGO's attitude could be put down to the 'early teething trouble of white collar trade unionism'.

The view that NALGO approached issues in a roundabout manner was endorsed by other Sheffield councillors. One of those took the view that while NALGO wanted a dialogue on the surface, underneath the union was sniping. The manual unions, on the other hand, were willing to sit down and talk on a constructive basis. An added problem, stressed by many Sheffield councillors, was that NALGO contained members of the Socialist Workers Party (SWP) among its shop stewards and they took a totally destructive attitude. The Council Leader argued that the F and C S NALGO Shop Stewards Committee was dominated by SWP members. For one councillor, the SWP presence in the union when linked to a conservative, traditional council officer section creates an explosive mixture, making council dialogue with the union very difficult. Another councillor, while accepting that NALGO and the Administrative, Professional, Technical and Clerical (APT and C) side representatives tried to drag issues out while the manual unions wanted to get on with solving problems, argued, nonetheless, that 'all unions were interested in representing their members as best they could. I'm very doubtful if NALGO approaches issues any differently from other unions'.

Other councillors stressed that NALGO did approach issues differently because of the unions' different histories and perceptions of their role. This view linked in with another that NALGO's approach represented the teething problems of white collar trade unionism. Only one councillor, the then Chair of the Personnel Sub-Committee, argued that the council's relations were not necessarily better with manual than non-manual trade unions. 'The problem is often that some councillors see NALGO as representing members with very good, cushy conditions and support blue collar workers as a result', in his view.

In Doncaster, councillors also saw manual workers as working more closely with the council than non-manual unions, like NALGO. The Leader of the Council said that while the manual trade unions would put the council's view to its members even if they disagreed with it, NALGO stewards would not. For him, professional workers, such as teachers, social workers and senior officers, made great demands on the council. In his view, the attitudes of the different unions on competitive tendering was a fair reflection of their attitudes and practices more generally: 'The manual unions are prepared to accept job losses through privatisation' he said. 'NALGO, on the other hand, is just unreasonable, wanting all APT and C jobs guaranteed by the council, even if the council loses contracts. That's a ridiculous position'. This view of NALGO, as more difficult to work with than the manual unions, was accepted by all the Doncaster councillors whom I interviewed. The common view was summed up in the comment: 'Manual trade unions work well with the council. They want to reach agreement. They don't make unreasonable demands. They are very patient'.

Trade Unionists

Among NALGO representatives, in both councils, there was a strong opinion that councillors do treat manual workers better and have a greater empathy with manual union representatives. For a number of

NALGO stewards in Sheffield, the difference was due to one of tradition. Traditionally, in Sheffield there have been very close links between the Labour Party and the manual trade unions. This close relationship has worked through to relations in the council. Another reason put forward by NALGO stewards, for the close relations of councillors and the council manual unions, was the dominance of the manual unions by full-time officers. For many NALGO stewards, the manual unions had a very poor level of membership involvement. Full-time officials were more willing to reach agreement with the council, were looking for solutions to problems which would avoid conflict with the council. This often resulted in deals being concluded with the council which were not really beneficial for the unions' members. This view was obviously very similar to that expressed by certain Marxists operating in the Trotskyist tradition, and others. It is premised on the notion that full-time union officers are removed from the day to day experience of their members and have an interest in bringing problems to a speedy conclusion as disputes only produce more work and stress for the full-time officer (cf., for example, Cliff and Gluckstein, 1986). Many NALGO stewards in Sheffield complemented this view by contrasting the position in NALGO. In NALGO it was lay branch officers and shop stewards who carried out negotiations with the council, took up member grievances and so on. That made NALGO a much more democratic union, many NALGO stewards argued, and, because they were in direct contact with the membership and accountable to them, NALGO stewards were able to accurately reflect the wishes of the membership. However, as will be shown in another section, this view of NALGO accountability was not accepted by certain manual worker representatives. The different views of the 'best' way to organize a union expressed by NALGO and manual union representatives could potentially present problems for the new union Unison. It is at least possible that the different views could produce problems at a time of worker militancy.

While the majority of NALGO stewards I interviewed in Sheffield argued that relations were better between the council and the manual trade unions, some did not accept that view. In a few cases it was argued that relations were sometimes better between the council and the manual unions because of the weakness of the manual unions. However, this position continued, there was little evidence that the council tried to treat manual workers better than non-manual workers. The manual trade unions did not take a single, uniform line on all issues, some NALGO stewards argued. The manual unions could be conciliatory on some issues and more 'aggressive' on others, it was claimed. To believe the manual unions acted as a monolith, one NALGO steward commented, was as wrong as believing that there were no differences in NALGO. There was a general view, among NALGO stewards, that NALGO stewards were less willing to take council proposals at face value. NALGO stewards were always trying to work out the real implications of what the council was proposing, unlike the manual representatives who were too willing to take matters as they found them. Finally, a NALGO steward was of the opinion that:

> The councillors do try to improve the terms and conditions for manual workers and this is often done at the expense of other workers. But this empathy doesn't feed through to managers. In recreation, management's relations with manual workers tends to be highly confrontational - not so with NALGO.

Among manual worker shop stewards in Sheffield the view that even if councillors did formally have some empathy with manual workers, this was not reflected in the actions of management, was strongly expressed. In some cases, such as recreation, the lead given by the committee chair was criticized. There was a strong feeling that managers were allowed to treat workers as they liked.

In Doncaster, the NALGO stewards generally endorsed the views expressed by their counterparts in Sheffield, although, if anything, they saw an even bigger difference in relations between the council and the manual unions and the council and NALGO. One steward said that NALGO's relations with the council were 'really bad'. For this steward 'The council is seen as on the side of manual workers rather than white collar'. Another NALGO steward believed the difference in the council's attitude was due to the failure of Labour councillors to see NALGO as a proper trade union. Historically NALGO has been 'a quasi non-Labour organization. Over the last five or so years that's changed to some extent. NALGO's tried to be constructive over this period, not just bloody minded'. This steward accepted that some older councillors still regarded NALGO members as not working-class but the younger ones did not take that view. It is interesting that NALGO stewards in Sheffield rarely mentioned councillor hostility to the union resulting from councillors not regarding NALGO members as working-class. There seemed little doubt in the minds of the Doncaster NALGO stewards that councillors treated NUPE better than NALGO. That the council liked NUPE full-timers far better than NALGO shop stewards was a generally expressed position. Again a reason given for this was the greater willingness of manual union full-time officers to accept council pronouncements at face value. This view, if not always expressed openly was implicit in many of the comments made by NALGO stewards. As one steward put it 'You know, NALGO now has good branch officers who no longer sell people out and this creates problems with the council'.

For those manual worker representatives interviewed in Doncaster, there was a strong feeling that the manual unions approached issues in a more responsible manner. NALGO made unreasonable demands, it was claimed, and the disputes or poor relations with the councillors sprang from this. The NUPE representatives stressed that the union had good political relations with the Labour councillors, something NALGO lacked. NUPE representatives were not unwilling to use political channels to make progress on issues, they argued. For those representatives, often issues where no progress has been made with management could be taken to the politicians and a better response achieved. However, this view must be set against that expressed by a GMB full-time officer who had negotiations with both councils, who argued that he had never known councillors in Doncaster oppose a management decision while that sometimes happened in Sheffield. While NALGO stewards virtually universally believed their method of negotiation and bargaining by lay stewards and officers was best, many of the manual union representatives believed that only full-time officers could gain the experience and knowledge needed to negotiate successfully with the council.

This difference represents a conflicting view of what trade unions should be like, their purposes and nature. On the one hand, is the view, expressed by NALGO stewards, that the union should be run and controlled as far as possible by lay members. This view, as Fairbrother (1984, p. 39) puts it, emphasizes the 'involvement of members in the development of policy, the process of collective bargaining, the conduct of industrial and political action, and the control of representatives and officials'. On the other hand, is the view, expressed by manual union representatives, that only trained and experienced union 'experts' can negotiate successfully with management. This view is well summed up by Fairbrother (1984, p. 38) as follows,

> servicing the membership means that a union is organized on the basis of a shrewd and sensitive leadership, a body of officials who owe their position to their knowledge and expertise, and maintain a steady downward flow of communication and information to the members.

Officers

On the officer side a variety of views were expressed. Some senior officers saw no real differences in the way different unions approached issues. For the then chief officer in recreation in Sheffield there had been 'no difficulties with NALGO and with the manual trade unions industrial relations have generally been good'. This view was endorsed by the then Director of Social Services who said 'The unions here are all working from egalitarian principles'. However, the then Director of Housing was of the opinion that different unions did approach issues differently and, as a result, relations with the unions differed. For him, NALGO representatives were not really representative of their members. NALGO shop stewards were dominated by members of the Socialist Workers Party. The greater financial insecurity of manual workers meant they were bound to take a different view to NALGO members, in this officer's opinion.

For the PIRO in the Sheffield Housing Department, relations were better with the manual trade unions than they were with NALGO. However, the position was improving on the NALGO side and becoming marginally worse on the manual side. Non-manual staff had been worried about the number of changes in the department recently and their fears were understandable, he said, even if their reaction often was not. In the past manual workers had been treated very badly and been poorly organized in the department. Recently, however, that had started to change, with real improvements in the position of manual workers being achieved. For him, in the past many managers had tried to impose solutions on the manual workers that they would never dream of doing with NALGO. This argument strongly reinforced that advanced by manual worker representatives and some NALGO representatives that, while Labour councillors may have a greater empathy with manual workers, managers generally do not. The argument also supported the contention that the manual workers may not, in practice, have been all that well organized.

For the other PIROs interviewed, one argued strongly that it was not true that the council had a different attitude to different unions. He accepted, however, that there were very close relations between the council and the manual trade unions. For this PIRO, manual and non-manual trade unions did have different cultures, but 'NALGO and the manual trade unions have a common sense approach in recreation, trying to resolve issues in a common sense way. NALGO only takes a hard line attitude in some departments'. For another PIRO, the manual trade unions did approach issues differently from NALGO. He argued it was easier for NALGO members who were concentrated geographically, than manual workers who were dispersed, to mobilize their members for industrial action. He also stressed the SWP domination of the NALGO shop stewards committee.

Senior officers in Doncaster believed that NALGO did approach issues differently from the manual unions. For one chief officer, NALGO generally sought confrontation too readily. As an example of this, he cited the flexitime dispute where NALGO encouraged members to strike, without holding a ballot. (The whole flexitime dispute will be considered in a later section.) The manual unions, however, were much more prepared to accept the reality of the situation, in his view. For another senior officer, some councillors had a natural affinity with the manual trade unions. He argued that no such affinity existed with the 'officer trade unions'. In his view 'If NALGO supports something, sometimes the council looks at it suspiciously. The council doesn't want to be seen as a well liked employer by the officers' trade union'. The manner in which NALGO organized industrial action was also disliked by some councillors, according to this officer. Some councillors believed all workers should be brought out if there is a strike, this officer said. NALGO, and other non-manual unions, however, tended to bring out selective workers only. The activity of some officers in the Labour Party, where they criticized the council, or individual councillors, could also create opposition from councillors, this officer thought.

A third senior officer viewed the manual unions as very constructive and helpful. He had 'never lost one day's production on the manual side'. Relations with the non-manual unions had deteriorated somewhat in recent times. For him, the non-manual unions were now facing problems the manual unions had faced in the past. Echoing views expressed by Sheffield councillors and officers, he said, 'The manual trade unions have more understanding of the problems the council faces'. While the white collar workers would regard him as weak, intransigent on privatization, he saw the problem as white collar workers having to face up to a difficult position for the first time. Many non-manual workers were worried about cuts, he said, and suspicious of the council's intentions. For the council Chief Executive, however, the unions generally approached issues in a similar manner. In his opinion, white collar workers, because they had different jobs from blue collar workers, had different concerns. For him, and this attitude was unique, the manual unions were less aware of the problems of the council. NALGO and NUPE, because it dealt with both APT and C staff and manual workers, had a wider view than the purely manual unions, the Chief Executive argued.

It can be seen, therefore, that there were differences between the three groups on this issue. However, there was widespread agreement, among councillors, trade union representatives and officers, in both councils, that council relations with the manual unions were generally better than with NALGO. On this subject, two points of general interest and applicability should be noted. First, many of those interviewed, especially trade union representatives but some councillors and a few officers as well, believed that councillor empathy with manual workers did not filter down to senior officers who were often as seen as treating manual workers badly or having bad relations with the manual trade unions. This tells us something important about councillor/officer relations. Second, relations were generally, in all three groups, seen as better with manual workers than non-manual workers in Doncaster Council as well as Sheffield. Whatever the reasons for this may be, it suggests that it is not just in 'left wing' Labour councils, as some have argued, that relations between the council and NALGO were far from harmonious.

Decentralization

One of the main aims of new urban left councils, including Sheffield City Council, was the decentralization of services and a concomitant devolution of power. As has already been shown, in many cases such plans faced major obstacles. While Sheffield City Council succeeded in introducing a system of area management in housing, in social services where the council had a long standing commitment to decentralization little progress was made. In this section the reasons advanced by those interviewed for the failure in Sheffield will be set out and considered. Particular emphasis will be placed on the extent to which respondents viewed trade union attitudes as an obstacle to change. The views of councillors will be looked at first.

Councillors

When interviewed, the then Leader of the Council argued that decentralization in the Family and Community Services Department was still very much a live issue. The progress that could be made was, however, limited by financial constraints. For him, the lack of progress in this area was due, in part, to trade union opposition. As the NALGO shop steward committee in F and C S was dominated by members of the SWP and took a totally negative attitude to everything the council tried to do it was hardly surprising, in his view, that more progress had not been made. As he saw it, the F and C S NALGO shop stewards committee 'never see any of the problems the Labour Group faces'. In housing, the setting up of each new area office was held back by NALGO demanding a thorough negotiation of all the factors, even though, in many cases, one reorganization was practically identical to the ones that had gone before.

For the then Chair of the Family and Community Services Committee, budget constraints were seriously holding back progress on decentralization. A number of pilot schemes, projects, had been introduced and in the last twelve months efforts had been made to 'sharpen up' on this, he reported. For him, the political will to advance on decentralization still existed. However, the 'problem has been trade union insistence on regrading and working conditions'. Opposition was not confined to trade unions but was found among both management in social services and councillors, he said. Some managers opposed decentralization because they saw it involving a loss of power and empires and the squeezing of hierarchies, in his view. The Director of Social Services supported decentralization in theory, he thought, but management hostility had been expressed by other managers. Whether the expression of that hostility was due to a real lack of commitment on the Director's part or to a lack of managerial ability he said he did not know.

Among politicians, there was some dislike of the whole idea of devolving power to the community, he said. Councillors were elected to make decisions and run services, was a not uncommon view, he thought. For him, a major problem had been the joining together of physical decentralization with the devolution of power. If the two were separated, progress could then be made in one area at a time. He said he would like to see physical decentralization first but the money to do this did not exist. He saw a need for a phased programme on decentralization. He was still committed to the devolution of power but argued it was better to decentralize physically before attempting to devolve power. He was very critical of NALGO's attitude and practice. NALGO's attitude was that the council should produce plans first, then the union would respond to them. NALGO wanted financial remuneration for all changes, he argued, echoing the views of the Council Leader. The manual trade unions, on the other hand, had been keen to become involved in the whole process. Many manual workers resented the manner in which their views were ignored or not taken seriously by the professionals, he believed.

The ex-Chair of the Family and Community Services Committee accepted that progress on decentralization had been held back by trade union opposition. For him, some unions, the manual unions, wanted to negotiate properly and reach agreement. Other workers wanted to keep things as they were in order to protect their positions as social workers. They influenced the attitude of NALGO to a considerable extent. He thus gave fairly strong support to the view that NALGO's attitude and practice had held up progress on decentralization. For the manual trade unions, decentralization was not a major issue, in his view. He saw progress being limited by the council wanting to win over the hearts and minds of workers rather than rushing into change. Another problem, slowing down progress, was the way in which the council changed tack on decentralization. A fourth problem area, for him, was the attitude of senior officers. While some senior officers in F and C S supported decentralization, others 'tripped us up at every stage'.

David Blunkett saw decentralization in housing as only partially successful. As he saw it 'managers were still referring everything up. Because of the nature of the managerial system in housing decisions weren't being taken at the lowest possible level, which is a fairly sensible management practice irrelevant of whether you are a socialist or not'. In F and C S, while trade union opposition was one factor limiting progress, it was not the only one. It was, however, very important at one time, in his view. He said that in the early 1980s, of the NALGO points on decentralization, one should have been conceded and then the decentralization programme implemented. While the Director of Social Services supported decentralization, Blunkett argued, other managers saw it as a diversion. Further information on David Blunkett's attitude to decentralization and the reaction of the trade unions can be found in the book he wrote with Keith Jackson.

Blunkett and Jackson (1987, p. 96) argue that initiatives on decentralization have not always been wholeheartedly welcomed by professional workers. White collar and manual workers have faced problems from council reorganizations. However, they argue, 'decentralisation provides the opportunity for new working relations between white-collar and manual workers (and their unions) and the customer, which leads to more job satisfaction'.

The then Chair of the Personnel Sub-Committee said NALGO was legitimately worried about the introduction of decentralization without the necessary resources being provided to make it work. He said NALGO was bound to protect the interests of its members - what else did trade unions exist for? The council needed to convince NALGO members that they would benefit from changes and not lose out, he said. In this comment he was reiterating the point made by NALGO stewards by admitting, albeit implicitly rather than explicitly, that the council had failed to win NALGO members over to their point of view.

Trade Unionists

Among NALGO stewards in Sheffield, there was a clear view that the council had not thought through its plans on decentralization and that was the basic problem. A steward in housing argued that decentralization in that department had been carried out in a piecemeal manner. For the union the problem had been ensuring the minimum number of staff were employed. This steward commented, 'Tenants think of decentralization as simply going to the local office to be told you can't have what you want, rather than going to the Town Hall'. Decentralization, on this view, had not given tenants any more control over the service or improved service quality. The workers in the housing area offices were very disillusioned, the steward argued. Workers felt frustrated and many felt let down by the council.

The views of this steward were in direct contradiction to those expressed in the council booklet, *Sheffield Putting You in the Picture*. In this document the argument is advanced that the introduction of area management in housing had greatly improved the quality of the service. The document states, 'The new housing teams have proved able and easy to work with and are far more approachable than the old centralized system. Rather than blaming each other for housing problems, the professionals and the tenants are beginning to meet and work as equals' (Sheffield City Council, 1986, p. 19).

A NALGO steward in F and C S said that many of the ideas on decentralization came from workers. A number of professional workers, for this steward, wanted to improve professional ways of working, to improve services and increase user control. 'But you can't ignore the need for administrative support', it was stated. For this steward, the council did not recognize the importance of administrative back up or take the plight of clerical workers, typists, receptionists and other 'support workers' seriously. NALGO was more committed to decentralization than many managers, the steward argued. Without proper funding and adequate resources, however, decentralization put people in a very exposed position, the argument continued. Sheffield Council, it was further contended, was not prepared to put any extra money into decentralization. This steward argued strongly that clerks needed regrading because decentralization would impose extra responsibilities on them. Another reason why decentralization had not gone ahead, it was further argued, was the problem of finding suitable accommodation.

Like councillors, this steward argued that managers did not give decentralization a high priority. In his view, management opposition was stronger lower down the hierarchy than it was at the top. He thought the Director had some reservations. His psychotherapeutic view of social work would not put decentralization as a high priority. The steward claimed that most NALGO stewards in F and C S, as socialists, believed services should be more responsive to users. 'We don't want to stay in here [Social Services Headquarters] any longer than we have to', was his comment. The attitude of councillors was also seen as creating problems. In his view, councillors found it hard to give up power. But, unless they were prepared to do so, decentralization could not possibly work. In line with the findings of other research, he said the NALGO F and C S committee in Sheffield was worried about users gaining control over issues such as the hiring and firing of staff. Problems around this area had to be resolved with the members themselves.

Another NALGO F and C S steward also argued that it was not true that decentralization in the department had been held back by NALGO opposition. NALGO was not opposed to decentralization in principle, although there were circumstances where decentralization could be more of a hindrance than a help. Those circumstances, the steward said, were if the decentralization was not properly funded and resources were not applied to enable services to be improved.

Officers

The views of senior officers in Sheffield Council differed on this issue. On the question of the aims behind the commitment to decentralization in Sheffield, an officer in the Central Policy Unit said that the aim in Sheffield had been to use decentralization not as a means of empowering people but as a means of increasing technocratic efficiency. By that he meant the aim of the council was to provide services less paternalistically, especially in housing. The objective was to treat tenants as customers shopping in a private store were treated, not to give them control over the running of the housing service or their estate. He doubted whether, in practice, this was a viable strategy.

For the Director of Social Services, the problem now was a lack of money to fund decentralization. This had not always been the case, however, he claimed. In the past the problem was more around the issue of agreeing appropriate management structures. Over the past eighteen months, he told me, the Decentralization Working Party had 'come up' with some good proposals. He did not accept that the trade unions, including NALGO, were in principle, opposed to decentralization. They were, however, worried about the decentralization being properly funded and staffed. He did not believe separating the devolution of power from the physical decentralization of services would aid the overall decentralization process. In his view, the council still wanted to decentralize physically and in terms of power. Discussions with the unions had covered both aspects. There were differences with the unions about the number of receptionists that should be employed in decentralized offices and for clear remits as to whom workers were accountable.

On the issue of the devolution of power to service users, he saw problems because of the statutory requirements surrounding social services. In principle, he supported the devolution of power but as a means to municipal socialism there were limits because of statutory obligations. He also saw potential problems with self-proclaimed politicians taking over any user committees which were established. Hence, in his view, a ward based electoral system was essential to ensure representativeness. He supported geographical decentralization strongly and hoped there would be progress on this front.

The PIRO in the F and C S department admitted decentralization had been slowed down by problems over the suitability of premises, the resources that could be committed to it and the health and safety of workers. The decentralization in the housing department had been completed at a mammoth cost. For him, the doubt in NALGO's mind revolved around fears about what user committees would mean for workers' terms and working conditions. While NALGO may take up strong initial positions, he said, the union always had a final position where it will reach agreement.

One can see, therefore, that there is no general agreement across the groups that NALGO opposition, or trade union opposition more generally, had been the only, or even the main, reason for preventing greater progress on decentralization. Although this may be an unduly cynical interpretation, the comment by the Chair of the F and C S Committee that the council should try to achieve physical decentralization before power was devolved, may support the contention of NALGO stewards that the councillors did not want to give up power. This view was tacitly accepted, as true of many Labour councillors, by the then Chair of the Personnel Sub-Committee. While one councillor saw the slow progress as due to councillors wanting to win hearts and minds, it was certainly the case, as another Labour councillor implicitly accepted, that the council, for whatever reason, had not succeeded in convincing NALGO members that the council's policies would be in the interests of NALGO members.

The issue of decentralization feeds into the question of whether NALGO, as a union, set out in Sheffield to protect the privileges of professional workers. As has been shown, that this is just what NALGO tried to do in left wing councils, is a view which is prominent in the published literature. The interview material will allow a detailed consideration of this contention to be undertaken in respect of Sheffield Council. The interview material will also allow the question of whether NALGO members tried to protect professional privileges in Doncaster Council to be addressed. This and a number of other themes will be discussed in the next chapter.

7 Industrial Relations 'Problems'

Professional privileges

Councillors

For the then Leader of the Sheffield Council, NALGO opposition to the council was partly, but only partly, due to the protection of professional privileges. In his view, NALGO tried to stop all change and was totally negative in its outlook. In many respects this view was endorsed by the then Chair of the Family and Community Services Programme Committee. He too said that the union wanted to hold onto all its positions and was not just concerned about protecting the privileges of professionals. For him, NALGO contained certain members of the Socialist Workers Party and others who took a romantic view of working-class struggle. In addition, the union contained conservatives, traditional local government officers, who were concerned with protecting professional privileges. When these two positions came together, as they did in 1984 in the strike, an explosive mixture is created which made constructive dialogue with the union difficult. (The strike of NALGO members in 1984 will be discussed, in detail, in a later section.)

For David Blunkett, NALGO's attitude could not be explained simply in terms of the union trying to protect the privileged position of professional workers. For him, the union was sometimes obstructive for few realistic reasons. However, he also stressed that workers, including members of NALGO, often took action to protect their interests for perfectly understandable and legitimate reasons, including the way they were treated by managers. The then Chair of the Personnel Sub-Committee also argued that NALGO was not concerned simply with protecting privileges. Of course, in his view, the union tried to protect the interests of its members, which was only to be expected. But it was not only professional or highly paid workers who tried to maintain job controls. In his opinion, all groups of workers tried to protect the controls over their work which they had managed to win - NALGO members were no different from other workers in that respect. This councillor also denied that most of the council's serious disputes had been with NALGO.

While he did not express this view when interviewed, David Blunkett seems to agree that all workers try to protect job controls or restrictive practices. As Blunkett and Jackson (1987, p. 212) wrote:

> Council employees can also be a barrier to effective local
> government... Long-standing habits of keeping the system
> going rather than improving it, and narrow definitions of
> professional responsibilities, may reduce accountability and
> responsiveness. Even among committed officers, professional
> detachment may mean too little account is taken of the need to
> produce results for the people they serve. Many officers and
> workers at every level do engage in self-protecting restrictive
> practices or abuse the power they hold when people depend on
> them for essential services and resources.

Which is not to suggest in any way that David Blunkett regarded all
efforts by workers to protect their positions as illegitimate or
backward-looking. Often workers take action because they have been
badly treated by management and such action, for David Blunkett, is
perfectly understandable and necessary.

It is clear, therefore, that among councillors in Sheffield, there was
no strong support for the argument that NALGO was a destructive
force in left wing councils *simply* because it was trying to protect the
privileges of its professional members. There was fairly common
acceptance that the council's 'conflicts' with NALGO locally sprang
from something more than the union trying to uphold professional
privileges.

Among councillors in Doncaster, there was a feeling that
professionals and senior officers made greater demands on the council
than manual workers. Professionals and senior officers, it was
contended by councillors, expected far more from the council. On
competitive tendering, for example, NALGO expected the existing
jobs of all its members to be protected whatever the outcome of the
tendering process. The argument found among councillors, was not so
much that NALGO protected professional privileges as that the unions'
members expected more because of their positions.

Trade Unionists

Among NALGO shop stewards, there was a general agreement that the
union did not uphold the privileges of its professional members. A
branch official, however, accepted that there was some element of this
within the membership of the branch. However, he argued, the branch
had called for flat rate increases in recent years which clearly would
benefit lower paid workers more than the traditionally negotiated
percentage increases. For him, a greater problem than NALGO
protecting professional privileges was the failure of the council to
recognise or accept that NALGO even had low paid members. In his

view, if NALGO was trying to protect the privileges of professional workers it was far from successful. This last point was specifically endorsed by another NALGO steward who said 'If NALGO is trying to protect professional privileges, it's not doing a very good job'.

Other NALGO stewards endorsed the general position described. For one steward, it was totally false to argue that the union was out to protect the privileges of some workers at the expense of others. NALGO's major aims, he argued, 'were to protect the interests of all our members and to keep trying and improve services'. He saw the two aims as mutually inseparable: the interests of members could only be secured if services were improved and the support of the public achieved. This last point raises important issues about the relationship between the interests of workers and the development of good services, which will be considered in detail in a later section.

Just as NALGO stewards in Sheffield generally rejected the argument that their union tried to protect the privileges of its professional members in a 'reactionary' manner, so too did their counterparts in Doncaster. For the Doncaster NALGO stewards, like their Sheffield counterparts, the union aimed to promote the interests of all its members and was committed to developing good services. In no way could the failure to improve services be put down to NALGO encouraging professional workers to be obstructive by trying to maintain their unreasonable privileges. A steward in the Social Services Department argued that before flexitime was introduced in the council, the office where he worked closed at lunch time. With the introduction of flexitime the workers in the office decided to keep the office open during the lunch break in order to improve the services provided. This steward also denied that the 'stand by' strike of social workers in 1980 could be seen as the union protecting social workers' privileges. The dispute, for him, was about the council trying to cut the number of social workers involved in out of hours duties from five to two. If the union had allowed that, the quality of service would have gone down alarmingly. The union believed the council should have established out of hours staff but the council was not prepared to spend the money to do so.

Once again, the issue of whether there is a conflict between workers' interests and those of good service delivery was raised by NALGO stewards. The NALGO steward concerned saw no such conflict and certainly denied that NALGO's praxis prevented the development of good services. However, to reiterate the point, the whole question of the relationship between union practice and service delivery will be discussed in another section.

Officers

The then Director of Social Services in Sheffield strongly argued that NALGO in his department did not support the status quo. The NALGO stewards did not oppose 'radical' changes in order to protect the position of their professional members. Protecting professional privileges 'was not implicit in NALGO's actions as a trade union'. He also commented that 'the unions here are working from egalitarian principles'. This view, however, was directly contradicted by the PIRO in the Housing Department who saw NALGO as wanting to uphold the status quo and as trying to promote and protect a fairly cosy life for its members. However, he said, there clearly was a more radical strand in the local branch. Echoing views expressed by councillors, he said that this radical strand was counterpoised by a strand representing more traditional local government officers who took a conservative line. One group believed council policy is not going forward with sufficient pace, another that changes are too fast. Therefore, to view NALGO as blocking changes because it is basically a 'reactionary' organization, implicit in the view that NALGO protects professional privileges, was too crude, in his opinion.

The PIRO in the F and C S department, however, believed it was true that NALGO did protect professional privileges. The union worked to maintain gains its members had already obtained. He said that from the 1970s, NALGO had seen itself as having the right to be involved in professional issues although in 1986 the union refused to discuss the issue of how the service should develop and the implications of that for professional practice. However, this PIRO did not suggest that NALGO's position had prevented radical changes being introduced.

In Doncaster, while officers believed that NALGO tended to approach issues differently from manual unions, there was no direct connection between this and NALGO trying to protect professional privileges. However, there was some argument that NALGO members had different interests and were now having to face problems which manual workers had faced in the past.

There was, therefore, some evidence of councillors and officers seeing NALGO as trying to protect the privileges of professional workers. However, among Sheffield councillors and some Sheffield officers this was not seen as the only or main reason for conflicts between the council and the union. All the NALGO stewards interviewed, in both councils, regarded the claim as misleading. Even some Sheffield councillors and officers saw the claim, when it was extended to argue that NALGO opposed radical policies because of its commitment to upholding professional privileges, as unsustainable.

Those interviewed on this issue raised some interesting questions about the relationship between trade union practice, on the one hand, and good service delivery on the other. After a consideration of a number of industrial disputes in both councils in the next section, these will be considered in detail.

Industrial relations

Three industrial disputes, one in Sheffield Council and two in Doncaster Council, will be considered in the following section. The disputes are the NALGO strike in the Housing Department of Sheffield City Council in 1984, which also involved some workers from other departments; the 'stand by' strike of NALGO social workers in Doncaster Council in 1980; and the flexitime dispute in Doncaster Council in 1988. The disputes have been chosen for consideration for two basic reasons. First, I was informed by the then Chief Assistant to the Chief Executive that there had been no disputes with manual workers in recent years in Doncaster Council. Hence, the only disputes that could be examined in respect of Doncaster Council were with non-manual unions. Second, a consideration of the disputes should enable important information about the relationship between the councils and their white collar workforce to be collected. The aim in considering the disputes, will not be to examine in detail how the disputes developed but to understand how those interviewed saw the disputes in retrospect and the significance of the disputes, for those interviewed, in explaining industrial relations in the two councils.

The 1984 'housing strike' in Sheffield City Council

The strike of NALGO members in Sheffield Council in 1984 lasted over ten weeks and involved NALGO members in the Housing Department and key workers from other areas. Ostensibly the dispute was about the introduction of new technology associated with the rent collecting system in the Housing Department. The dispute ended towards the end of 1984 with the existing negotiating agreement for the introduction of new technology in the council being abolished and with the new rent collecting system in the Housing Department in operation.

Councillors

When asked, the then Leader of the Council, who was Chair of the Housing Committee at the time of the strike, argued that the strike was not connected with the reorganization of housing services on an area management basis which had taken place in 1983/1984. Instead, he said, the strike was about NALGO trying to block completely the introduction of new technology in the council as it affected white collar jobs. The dispute was directly connected to the council's efforts to change the council house rent payment system. The dispute, for him, 'was purely and simply about the council wanting to end NALGO's veto over the introduction of new technology, for NALGO was refusing to negotiate sensibly over the issue'. Changes were needed, he argued, to improve services for tenants.

For another Labour councillor, the dispute was not about matters specific or peculiar to housing. The dispute was rather about the introduction of change and affected all council departments. The dispute, in his view, could have occurred in other departments. The question of the introduction of new technology just 'reached a head' first in housing and that consequently was why the dispute occurred there. Again, NALGO intransigence was seen as the reason for the dispute.

However, another councillor saw the dispute in a broader context. On the council side, he argued, there was a feeling that administrative workers in the housing department were making unreasonable demands. For him, some NALGO stewards in the dispute did act unreasonably. He believed a similar dispute would not occur at the time of the interview. For both the council and NALGO had learned from their experience of the strike. As a result, both sides 'would approach a similar issue very differently'. However, he admitted that certain Labour councillors 'are still very angry with NALGO for the dispute'. For him, both sides were to blame for the dispute which could have been avoided.

NALGO Representatives

Not surprisingly, NALGO stewards saw the dispute in very different terms from the councillors. For one branch officer, the dispute concerned the council trying to tear up unilaterally the existing new technology agreement. The dispute arose directly as a result of the Director of Housing disciplining workers for refusing to use new technology. For him, 'more progress towards resolving the dispute was made when David Blunkett was involved in the negotiations than when Clive Betts took over if Blunkett was away. When he was away and Clive Betts took over, little progress towards ending the dispute was made'. This NALGO officer accepted that the union did not think enough about how it could gain improvements for its members from the introduction of new technology. He tentatively put forward a set of proposals, including a shorter working week, but the idea of winning gains in other areas in response to agreeing to work with new technology, was never really promoted by the union. He said the council opposition to the existing agreement was ironic given the use made of the agreement by the TUC. The TUC publicised the agreement as the type of new technology agreement for which unions should be aiming.

For a NALGO steward in the Housing Department, the dispute was about how agreement between the unions and the council was to be achieved. Under the then existing procedure, if management wanted to change anything they needed to secure the unions' consent. The agreement, therefore, it was argued, prevented management acting unilaterally. The new agreement had given management the right to impose change once the formal machinery has been exhausted. This steward, like some councillors, believed the dispute could have been in some other department. The catalyst in housing, it was argued, was the attitude of the Director of Housing who took a very aggressive attitude to NALGO members. The Director of Housing did not work alone but had the backing of the councillors in his stance, the steward argued. This steward said that many Housing Department workers, who had joined the council because of its socialist reputation, were let down by the council who pursued a very authoritarian line. This view is endorsed by Darke and Goulay (1985), two members of NALGO in the Housing Department at that time, who saw the attitude of the council managers as totally out of place in a socialist council. This steward, like the branch officer, believed more progress was made when David Blunkett was involved in the negotiations aimed at resolving the dispute.

Officers

For a senior officer in the Central Policy Unit at that time, the strike was absolutely crucial in changing the attitudes of councillors. The strike was responsible for souring relations with the trade unions, or at least NALGO, and dealt a body blow to ideas of worker involvement. From that point, according to this officer, councillors became much more concerned about the requirements of, and need for, strong management. In many ways, this officer argued, the strike 'knocked the stuffing' out of councillors. The strike, he pointed out, was not just a Sheffield phenomenon but part of a number of disputes at that time between NALGO and left councils. By this the officer was not suggesting that the strikes were a co-ordinated affair, either by NALGO or the councils. Rather, he was trying to put the dispute in Sheffield into some sort of context. The officer was of the opinion that after the strike it became increasingly difficult for him and others to keep questions of radical change on the council agenda.

For the then Director of Housing, the dispute represented two conflicts rolled into one. At one level, the dispute was council wide and concerned with the introduction of new technology and NALGO opposition to that. At Departmental level, the dispute revolved around the effects of his efforts to change the way in which the Housing Department worked. The dispute concerned workers' feelings in Housing that they were being pushed around and was a response to the introduction of area management, regrading issues and other matters. For the Director of Housing, the whole ethos of the Housing Department had to be altered to be more service orientated and this was actively opposed by some union representatives. The strike, he argued, was a direct result of resistance to change, which was the prevailing attitude of NALGO officials. The dispute was triggered by a decision of NALGO members not to co-operate with normal procedures for collecting rents.

The PIRO in the Housing Department took a similar view about the causes of the strike as the Director of Housing. The dispute, in his view, was fuelled by a fear among NALGO members about what the various changes recently introduced in the Housing Department would mean for them. The issues involved far more than simply the introduction of new technology. NALGO members felt frustrated about the failure of the Plan 'B' proposals to try to restrict council house sales. Plan 'B' was a scheme whereby in return for paying higher rents council tenants would be eligible to claim the costs for repairs and home improvements they carried out, from the council. The aim was to encourage the 'better off' council tenants to stay in their council accommodation and remain as council tenants. In that way two aims would be achieved: council house sales would be limited and a broad mix of council tenants maintained. However, NALGO had grave doubts from the beginning about the workability of the scheme, the PIRO said, and, when the proposal was effectively barred by the central government, felt frustrated and angry with the council for having tried to introduce the plan. NALGO members were also very worried about the affect of decentralization on their working conditions, in the PIRO's opinion. The PIRO accepted that a 'crunch' was bound to occur on the issue of new technology as the positions of the council and NALGO were so far apart. However, he felt it was a great pity that the issue became 'tied up' with all the other matters. In retrospect, he acknowledged that the dispute was not well handled by management. However, it was not possible to reach a directly negotiated compromise between the positions of the two sides. In the end, for him, the dispute ended out of tiredness and the approach of Christmas.

One can see, therefore, a big difference in the position of people in the different groups. Most councillors saw the dispute as limited to new technology and/or NALGO obstructing change. A very interesting point was raised by the officer who saw the strike as contributing, in a crucial manner, to the 'killing off' of radical council initiatives, especially on the industrial relations front. This point was stressed at a CSE (Conference of Socialist Economists) meeting by a number of Sheffield academics and political and trade union activists, both inside and outside the council. It would certainly seem possible, to put it no stronger, that the dispute made it more difficult for Sheffield councillors to win the whole-hearted support of NALGO members during the 1984-1985 anti-rate capping campaign. It may also have led NALGO to view council proposals with distrust and for councillors to view NALGO attitudes and practices with a similar distrust.

If the dispute did reduce interest among Labour councillors in promoting worker involvement, then that ties into the conclusion reached by Laffin (1989) in his analysis of a strike between NALGO and the new urban left council he termed Labton, over the dismissal of a NALGO member. For Laffin that dispute soured relations between the council leadership and the NALGO branch and showed that the interests of a radical Labour council and the council workforce may not coincide. Laffin's analysis also shows the importance of personalities in the development of the dispute in Labton.

It is also interesting to note the way NALGO activists felt let down by the council because of the attitude of senior council management in the Housing Department. Whether the criticism made by those activists is justified, the fact that they felt that management's attitudes were incompatible with Sheffield Council acting in a socialist manner shows how little the council succeeded in convincing, even potentially supportive, white collar workers that the council was acting in a manner compatible with socialist principles.

The dispute, of course, raises a whole host of questions about how social change is to be introduced in left-wing councils and the praxis of white collar trade unionism. It does seem that there may have been some differences between leading Labour councillors about the council aims in the dispute. If it is true, as NALGO stewards argued, that the then Leader of the Council took a different attitude during negotiations from the then Chair of the Housing Committee, then that may suggest some important differences of outlook within the Labour

Group about how change was to be achieved. There may have been more of a willingness in some parts of the Labour Group to try to 'win over' NALGO members than in other parts, where the need to overcome or defeat NALGO's obstructiveness, was the prime concern. Certainly, it seems, from comments made by officers and Labour Party activists - expressed at meetings and during informal discussions, that, while the Labour Group Executive remained formally united during the strike there were strong tensions within the executive. There were also tensions between the Labour Group Executive and the District Labour Party over the council's handling of the dispute. While his comment does not relate directly to the 1984 strike, David Blunkett's statement about his relations with Clive Betts probably gives some insights into the type of tensions that existed in the Labour Group:

> You will appreciate partly why I failed personally and others around me to do that when you see that my successor was then the Chair of Housing. There was always quite a strong, not personal friction, because I always got on very well with Clive Betts, difference of perception about the role of managers and the value and methodology of decentralization. The relationship of the chair of a committee and chief officer is obviously important and the Leader of the Council is limited in terms of how he or she can intervene without challenging the otherwise competent and acceptable role of a senior colleague.

The comment of the NALGO branch officer that NALGO did not use the issue of new technology in an imaginative way to try to win improvements for its members, in areas like shorter working time, raises issues about the 'defensiveness' of the union branch and of the trade unions more generally. If it is true that the NALGO branch simply tried to maintain the status quo over new technology, as seems to be the case, then this sheds important light on the attitude of unions when they feel their members' interests are threatened. Of course, it would be wrong to read too much into a single dispute in a single local authority. But the 'failure' of the NALGO branch to take up a 'positive', 'forward-looking' position during the build up to, and during, the 1984 strike does suggest that if workers feel threatened by change, they and their union representatives are unlikely to react positively. If that hypothesis has any basis to it, then it suggests Labour councillors need to work very hard to produce the right climate in which workers and their unions will be positively responsive to change. Councillors also need to take time convincing workers, 'winning them over', to the proposed changes by showing that, far from threatening the workers involved, the changes will represent an advance for those workers. To do that the workers also probably need to be involved in devising the changes in the first place. That, for whatever reasons, seems to be something the Sheffield councillors failed to do.

The 'stand by' strike in Doncaster Borough Council, 1980

Councillors

For councillors, the strike of social workers over 'stand by' duties was a prime example of professional workers making unreasonable demands on the council. The dispute showed the unwillingness of NALGO to work with the council and accept the problems the council faced. The council was trying to rationalize the use of staff so that the best social work coverage commensurate with funds were obtained. The union, NALGO, simply refused to co-operate. For the Leader of the Council, NALGO just 'buried its head in the sand' over the issue and refused to face reality.

Trade Unionists

For a NALGO shop steward in the Social Services Department, the dispute revolved around the council wanting to reduce the number of social workers involved in out of hours duties. The council, he said, wanted to cut the number of staff from five to two. They believed that could be done without the standard of service provided being adversely affected. The union, on the other hand, knew that if the number of staff were reduced as the council suggested, the standard of service would necessarily fall. Instead of reducing staff, NALGO called on the council to establish a proper system of out of hours working and to establish out of hours staff. However, the council was not prepared to fund such a development, the steward said. Thus, for this steward, far from being unconcerned about the quality of service, NALGO was deeply worried that the council's proposals would greatly harm the service provided.

Officers

The Chief Assistant to the Chief Executive said the dispute concerned social workers refusing to carry out stand by duties which the council saw as an abrogation of their contracts. The strike lasted one week. He gave little indication of the real, underlying cause of the dispute, however. Another senior council officer said that between 1979 and

1983 there were a number of disputes in the department but only one was purely local - the stand by dispute.

This dispute, then, shows white collar workers feeling undervalued by the council. As in the disputes in Sheffield, there was a feeling among NALGO shop stewards that the councillors disregarded the position of NALGO members and acted in an overbearing manner. The councillors and management made little effort to try to work constructively with the union in order to improve the service provided, according to NALGO. From the councillor side, however, came the contrary view that NALGO acted unreasonably and failed to take the council's position into account.

The 1988 flexitime dispute in Doncaster District Council

Councillors

The dispute, for the Leader of the Council, was due to the abuse of the flexitime scheme by white collar workers. As he put it 'White collar workers had had it for six months. It's been abused'. The council policy, he said, was to abolish the scheme as it was not working well. NALGO wanted the scheme to remain exactly as it was, despite the problems associated with it, he commented. That showed NALGO's general negative attitude, he said. NUPE, on the other hand, came forward with proposals for change in a constructive manner. The changes proposed by NUPE proved acceptable to the council. The whole issue showed the differences in perspective of NALGO and NUPE, in the view of councillors.

Trade Unionists

A NALGO shop steward argued management had unilaterally changed the time people could take off, from the credits they had acquired through working longer than the standard working week, from one and a half days to just one day a month. For this steward, councillors clearly felt the system had been abused and management, as a result, wanted to see the scheme ended. In response to the council's opposition to the scheme, NUPE proposed reducing the time people could take off in a month to one day while NALGO wanted to keep the system going as it was. NALGO did not accept that flexitime working was affecting service delivery adversely. Another steward denied that the union had forced members to go on strike over flexitime. All the union did, it was claimed, was to encourage members to go on strike to protect the flexitime scheme. The dispute revolved around councillors wanting to scrap the flexitime scheme, in total. In the end, the council compromised. This steward doubted whether this would have been the case without NALGO's firm action. It was sad, for this steward, that NUPE had taken a different view over the issue from NALGO. For this steward, NUPE's position meant that, as well as reducing the time workers could take off work at one time, all workers must start work by 9.00 a.m. instead of 10.00 a.m. as was the case. The council had wanted to reduce the latest time at which workers could start work to 9.00 a.m. With greater unity, the council's objectives in this area could have been defeated, this steward argued.

For a third NALGO steward, there were a number of strands in the council's opposition to the flexitime scheme. The council, for this steward, wanted to withdraw the scheme because it prevented chief officers being as available to councillors as used to be the case. Moreover, staff were seen taking children to school which annoyed some councillors. A councillor also saw half of a department at a bus stop at 4.00 p.m. one afternoon and deduced from this that the department's work must be suffering. However, as shown in an earlier section, this steward said that, after the introduction of flexitime, the workers in his office agreed to open the office at lunch time, something which had not happened before.

A NUPE representative argued that NALGO's approach to the flexitime issue had been unnecessarily militant, as acceptable adjustments to the scheme could be agreed with the council. NUPE had not encouraged its members to cross NALGO picket lines, they had done so of their own volition.

Officers

For a chief officer, the dispute resulted from councillors' belief that the scheme was being abused. NALGO not only opposed the council's position on flexitime, he said, but encouraged members to strike without a ballot of the membership, which was totally unconstitutional. NUPE, on the other hand, took the council's worries about flexitime seriously and tried to reach a compromise solution. In the end a solution was reached based on NUPE's proposals, he said. NALGO's unconstitutional action angered a lot of councillors and did the union's reputation much harm, this officer claimed. Whereas NUPE's conciliatory approach won the union respect from councillors, he said. Over the flexitime issue, managers, this officer argued, tried to prevent workers going on strike. Like everyone else, a manager's first duty is to the employer, he said.

A senior officer said that the action over flexitime was at a lower level of intensity and involvement in his department than in other departments. The dispute did not disrupt things too badly in the department where he worked. The Director of Housing also said that there were no problems over flexitime working in his department. The workers in the Housing Department, he said, were conscientious and hard working and had not abused the flexitime scheme.

There were, therefore, differences in the attitudes of members of the different groups over this issue. The dispute may well have reflected a lack of trust between councillors and NALGO members, especially shop stewards. It clearly suggests that councillors did not have faith in their white collar workers not to abuse the flexitime scheme. This tells us a great deal about the relations between the council and its workforce. For it shows that there was little feeling of common purpose between councillors and workers.

Trade union practice and socialism

There has been much discussion in the published literature about the relationship between the practice of trade unions and the development of good service delivery in local government and the public services more generally. It is argued, as has been shown, that the two are liable to conflict, as trade union aims of protecting the interests of their members are incompatible with the objectives of improving the delivery of public services. Examining how the different people I interviewed saw this issue is important, as in this way, some light may be shed on the question of the relationship between trade union practice and service delivery. As before, the views of councillors in Sheffield will be set out first.

Councillors

For the then Deputy Leader of Sheffield City Council, there was an inevitable conflict between the defensiveness of trade unions and the introduction of socialist change. He argued that it took a great deal of hard work to convince trade union members that changes were a good thing. Once trade unionists were so convinced, he said, they tended to be very supportive of any changes introduced. Another Chair of a council committee agreed that trade unions were conservative organizations but with a small 'c' only. Trade unions, in his view, were wary of change, suspicious of what it would mean for trade union members, that is, workers. There was no use denying, he said, that trade union conservatism could create real problems for a council wanting to introduce radical change in order to improve the delivery of services.

A third councillor also believed that trade union attitudes and good service delivery could conflict. While he supported free collective bargaining, he recognized its operation could create real problems. For him, the crucial point was to convince workers that any proposed change was in their interests. This necessarily took time and could create problems. The important point to recognize, he said, was that improving industrial relations was a marathon and not a sprint. Progress, to be secure in the long term, would necessarily be slow at the beginning.

The basically defensive nature of trade unionism was accepted by another leading Labour councillor. For him, 'In the main they [trade unions] are primarily defensive'. Trade unions, in his view, are out to protect gains already made. As a result, the argument continued, getting trade unions to take a proactive stance was difficult. For him, this was particularly true in the climate then prevailing, when the trade unions felt, and were, under attack from central government.

For the then Chair of the Personnel Sub-Committee, it was a totally false idea that sensible personnel policies obstructed good service delivery. For to achieve good service delivery the commitment of the workforce was essential. 'While trade unions have been forced to adopt a defensive stance in present circumstances, I don't believe trade unions are necessarily defensive organizations'. Like the councillor whose views were reported above, he said, 'it takes effort and patience to win trade unions over and get them to adopt a proactive stance. But once the trade unions recognize their members are not being attacked trade unions are happy to play a constructive, active role'. From his experience, many workers, even at low levels, were happy to look for ways in which service delivery could be improved. Often however, they were frustrated by the bureaucratic hierarchy which blocked their initiatives. There was no play off, in his view, between giving people decent pay and conditions and providing good services. On the contrary, in his view, the two went together.

The then Leader of the Council also argued that there was no difference in the aims of the council and of the council trade unions. For him, both sides 'want a lot of everything - good working conditions and pay and good services'. There may be, however, in his view, differences of emphasis and priority between groups within the overall objectives. Moreover, the unions, in his view, had not always given the promotion of good services the priority they deserved.

For David Blunkett, the interests of trade unions and good council service provision could conflict. So too, in his view, could trade union actions and a council trying to introduce socialist change. Often it may seem that the immediate interests of workers lie in keeping things exactly as they are. However, he argued, when one looks deeper it becomes apparent that that is not the case. 'For workers and councillors both have an interest in ensuring service provision is as good as possible'. Only in that way could the jobs and conditions of council workers be made secure, as only in that way can the support of the general public for local councils be achieved.

One can see, therefore, a high level of agreement among Sheffield councillors that trade union attitudes and the provision of good council services can conflict because of trade union defensiveness. There is also a high degree of agreement that such conflicts can, in principle, be overcome if councillors succeeded in convincing workers that changes did not threaten their interests. However, there was also a strong feeling, expressed in answer to questions on other topics, that winning over the trade unions, and the members they represent, may, on occasion, prove very difficult, if not impossible. There appears, on the face of it, to be a conflict between the attitudes of some individual councillors. For, on the one hand, they believed it was possible to win the support of trade unions for change, in principle. While on the other hand, they believed it was often, in practice, impossible to achieve such trade union support.

Of councillors in Doncaster, the general view was that sometimes unions could make demands which interfered with good service delivery. The actions of trade unions and good service delivery did not always automatically coincide. There was a common agreement that where trade union action was seriously adversely affecting service delivery the council would have to take strong measures to remedy the situation. That showed that councillors in Doncaster did not believe there was a unity of interests between the council and its workforce. However, the Leader of the Council made clear, while the council would take action against workers who were adversely affecting service provision, the council would never bring in private firms to defeat council unions with whom the council was in dispute.

Trade Unionists

A NUPE representative in Sheffield argued that the defensiveness of trade unions was a real problem. Such defensiveness could make the introduction of socialist change very difficult indeed. For him, the culture of trade unionism needed to change so that trade unions could become more proactive and less reactive. In Sheffield, he argued, 'Trade unions have not been prepared to accept change'. The main priority of the Sheffield Council trade unions had not been improving council services. However, he hoped, with the introduction of compulsory competitive tendering that situation would change. Too often the council, councillors and officers, had been too concerned about worker reactions to press hard enough for change, he said. For a NUPE shop steward, the trade unions had traditionally responded to initiatives from management. Little emphasis had been placed on trade unions putting forward proposals. In his view, this needed to be changed. 'There's a tendency just to respond' and that was a bad thing to do. For him, the problem of trade union defensiveness sprang from the way in which unions carry out their training. 'If we want to win over the public we can be involved with them by putting some of their things which correspond with trade union aims'. He thought management would dislike that. However, with political backing for such initiatives, management would not be able to stop such developments.

For another manual worker steward, trade unions were not just defensive organizations. If they were they would have no gains to protect, in the first place. For him, there were times when the trade unions were defensive as a result of circumstances, other occasions where they were more proactive and trying to win improvements. The circumstances in which trade unions had to operate were crucial in determining whether or not unions were defensive at any particular time.

Of the NALGO stewards interviewed, one was of the opinion that while they often were, trade unions should not be, defensive organizations. While they were not organizations fighting for socialism, unions had to become more offensive, fighting for positive improvements and gains. Another steward saw no conflict between trade union demands and good service delivery. For that steward, you could not hope to improve services by exploiting workers ever more strongly. Better pay and conditions would encourage workers to feel committed to the council and will consequently, this steward argued, create better service provision.

A third NALGO steward was of the opinion that when resources were being cut, there was bound to be a conflict between trade union interests and the development of good services. The attitude was that 'you can't hope to get a quart out of a pint pot'. This steward accepted that trade unions were reactive organizations, tending to respond to initiatives and actions introduced by others. If they were to affect significant changes at work, trade unions must become more involved at an earlier stage. For him, some conservatism in trade union attitudes and reactions was only to be expected given their position in the employment relationship. He stressed strongly, that if councillors hoped to bring about change they would have to spend time winning workers over to their views.

Another NALGO steward accepted that workers' demands and service provision were bound to conflict. The important point, for him, was how you dealt with those conflicts. The central problem, as he saw it, was how much time you spent talking about issues and how much time actually getting something done. In his view, trade unions were not sufficiently versed in policy matters. This was an area the unions needed to take more seriously.

Trade unionists in Doncaster generally believed that any conflicts between trade union attitudes and service delivery could be overcome as they were not inherent in trade union practice. One steward, for example, said that over the flexitime dispute the Council Leader had said the council existed to provide good services and trade union demands often ignored this. For this steward, the councillors often saw NALGO as on a different side from them. The union was seen by councillors as oppositional. For this steward, however, that need not be the case if councillors would involve the trade unions earlier in discussions about important issues. It was when the trade unions were presented with a fait accompli, by councillors, it was argued, that trade unions became defensive and service provision could be harmed.

Another NALGO steward stressed the commitment of most council workers to improving services. But they also wanted good pay and working conditions. As an example of worker commitment to good service provision, he instanced the social workers in his office accepting the office staying open during the lunch break. For this steward, it would be impossible to improve services when the council was trying to implement financial cuts. In that situation, which had prevailed in Doncaster for some time, he said, conflicts between trade union demands and service provision were bound to occur. But the unions were not to blame for the conflict which was the result of council imposed cuts.

For a NUPE official and a NUPE shop steward, trade union demands and good service delivery could, and did, clash. That would happen, they agreed, especially in a period of financial constraints, like the one then facing local government. For them, trade unions were not the opponents of councils. The aim is to agree common solutions to problems. In the current hostile climate, the need was for trade unions to survive and win something for their members, it was agreed. In the process, service quality might also be maintained.

A GMB full-time officer said the councils faced a dilemma between employing a larger number of workers at lower rates of pay or employing a smaller number of workers at higher rates of pay. On the whole, he seemed to support the second option.

A national full-time NALGO official said that NALGO branches locally should forge links with tenants and other service users. In that way, he said, it would be possible for joint demands to be placed on councils. The NALGO branch in Wandsworth had tried to do this but the Conservative controlled council was not interested. For this officer, the interests of council workers and service users were clearly compatible.

Officers

In Sheffield, an officer in the Central Policy Unit argued that a conflict between trade union attitudes and good service delivery was almost inevitable. Such conflicts were not confined to local government but 'infected' all public services, in his view. A good example of the clash, he argued, was the attitude and actions of COHSE in the health service. For in the health service, COHSE was holding back and opposing a number of important radical ideas. A chief officer also accepted that there was a conflict between workers, trade union, demands and service delivery. For him, good industrial relations and service delivery were not one and the same thing. Of the two, when they clashed, service delivery must be given the top priority. Another chief officer saw the two factors as not intrinsically incompatible. If the two conflicted it was because of trade union intransigence. If the trade unions acted reasonably then their demands and good service delivery would not be in conflict. A PIRO argued that there was no conflict between good industrial relations and good service delivery. For him, the two were mutually supportive. To achieve good service delivery you needed good industrial relations. For him, if the council achieved good industrial relations, service provision must benefit. Another PIRO disagreed with that view. In his opinion, conflicts between trade union demands and management objectives were inevitable. The important point, for him, was how you tackled such conflicts. But, in his experience, trade unions always tried to compromise between meeting the needs of their members and of their clients, as the needs of those groups are not one and the same.

Among officers in Doncaster, there was agreement that the interests of trade unions and of service provision can conflict. In any such conflicts, one chief officer argued, the interests of consumers must be paramount. However, in the long term, for this officer, workers and management both had an interest in keeping the customer happy, as their jobs ultimately depended upon it. Another officer in Doncaster saw a conflict between trade union demands and service delivery. For him, this resulted from trade unions wanting to get better working conditions and pay for their members. Hence, in his view, if resources were limited and unions pushed for more pay and better working conditions service provision was bound to suffer. The Chief Executive accepted that good service delivery and trade union demands could, and did, conflict, especially when council resources were scarce.

The views expressed, although far from unanimous, are important for a number of reasons. First, they lend some support to the view that unions are defensive and reactive organizations, at least in certain circumstances. Second, the views suggest that when unions are defensive it is because they feel their members' interests are being threatened. Third, and following on from the above point, there was some support for the view that the Labour councillors had failed to convince the trade unions and their members that proposed changes were in the interests of the unions' members, a point raised in respect of other issues. Fourth, the belief that unions and workers can act in a positive manner if given the opportunity, expressed by trade union representatives and some Sheffield councillors, suggests that unions are not simply defensive organizations. Fifth, in so far as there are differences of interpretation, those differences tend to reflect people's different positions in the employment relationship. For example, unionists tended to see conflict in this area springing from bad industrial relations and workers being treated badly by employers. Councillors tended to see conflicts as built into the incompatibility of union demands and good service delivery (although many Sheffield councillors, to varying degrees, denied this). Officers tended to see conflicts resulting from unreasonable union demands. Sixth, councillors and some officers in Doncaster remarked upon the different attitudes of NALGO and NUPE. While NUPE acted responsibly and constructively, as over the flexitime dispute, NALGO acted in a totally negative, unreasonable and often hostile manner. This could tie in with the argument that white collar workers either made greater demands on the council than manual workers, or that manual workers had unreasonably low expectations, depending on one's point of view.

Managers' I.R. practices and attitudes

There have already been suggestions from the analysis of other themes that managers may not have exactly the same attitude towards industrial relations as councillors. Moreover, from the earlier theoretical analysis this is what one would expect. In the next section, the views of those interviewed on the attitudes and practices of managers will be considered. The views of Sheffield councillors will be set out first.

Councillors

The then Deputy Leader of Sheffield City Council said there had been a tradition in the Recreation Department of managers simply telling workers what to do. Workers had then done as they were instructed. This was a harmful approach, in his view, and needed to change. For another leading Labour councillor, managers in the F and C S Department were too accommodating to trade unions. Managers in that department wanted to avoid unpleasantness and trouble and went out of their way to do so. While in many ways this councillor thought that was an admirable trait, it could mean that difficult problems were not always tackled promptly or effectively. Another councillor also believed that different departments had their own special ethos which affected the attitudes and practice of managers. The different ethos resulted from the nature of the service provided. The then Chair of the Personnel Sub-Committee said some senior officers saw industrial relations as a diversion. For him, they saw industrial relations as a side issue which conflicted with their search for efficiency. He believed that view was short-sighted and mistaken. For him, good industrial relations and efficiency did not clash.

For councillors in Doncaster there were differences in the attitudes of managers. The Council Leader accepted that personalities were important. Doncaster councillors stressed that the council organized training courses for managers on industrial relations in order to try to create good attitudes among council management. For the then Chair of the Housing Committee, the managers in the Housing Department all gave industrial relations the right priority and tried to deal constructively with the grievances and problems of workers.

Trade Unionists

A NUPE representative in Sheffield said that while the terms and conditions of employment of managers had improved greatly over the last ten years, in some areas the standard of management was no better now than it had been then. He cited the management in the Cleansing Department as an example of what can be achieved if managers were forward looking and committed. He commented 'With managers of vision so much more could have been achieved' in other departments as well. A NUPE shop steward in F and C S agreed that departmental managers were beginning to talk to the workers more. But particularly senior managers were not aware of the situation at grass roots level. For this steward, managers were aloof from the day to day experience and concerns of workers. Other manual worker representatives stressed the importance of middle and lower managers, the people who deal with most industrial relations matters, in determining the industrial relations climate in a department.

A manual worker trade union representative said management opposed everything. *The Job Satisfaction Survey Report* recommendations in Recreation, in his view, had been blocked by management. While, he argued, 'there was often support at the top of the council, at departmental level good proposals are being strongly opposed by management. Management don't generally delegate decision making', he said. That created problems. Both shop stewards and middle managers criticized the lack of 'bringing down' of decision making. A joint seminar of shop stewards and managers in the Recreation Department was held not long before the interview to try to improve relations in the department, he said. Since then, there had been a slight change but 'I'd feel Peter Price [Chair of the Leisure Committee] hasn't pushed this very much'. This steward agreed there were differences between managers at different levels. Some lower level managers were more understanding than others. Generally, however, this steward did not have a high opinion of managers. On the whole, he said, managers tried to make workers feel degraded by stopping them having tea breaks and generally treating them badly. For him, managers wanted to control workers.

A GMB full-time officer and a GMB shop steward in Sheffield Council both saw the attitude of the chair of committee as crucial in determining the industrial relations climate in a department. Where you had a good Labour councillor as committee chair, managers generally took a reasonable attitude, they argued. Where the Chair of Committee was not so good, managers tended to have a more antagonistic attitude towards workers, in their view.

For a NALGO shop steward in Housing, industrial relations in the department had never been good. However, they had deteriorated recently. For this steward 'Senior managers below Director level seem to take pleasure in saying no to shop stewards and failing to give even basic information'. They took their lead from the Director, in this view. For a second NALGO steward, middle managers in F and C S were very mediocre. They were incapable of taking decisions on anything. For this steward, managers needed a great deal of training. A person could not just become a good manager overnight. For this to happen, it was argued, councillors ought to be promoting management training in a much more positive manner. In F and C S, relations between shop stewards and top managers had traditionally been very good, this steward said. With the budget cuts, however, these good relations were under threat. There were signs, it was argued, that the Director of Social Services was beginning to feel he had no say in many issues and hence saw little need to negotiate with the trade unions.

For another NALGO steward, there were big differences in the attitudes of managers. While some managers, he argued, were good at communicating, some are not. He said, there was one officer in his department who listened to what you said as a union representative and then did what he wanted. He knew of middle managers who were good at communicating, a skill which, for him, was crucial, and in getting the job done. But managers, generally, had not tried to win workers over to change.

A NALGO steward in Doncaster said the attitude of managers differed according to circumstances. From his experience, when the going was good managers were not too bad. Their attitudes and actions were reasonable in such circumstances. But if circumstances were difficult, then managers were terrible. This steward said that NALGO stewards in the Housing Department were quite happy with the attitude of the Assistant Director of Housing who dealt with all but the most important industrial relations matters.

A NALGO steward in Social Services in Doncaster, said middle managers paid little attention to industrial relations in their day to day work. The consultative machinery was the place where most industrial relations issues were 'taken up'. Since the new Director of Social Services took over there had been a change in attitude. At one time the old Director was willing to meet the shop stewards committee whenever they wanted. Towards the end of his time with the council, however, he wanted to reduce the frequency of the meetings as he was out of line with other Directorates. The new Director, this steward said, was opposed to regular meetings. In the new Director's view, meetings should take place as and when required, over specific matters. NALGO, on the other hand, wanted to have regular meetings with the right to call specific meetings on particular issues.

A NUPE representative said many officers had a bad attitude towards manual workers. For him, senior officers are a professional group of people with a superior view of their positions. The Chief Executive and Directors and Assistant Directors of Services tried to squeeze manual workers, all too often. They also did things, this representative argued, about which councillors do not know, and would probably disapprove if they did. He said that some senior officers were worse than others. 'Some are full-time bastards'. He saw professional and career advancement as very important for those people and affecting the way they operated. Officers had a very big input into policy. They put reports to councillors and, as part-timers, councillors did not have the time to scrutinize such reports properly. Trade unions do not have the right to make reports to councillors, he said. Officers, he said, set the pace by coming forward with suggestions and councillors responded to those suggestions. These views raise issues about the policy making process in local government to which I shall return in a later section. The NUPE representatives I interviewed agreed that differences within departments did exist. Such differences, they claimed, were due to the different personalities of managers and leading councillors.

The findings in respect of trade union representatives do not fit in with the results of the study of the attitudes of local government shop stewards unearthed by Marchington and Armstrong (1982, p. 42). While they found manual shop stewards in local government most deferential towards management of those interviewed, my research found manual worker representatives very critical of management. An interesting point is that while many councillors were critical of council managers, few seemed to see the need to devise a strategy to change the attitudes of managers although councillors in Doncaster did mention the training the council organizes for managers on industrial relations.

Two other points of wide significance are the importance many trade unionists placed on the position of middle managers and their attitudes and the view of councillors that departments have their own ethos springing from the type of service provided. The first of those points, suggests, if it is correct, that the strategy of councils like the GLC from 1981-1986 in bringing in officers in high positions to try to get new supportive channels of advice and action may not be enough to change the way councils operate. If the attitudes and actions of middle managers are as important as some trade unionists suggested, then there is clearly a need for councillors to work not just to change things at the top of the managerial hierarchy but to bring about changes at lower levels as well.

The second point may have some substance to it. For example, it may be one of the factors explaining why the strike in 1984 in Sheffield City Council occurred in the Housing Department and not in the F and C S Department. However, that does not explain why there was the stand-by strike in Social Services in Doncaster in 1980. Without a more detailed and major study of councils it would be impossible to comment categorically on that point but it would seem to be open to very serious doubt. For example, manual worker stewards and NALGO stewards in F and C S in Sheffield did not believe the attitude of managers was particularly good and much criticism was levelled at top managers in the department by a manual union shop steward though not by NALGO stewards.

Relations between different trade unions

An issue which is of importance in understanding industrial relations
in the councils, concerns the relations between the different council
trade unions. Understanding whether the unions worked together on
issues or whether there were conflicts between them and strained
relations is important for understanding the dynamics of industrial
relations in the councils. It is also important in understanding the
'nature' of trade unionism. Hence the current section will look at the
views of the trade union representatives I interviewed, on this issue.

Sheffield Trade Unionists

A NUPE representative in Sheffield argued that traditionally relations
between the trade unions in Sheffield City Council were poor.
Relations between the two main general unions in the council - GMB
and NUPE - have historically been frosty. One reason for this, he
suggested, was the competition for members. The two unions were
trying to recruit the same council workers and that, in his view,
necessarily created tensions. For him, relations were very poor
traditionally between NALGO and the manual unions in the council.
This was especially true, he said, of relations between NALGO and
GMB. He considered NALGO's structures as very unrepresentative.
Preparing for competitive tendering had brought the manual and
non-manual unions together, to some extent. In other areas, however,
he said, conflicts between the unions still existed. There were
problems between NALGO and NUPE in Housing, for example, where
NUPE had a number of members who had changed from NALGO,
over representation on the Joint Consultative Committee.

For a NUPE steward, the union, at her level, worked quite well with
NALGO. She believed friction occurred at higher levels where
workers did not have contact with the public. NUPE's relations with
the GMB had improved slightly in her department, partly because of
competitive tendering. On competitive tendering, NALGO opposed
equal white collar, blue collar job losses, she said.

For a third manual worker union representative, NUPE relations with
NALGO were not very good. For him 'manual workers see NALGO as
being a bosses' union generally ... NALGO are in charge of a pyramid
of promotion which goes on for ever'. NALGO members opposed
taking their fair share of cuts, when they were proposed, he said. He
did not believe that compulsory competitive tendering had brought the
unions together. In his department, there was little contact between
manual and non-manual trade unions on compulsory competitive
tendering. He was worried about the ability of the council to compete

on competitive tendering but argued 'There's no attitude to change that situation [from NALGO]. There's no holding back on salaries.' At shop steward level, he said, relations with the GMB were quite good. However, there were greater problems now then there had been but that was due to personality differences.

A GMB shop steward while he accepted there were differences between the manual and non-manual unions, did not agree with such differences and splits. For him, while it was in the immediate interests of the manual unions to work with NALGO, it was not obviously apparent that that was the case the other way round. He said the manual side of the council's activities had been pruned to the bone but there was still some fat on the non-manual side.

A GMB full-time officer and a GMB shop steward both saw relations with NUPE as far from ideal. In line with the view expressed by the NUPE full-time officer, they argued that the two unions - GMB and NUPE - were chasing the same potential members and that produced problems. Relations with the Transport and General Workers Union, for them, were good. The shop steward saw the relations between the GMB and NALGO in F and C S as very good. The two shop stewards committees met on a monthly basis.

With regard to NALGO stewards in Sheffield, opinions differed. One branch officer said that six months ago relations between NALGO and the manual unions were terrible, since when they had improved. In some departments, he said, at rank and file level relations were not too bad. For him, a situation existed where, on the one hand, manual workers saw NALGO as a bosses' trade union and regarded white collar workers as lazy and 'on the backs' of manual workers; while, on the other, professional workers saw manual workers as bad workers, lazy and not pulling their weight. There were also problems with NUPE poaching NALGO members, which created tensions. A NALGO shop steward in Housing said that the manual unions and NALGO get on well in that department. The problems occurred at council level where NUPE poaching of other unions' members is a real problem. Another NALGO steward saw relations between NALGO and the other trade unions varying. Many manual workers saw NALGO as privileged, as getting unfair treatment, better conditions and so on. That could cause friction between the unions.

In Doncaster Council a NALGO shop steward said relations with NUPE were terrible. NUPE had poached members actively in one area, it was stated. NUPE members crossed NALGO picket lines over the flexitime strike. For this steward, the hierarchy in NUPE got on badly with the hierarchy in NALGO. For NALGO, NUPE 'sold out' over flexitime. Apart from NUPE, it was argued, relations with other council trade unions were good. Another NALGO shop steward agreed that NALGO's relations with NUPE were very poor. A third NALGO steward argued that relations with NUPE were uniformly bad. The two unions were a long way from overcoming their internal differences. In the past, he said, NALGO has not wanted other unions involved in the agreements it has negotiated. Now, however, NUPE was adopting the same attitude. He disliked this situation, believing that all unions should work together. Over flexitime, for instance, the council had exploited union differences, in his view.

On the general question of NUPE poaching of members of other unions, it is interesting to note that between 1970-1985 NUPE's membership grew from 439,890 to 752,130 (cf. Fryer, 1989). There is no suggestion that NUPE's membership growth was the result of poaching members from other unions. However, the growth does suggest a strong, vigorous recruitment drive by the union. The comments on NUPE's poaching of members also suggests that it may be difficult for the component parts of the new union Unison to work together. Moreover, given the different histories and the operating styles of the different parts of Unison, some tensions may be unavoidable. On the other hand, forming a single union may bring different workers together and create a situation where the necessity of overcoming divisions 'forces' manual and non-manual workers to work together. Obviously, forming one union will eliminate any problems of poaching.

A NUPE representative in Doncaster Council saw relations with NALGO as reasonable. Problems were not nearly as bad, he said, as NALGO locally suggested. For him, NALGO's attitude sprang from the part-time, lay position of its negotiators. In his view, workers needed full-time officers to negotiate with management, as part-time, lay representatives lacked the necessary experience and knowledge. Over the last eighteen months, he said, many APT and C staff had joined NUPE. They had changed unions voluntarily, NUPE had not directly encouraged them to do so. Hence, for him, NALGO had blown up the poaching issue out of all proportion. This officer did say, however, that he would like to see a single union -NUPE- covering all manual and craft and APT and C staff. Relations with other manual worker unions, GMB, UCATT (Union of Construction and Allied Trades and Technicians) and the TGWU were very good, he commented. All those unions work well together.

There would seem, therefore, to be some tension between the unions and especially the manual unions and NALGO. There was some evidence to support the findings of the study by Marchington and Armstrong (1982, p. 46). Their research showed that mutual suspicion between manual and non-manual shop stewards in the local authorities they studied was strong. However, my research does not entirely support that finding suggesting a more complex picture. A number of manual union representatives saw a conflict between the manual unions and particularly the GMB and NUPE as well as between the manual unions and NALGO. There was quite strong support for the opinion that manual workers viewed NALGO as a bosses' union, getting preferential treatment. However, NALGO stewards in Doncaster were strongly of the opinion that NUPE was 'in the council's pocket'. It would appear that there is some reason to believe that relations between unions differ from department to department. Certainly NALGO and the GMB union representatives in the F and C S Department in Sheffield seemed to get on very well. It is interesting to note the number of those interviewed who believed any conflicts and differences between the unions were a bad thing. A number of NALGO and manual worker representatives wished the unions did work together more closely. However, the overall conclusion is that there were conflicts at different levels and of different intensities and that these are not just between NALGO and the manual unions but also within the manual unions. This suggests that trade union sectionalism was a very active ingredient in the two councils studied. Whether the formation of Unison will help to overcome such sectionalism remains to be seen.

Attitudes of councillors

An issue which is of prime importance in determining the nature of industrial relations in local councils is the attitude and approach of councillors, especially leading councillors. Trade unionists and officers were, therefore, asked how they thought councillors approached the issue of industrial relations. Some councillors were also asked how they saw the role of the councillor in industrial relations. The respective views will be set out below starting, for once, with the views of Sheffield trade union representatives.

Trade Unionists

A NUPE representative in Sheffield commented 'Politically industrial relations even in Sheffield is not taken as seriously as it could be'. He said Appeals Panel hearings were often cancelled because councillors failed to turn up for them. This situation had improved somewhat recently with councillors taking a more responsible approach. But the Local Joint Committee (LJC) was often inquorate on the council side. Recently, he said, senior councillors from the Labour Group Executive were attending the LJC, which represented an improvement on the past. However, his comments strongly suggested that councillors, at least until the late 1980s, had not given attendance at LJCs and Appeals Panels a very high priority, even allowing for the constraints on councillor's time. This officer said relations were better between the politicians and the manual trade unions than they were between the politicians and NALGO.

For a NUPE shop steward, councillors in top positions on the council still treated workers as dirt. For this steward, councillors were too concerned about 'saving their skins', too cut off, removed from what is happening at 'grass roots level' to play a constructive and helpful role. There was a lack of concern among councillors, in this view, about the experience of workers at grass roots level. Hence councillors were not aware of the problems workers faced and did not take workers' worries seriously. For this steward, councillors, because they were removed from the everyday experiences of workers, were in much the same position as top council management.

Another NUPE shop steward was of the opinion that on the whole industrial relations problems could be resolved at departmental level. He said 'Speaking personally, the main problem is at the political level', with councillors often doing things for political reasons rather than for reasons connected with industrial relations. This steward commented 'I think there's less political involvement overall now, it's down to individual politicians'. Not all councillors approached industrial relations in the same way, he said. That meant managers in different departments had different scope for action, depending on who chaired their committee. He criticized councillors strongly, 'A lot of councillors think they'll go along with trade unions ... but they don't put a lot of work in to see things are followed through'.

As already shown, a GMB full-time officer and a GMB shop steward both felt that the chairs of committees were very important in determining the industrial relations climate in departments. The steward said the chairs in F and C S recently had given a strong lead to management. While for the full-time officer, in Recreation, where he thought industrial relations were the worst in the council, a strong political lead was lacking. For them, there had certainly been a change in the council's attitude since David Blunkett left. However, the full-time officer was not sure whether things would have changed as they have if David Blunkett had stayed, as the circumstances in which the council was operating had changed.

For a NALGO shop steward, David Blunkett was probably sincere in what he wanted to do. However, because of his politics and particularly his attitude on rate capping, 'you end up with window dressing', it was argued. The situation had not changed markedly since he left and had he stayed, this steward commented, similar policies to those being introduced now would have been employed. Another NALGO steward said councillors made many strategic decisions behind closed doors then negotiated with the trade unions on important issues afterwards. Councillors, this steward believed, wanted to make policy without a trade union input. For him, the position had deteriorated recently, with growing secrecy. While this steward did not link the change with David Blunkett's leaving the council, his comment suggested there had been a change in recent times. This may or may not be connected with Blunkett's removal from the council. He said councillors 'rubber stamp' management's positions and did not take a line independent of management, in many cases. For this steward, while there were differences in the attitudes of councillors, it would be wrong to make too much of personalities in discussing this issue.

A NALGO steward in Recreation thought Sheffield councillors were very good at making 'right on' statements but not nearly so good at seeing the statements were put into practice. The policy process was piecemeal, in his view. Councillors worked out what to do, then left it to managers to implement the agreed policies. Little effort was made by councillors, in this view, to ensure its policies are implemented in the way desired.

For a NALGO steward in Doncaster, the council acted in a very conservative fashion. Labour councillors' seats on the council were safe and, as a result, there was a lack of vigour in their approach. Councillors, it was argued, had become complacent and failed to take a serious approach to industrial relations, or other matters. Councillors did not take the views of the trade unions seriously when deciding issues and expressed a high degree of arrogance. Another NALGO steward said councillors treated NUPE better than NALGO. Councillors liked NUPE full-time officers much more than NALGO shop stewards, he said. Councillors, therefore, favoured NUPE as a union and gave its proposals and actions a higher priority than those of NALGO. A third NALGO shop steward saw councillors feeling a greater empathy with manual workers and treating manual workers better. Councillors tended to view NALGO members as a threat and were wary of them, as a result, he said.

For a representative of NUPE in Doncaster, his union had a better relationship with councillors than NALGO because of the union's political ties to the Labour Party. Because NUPE was affiliated to the Labour Party nationally and locally and could show its commitment to the Labour Party it was able to work more closely with the Labour councillors. Sometimes, he said, NUPE would use political channels to make progress where managers had blocked matters. NALGO, which had no direct links with the Labour Party and had only recently established a Political Fund was distrusted by the council and was unable to make use of political channels in the way NUPE could. There was no doubt, for this officer, that the manual unions, and not just NUPE, had better relations with councillors than NALGO. However, a GMB full-time officer did not accept that manual unions could gain a better response from councillors. He said he had never known a management decision to be overturned when it reached Doncaster councillors.

The responses of trade union representatives, then, raise certain questions about the commitment of councillors and their partiality in dealing with different trade unions. For whatever reasons, there does seem to be a strong view among union representatives that Labour councillors, in both councils, treated manual unions and their members better than non-manual unions and their members. Or at least, councillors were seen as having a greater empathy with manual than non-manual workers. This point, of course, has already been expressed in another section, the analysis here simply reinforces the point. Many trade union representatives in Sheffield questioned the commitment of councillors to put their expressed objectives into practice. There was an agreement, certainly among union representatives in Sheffield City Council, that the 'personalities' of individual councillors in top council positions could make a difference to industrial relations. There was an interesting disagreement between NUPE and GMB full-time officers about the 'responsiveness' of councillors in Doncaster, as well as differences between the NUPE full-time officer and NALGO shop stewards in their attitudes in that council.

Officers

Most officers approached this issue very differently from the trade union representatives. For them, the issue revolved around the extent to which councillors interfered in the running of departments. The issue of councillors' attitudes to industrial relations was linked to the question of councillor involvement in the running of departments, in the interviewing of council officers, partly because of the way I phrased the questions. Officers were often asked about councillor involvement in the running of their departments and the connection between this and councillors' attitudes to industrial relations. In one or two cases, however, officers made the link themselves.

Most officers believed there should be a demarcation line between the concerns of councillors and of officers. A good example of this attitude was the position adopted by the then Director of Social Services in Sheffield. For him, most industrial relations responsibilities in departments rested with management. Councillors were involved, he said, in the formal procedures, such as monthly Joint Consultative Committees, dispute procedures and so on. He saw nothing to be gained by councillors becoming involved in day to day industrial relations matters, as that would only blur the lines of responsibility.

That view was endorsed by another chief officer in Sheffield Council who argued, as well, that councillors who were trade union representatives often had a struggle coping with the responsibilities of management. For him, councillors had had too much input in administration in the past. If the chief officer did not do the job, ultimately his or her contract should be ended, he said. Otherwise they should be free to get on and do the job for which they were paid.

The PIRO in the Housing Department, argued that in a council like Sheffield which is so 'up front' about wanting change, councillors must be involved in industrial relations. He said that the then Leader of the Council was much more involved in the day to day running of the department when he was Chair of the Housing Committee, than is the case with the current Chair of Housing. For him, major issues are too important to be left with the vagaries of a procedure which relied upon advocacy skills rather than negotiations. He said,

> It is a nonsense to ask 'neutral' councillors to sit in judgement for a couple of hours on issues which are very complex and which had months of negotiations at departmental level. Furthermore, a procedure based upon advocacy emphasizes the procedure itself rather than negotiations. I think that the procedure should be changed to concentrate more upon the negotiation process and Councillors (as the employers) should, where needed, be involved in those negotiations, instead of being asked to act as quasi judges.

For the PIRO in F and C S, chairs of committees are very important in setting the industrial relations attitude in departments. For him, councillors have an important role to play in industrial relations at departmental level, but not in the day to day running of departments.

In Doncaster, a chief officer said councillors tended to favour manual workers in Labour councils. He said politicians were getting more involved in the running of departments. Today, he said, the chair has a right to be consulted on issues which in the past managers would have decided on their own. Councillors, in his experience, did not believe they knew all the answers and recognized they were dispensable, as were chief officers. The Chief Executive said many trade unionists believed politicians were more sympathetic than officers. Another officer said that if a dispute was taken to appeal by a union, especially on a disciplinary matter, the officer concerned had to be sure he or she had a cast iron case, otherwise the council would not support him or her. That view directly contradicted the statement of a manual union official, reported earlier.

One can see, therefore, that there were differences in the approach of individual officers. While many officers were worried that councillors should not become more directly involved in industrial relations in day to day matters at the departmental level, others believed councillors should accept that they are part of the management side and act accordingly. However, that idea raises a host of issues relating to the extent to which the aims of councillors and managers are the same. How far do managers accurately reflect the policies and outlook of councillors? Should councillors take the side of managers even if they disagree with managers' stance? Clearly, the officer in Sheffield Council who said that councillors cannot be neutral on issues which have resource implications for the authority was right. But it does not seem self evidently true that in a council where the councillors are trying to change the way the council operates, councillors should be automatically on the side of management in disputes with workers. The officer concerned seemed to be calling for an earlier and greater involvement of councillors in industrial relations issues so that councillors can ensure the managers' position is acceptable to them. However, many other officers, from their remarks, would clearly regard that as unacceptable. In this respect, it is interesting that the then Chair of the Personnel Sub-Committee in Sheffield believed councillors should be involved less in the details of industrial relations. For him, councillors should lay down aims and objectives and leave it to officers to put the aims and objectives into practice. It is also interesting that a number of officers believed, like many trade unionists, that the attitude of the committee chair was crucial in determining the industrial relations climate in a department.

How policy is made and chief officer power

Arising out of the above discussion it is important to consider how policy is actually made within the two councils and the respective roles of councillors and officers in policy formation. Councillors and officers were asked about those related issues. Their replies should enable any differences in opinion between the two groups to be made explicit. It should then be possible to offer explanations for the differences, if indeed any exist.

Councillors

The then leader of Sheffield City Council said that he now realises the chief officer machine was very formidable. After the new leadership took over in 1980, however, there was a feeling that 'We can make chief officers do what we wanted'. There was no clear strategy among the new leadership, he said, to overcome the opposition of chief officers or their potential hostility to what the new leadership wanted to do. At that time he was Chair of the Housing Committee and found the then Director of Housing had little or no interest in the type of changes and issues which concerned him.

David Blunkett also argued that there was no automatic movement from councillors passing policy and chief officers simply ensuring it was implemented as intended. He commented,

> there is a belief that councillors pass resolutions and the bureaucracy simply jumps. Well, I think we have an enormous amount to learn, as we have at national government level. I agree with Tony Benn strongly about the question of addressing the issue of how you deal with the civil service and the same applies at local level.

Blunkett related this to the need to win people over and gain their support if the aims of councillors were to be achieved. This was something, he admitted, the council failed to do while he was leader. Other Sheffield councillors also believed officers had the ability to make the implementation of policy difficult, if they disliked what the council was trying to do. However, it was argued, it was not just chief officers but managers at lower levels as well who had that ability.

Among councillors in Doncaster, the view was that councillors make policy and officers then carry it out. The two tasks, policy making and implementation, were linked but separate. The general view of councillors was that there was no real problem in Doncaster with managers trying to move beyond their proper role.

Officers

Among officers, opinions varied. One officer, in the Sheffield Central Policy Unit, when asked, said that most senior officers in Sheffield wanted some excitement and to feel the local council was moving forward. Hence, he said, officers in Sheffield were not opposed to the policies and strategy of the council after 1980. There was certainly no concerted effort to block the council's policies in the early years of the new leadership, in his opinion. This was a very different situation, he said, from that which existed in the GLC. In the GLC, senior staff were very much like civil servants. They were in a patrician mould. Hence, the arguments of Livingstone and Robin Murray that officers in the GLC tried to actively stop the implementation of the 1981-1986 council's policies, about which he was questioned, could not simply be re-applied to Sheffield. While people like Robin Murray were brought into the GLC as intermediaries between chief officers and councillors, that was not the case with people, like him, who were appointed in Sheffield.

The then Director of Social Services in Sheffield council said that the council did give officers a role in policy formation. Officers in Sheffield, he said, were not simply involved in implementing and carrying through policy. Senior officers, he commented, gave advice and made recommendations to councillors. Councillors, however, in his view, made final policy decisions. In his opinion, there was a clear cut off point where the officers' involvement ended and councillors 'took over' in the policy process. The then Director of Housing said policy ideas came equally from the Labour Group and from the chief officers. Councillors, however, he said, made the final decisions, wherever policy originated. For him, his job was eighty per cent administration and twenty per cent political and for politicians the percentages were reversed.

In Doncaster, the Chief Executive was of the opinion that the vast majority of proposals come from officers, not councillors. However, as with Sheffield officers, he said that, while recommendations on policy come from officers, councillors made the final decisions. He said councillors in Doncaster were not very good at thinking about long term issues. He said he did play a big role in policy formation and wished Labour councillors would give more attention to longer term planning.

A chief officer in Doncaster said he was accountable to the Chief Executive and the council Corporate Executive, as well as the Chair of the Committee covering his department. At first he said councillors made policy, he simply implemented it. But when further questioned, he said that generally policy initiatives were made by professional, employed staff. The main drift of policy initiatives came from officers and, in his view, that was the way it should be. For another senior officer in Doncaster, the councillors left officers to decide what to put on committee meeting agendas. He argued that most policy initiatives came from officers. Officers were reviewing services, making recommendations and preparing reports from those activities. But, while the first move on policy was made by officers, he said, the final say lay with councillors.

It seems, therefore, that officers generally recognized that they did play a part in policy formation but believed final policy decisions were taken by councillors. That view was common in both Sheffield and Doncaster Councils and accepted by Doncaster councillors. Sheffield councillors, however, recognized that senior officers might not always play a particularly benign role. Officers had the ability to block council policies, was the view of Sheffield councillors. There was, therefore, an important difference between Sheffield councillors and council officers on this issue. It may well be true, as officers argued, that councillors generally make the final decisions on most policy matters but that does not mean, as was generally implied, that councillors, therefore, make policy. For the options from which councillors chose policy may be limited severely by the recommendations which officers present to them. The agenda, in terms of what is and what is not possible, may be crucially controlled by senior council officers. This view, as has been shown, was advanced by a full-time NUPE official in Doncaster. There was little support for the view that councillors were becoming too involved in the day to day running of council departments and that the roles of councillors and officers are becoming blurred, a view expressed by chief officers surveyed by Laffin and Young (1985).

Moreover, as Sheffield councillors remarked, once policy was agreed by councillors, there was no guarantee that it would simply be implemented by officers as councillors intended. The neat split between policy making and policy implementation may be, in reality, artificial. As the officer in the Sheffield Central Policy Unit argued, there may not be a concerted effort by senior officers to directly block the implementation of radical council initiatives, where they occurred, in most councils. However, as policy often has to be interpreted before it is implemented, senior officers have considerable scope for autonomous action. The general role of senior officers in setting the agenda and giving technical advice also gives them power.

Two other points are also worthy of comment. First, the Chief Executive in Doncaster clearly believed councillors in Doncaster have a limited interest in policy development. Most councillors, in his view, were happy letting policy ideas come from officers. If true, then this says much about the conservatism of leading Labour councillors in Doncaster. It also gives support to the views of NALGO stewards that the councillors are very conservative with a small 'c'. Second, it is interesting that a senior officer in Doncaster had the view that it was right that most policy ideas come from council officers. This suggests that he saw the policy process as mainly a technical activity where expert technical advice was crucial to making good policy, rather than a political activity about social aims and objectives and how you achieved them. This view was strengthened by the opinion of this officer that senior council officers should be politically neutral.

Having dealt with a number of themes which largely have relevance for both councils, I will next consider some themes which are of direct importance for, and spring from the experience of, Sheffield City Council and not Doncaster Borough Council. Those themes relate to the development of socialist management and industrial democracy, which were expressed as aims by David Blunkett and which have been included in Sheffield District Labour Party manifestos over the years, the working of council initiatives like the Low Pay Supplement, the *Take Ten* education initiative, the Equal Opportunities policy, the Job Satisfaction Survey recommendations in the Recreation Department, the Passport to Leisure scheme and the introduction of Elderly Persons' Support Units. I will begin by looking at the issue of socialist management and industrial democracy in the council, in the next chapter.

8 Sheffield's Radicalism

Socialist management and industrial relations

Many of the pronouncements of David Blunkett, former leader of Sheffield City Council, showed that in the 1980s promoting a new socialist management and industrial democracy in the council was one of his prime aims. Many of the statements in which Blunkett made this commitment are to be found in earlier chapters of the work and they will not be repeated here. The commitment of the council Labour Group to promote industrial democracy in the council was also clear from various District Labour Party manifestos issued during the 1980s. The 1983 manifesto, for example, said 'This fundamental commitment to extend democracy in the workplace and the economy has led us to re-examine the ways in which departments operate' (Sheffield City Council, 1983, p. 6). The 1984 manifesto also said:

> We are committed to working jointly with Council employees and those who use Council services to improve the quality and value of those services and to extend democracy in a way which provides real choice for those who otherwise would be denied access to power and decision making (Sheffield City Council n.d., p. 6)

It also said the council would 'Increase employee participation through a series of joint committees and by supporting the development of effective joint stewards organisations' (City Council, n.d., p. 33).

In addition, the 1987 manifesto said the council would 'Develop Socialist ideas of Industrial Relations democracy and how they apply to Sheffield Local Authority' (Sheffield District Labour Party, 1987, p. 35). The document committed the council to 'actively seek a constructive and open dialogue with the workforce, through their elected Trade Union representatives, about the development and implementation of Manifesto commitments' (Sheffield District Labour Party, 1987, p. 35). Also in 1987, the council adopted a document which recommended that service users and workers should be consulted about service aims and objectives and departments made more accessible to the public. Departments should evaluate annually their success in achieving greater public access (Sheffield City Council, 1987).

It seems clear, therefore, that the Labour Group had firm, if unspecified, commitments to introduce industrial democracy and change the way the council operated to achieve that. But how far did those interviewed believe the commitments had been achieved or furthered? The views of councillors will be discussed first.

Councillors

A chair of committee said industrial democracy is not something different from that which the council was doing in its negotiations with the trade unions. For him, there were plenty of opportunities for workers to be heard, through their trade unions, in the council's industrial relations structures. On the question of whether workers should have representation on council policy committees, another councillor said that a stage had not yet been reached where worker representatives on council committees was possible. Councillors were accountable to the electorate, he said, and if workers had seats on committees that must not be at the expense of electoral accountability. He said, 'It's a very sensitive area to give people seats on committees just because of their jobs'. For him, access through consultative meetings probably gave workers as much involvement as workers having seats on council policy committees without voting rights. He saw no way in which workers could be given seats on committees with voting rights.

For David Blunkett, the council had not succeeded in working out a socialist management practice. But, then, he argued, neither had anyone else. At national level, he said, there were now some moves afoot to try to do that. He said 'We recognized it', the need to change the way the council worked and tried to change structures. The changes included altering the Corporate Management Unit into the Central Policy Unit. Changes were also introduced in the Personnel Department which were important. However, he recognized that if changes were to be secured and to be long-lasting, they needed to go deeper than instructing chief officers to do certain things. It was crucial, Blunkett said, to win over people at all levels to your way of thinking. He also said he supported workers having seats on council policy-making committees. This had been offered to the trade unions, who had turned down the offer.

While he accepted that little positive progress had been made in promoting worker and user involvement in the development of services, the Chair of the Personnel Sub-Committee said that, for him, making progress in that area was still a major issue. He accepted promoting worker and user involvement was not the most important issue for all Labour councillors but a large number still gave it a high priority. For him, the lack of progress on industrial democracy was due to a number of factors. These included the council having to fight so hard simply to keep services going due to central government opposition and the tendency not to do anything unless it could be introduced right across the board. The way forward on industrial democracy, for him, was through the introduction in personnel policy of pilot schemes which he thought would lead to bigger and more widespread initiatives, if they were successful. He gave the strong impression that he would hope to introduce pilot schemes in the not too distant future.

The Job Satisfaction Survey in the Recreation Department had as one of its proposals the involvement of workers in the appointment of managers. While the majority of *The Job Satisfaction Survey* recommendations and findings will be discussed in a separate section, the attitudes of the Chair of the Leisure Committee, the Director of Recreation and shop stewards on this recommendation will be discussed in this section. The views of the Chair of the Leisure Committee will be discussed directly below, while those of the Director of Recreation and shop stewards will be set out in the appropriate place later on.

The Chair of the Leisure Committee argued that workers having a direct say in the appointment of managers was not always a good thing. He said that while he was chair of social services, when senior appointments were made workers had a say but were not on the selection committee. The problem with worker involvement was that they did not know external candidates as well as internal ones. At the moment, he said, workers did not have a say in the appointment of senior personnel in the Recreation Department. He thought, however, that some scheme could work in areas like sports halls and sports management but not in other areas covering a bigger number of workers, where size made it impracticable.

For councillors in Doncaster, the general view was that negotiating procedures gave workers a sufficient input into issues which directly concerned them. The Council Leader said that the council used suggestion boxes to get workers' views. 'Perhaps we should look at how we can do more of that kind of thing', he commented.

Trade Unionists

For a manual worker shop steward, shop stewards have come forward with some ideas but the shop stewards committee has not been active enough in promoting those ideas. Shop stewards, he said, had put forward a twenty eight point plan for savings, none of which, however, were implemented by the council. The shop stewards committee did not follow up this issue with any vigour. He said, 'The Shop Stewards Committee has never acted in a cohesive fashion... It's not been able to do much on this'. For him, the Central Policy Unit (CPU) had been set up to develop worker participation and worker democracy in the council. It met opposition, however, he said, from chief officers and some chairs of committees. The CPU failed to beat that opposition and changed course in what it was doing, as a result. If this steward had a criticism of David Blunkett, it would be that he should have done more to ensure the victory of the CPU in its efforts to promote industrial democracy. This steward also believed that full-time union officers did little to ensure the CPU was successful in its original objectives. This was because the full-time officers wanted to maintain their power.

Asked about the desirability of workers having representation on council committees, a NALGO shop steward said that would only be useful if it enabled workers to gain information. For this steward, worker representatives on council committees was simply tokenism and could give the council the chance to argue that the trade unions were party to a decision when they had not been in any real sense a party to the decision at all.

Another NALGO steward said the problem for the union revolved around whether it wanted to be involved in policy formation from the start or to negotiate on a package brought forward by the council. There were different views in the union, he said, on this issue. For him, if workers having representatives on council committees gives workers the chance to gain information and to impart it, then worker representatives on council committees may possibly be a good thing. However, this steward was emphatic that the unions did not exist to manage the local state. For him, socialist industrial relations was not about councillors giving up power on committees but councillors taking the trade unions into negotiations about how the council's aims can be realized. Trade unions, he said, should always reserve the right to oppose any changes, no matter how closely they were involved in formulating them in the first place. It was quite legitimate, for this steward, for a council to come to a union and say 'We want to decentralize services but have only so much money, what should we do?' It would be right, he said, for the union to respond to such an approach while maintaining its independence of formal council committee structures. For this steward, Sheffield council did not do enough to involve workers.

A third NALGO representative said worker representation on council committees could be a good thing for trade union input. But in terms of press reaction, which would be universally hostile, he said, it was not worth the trouble. Another NALGO steward said that while NALGO had been involved on a social services committee the council had unilaterally decided to remove NALGO representatives from the committee because the council did not like what NALGO was proposing.

While the Labour Group had no commitments to promoting industrial democracy in the council, trade union representatives in Doncaster were still asked for their views on this issue. A NALGO shop steward was very much in favour of workers having representatives on council committees, at all levels. This would enable problems to be sorted out earlier, sometimes even before they arose, it was argued. Workers ought to have an input, this steward argued, before major policy decisions were made. However, the steward accepted that trade union representatives should have seats without votes on main policy committees. A second NALGO shop steward said that trade union representatives on policy committees should not be necessary. However, workers should have representatives on the Personnel Sub-Committee, although without a vote. On policy committees worker representatives would only be useful as a means of workers giving and receiving information and that would not be a marked gain, he said. He supported the establishment of a joint committee of tenants, councillors and workers.

For a third NALGO steward, trade union representatives on policy committees would be a good thing. However, he did not believe it would happen. In his view, the council ought to be looking for ways of involving workers at decision-making levels, even if on a limited, non-voting basis. He said NALGO had worked hard to maintain the Joint Consultative Committees and Joint Staffs Committee but had perhaps not done enough to expand those limited forms of worker involvement. This steward said that in his directorate there was occasionally a chance to put forward ideas for improving services or the running of the department. For example, when the initial round of cuts started workers were asked to put forward ideas for cuts. The steward saw that as a very negative form of worker involvement. Worker involvement was not a regular process, he said. The implication, although it was not 'spelt out' by the steward, was that management and councillors wanted the involvement of workers on issues of the management's and councillors' choosing, only.

A NUPE full-time officer in the council said that whenever he has seen industrial democracy in action workers have come out slightly worse off. For him, industrial democracy, by which he meant limited worker representation on council policy committees, is a double-edged sword. He supported consultation with negotiations. He saw industrial democracy as dividing trade union leaders from union members. Industrial democracy, for him, could enable workers to have an input but could also have drawbacks. For him, trade union democracy must involve mass membership meetings where full-time officers report-back to the membership. In present circumstances, workers have to be heard a little, but council officers generally do not want workers to have ideas.

Officers

The Director of Recreation in Sheffield said that it was impracticable for workers to be directly involved, in a voting capacity, in the selection of senior council staff. However, in the same vein as the Chair of the Leisure Committee, he thought that the views of workers could be canvassed informally. On the broader issue of worker involvement, he felt that shop stewards often did not understand the consequences of their proposals. In the Recreation Department, a shop steward had been seconded to the Strategy Unit to see how proposals are processed and to help workers understand the problems managers face.

The PIRO in the Recreation Department did not believe that workers having a say in the appointment of supervisors was feasible. Like the Director of Recreation and the Chair of the Leisure Committee, he saw no reason why potential candidates should not be seen by a group of workers before an appointment was made. However, he believed that management must have the right to manage. He did not believe there should be a worker representative or representatives on the selection committee as this could work against the interests of workers if workers later were involved in a conflict with that manager.

With most officers the question of the council's commitment to industrial democracy and its progress in moving towards the stated objectives was not directly and specifically raised although the broad issue of worker involvement was.

An officer in the Central Policy Unit in Sheffield said that in the early to mid 1980s leaflets were sent out twice a month to the workforce. Those leaflets stressed that the council wanted to open up a debate with its workers about how the council should develop. Until 1985, he said, there was much talk about uniting workers and service users. For him, much of that talk was no more than propaganda as it glossed over a number of the contradictions in the interests of workers and of users. The council never really, for this officer, tackled the tension between extending worker control and the control of council service users.

The Director of Social Services in Sheffield said that he was worried about compartmentalization at work and supported efforts to create conditions in which people could work co-operatively. He believed power had been too concentrated in the past. There were efforts now to involve workers more in decision-making in the department. He said efforts were in hand to encourage residential social workers to work more with domiciliary staff. In his experience, trade unions were not opposed to this.

A chief officer in Doncaster said there were no formal monthly meetings with union stewards as in Social Services. However, he said, he had an open door policy, where by appointment he would see trade union representatives and any staff. A senior officer in Doncaster said that there were regular quarterly meetings between the manual trade unions and councillors and management. The meetings were cordial. Meetings between the trade unions of officers and managers and councillors are irregular and at arm's length. Management in social services met officer shop stewards every two months or so, he said. NALGO had allowed negotiations with councillors to become an infrequent occurrence. The union, he said, could be criticized for allowing that position to develop. In theory, he said, workers in the council and the department where he works are encouraged to come forward with ideas about improving service delivery and the ways in which the department worked. His contact with the trade union tends to be 'problem centred', however.

It can be seen, then, that most trade union representatives, in both councils, did not believe they had an adequate input into major policy decisions. However, there were very big differences among stewards on the question of whether workers should have seats on the council policy committees. However, whatever their views about workers having seats on council committees, there was strong agreement among union representatives that workers had too little involvement in major policy issues. This suggests that the objectives of Sheffield Council of bringing workers more into the process of deciding how manifesto commitments would be achieved had largely failed. It is also interesting that workers in Doncaster would have liked more input.

Among councillors, attitudes varied. Councillors in Doncaster saw the issue of worker involvement simply in terms of introducing suggestion boxes. However, even among Sheffield councillors who believed workers should have more involvement in policy development there was a strongly held general view that final policy-making should rest with councillors alone. That suggests that councillors were unwilling to relinquish their formal policy-making powers.

Officers, in both councils, Sheffield as well as Doncaster, either believed that schemes to involve workers in the running of the department were unnecessary or undesirable. The responses of Sheffield officers raise the question, once again, of the extent to which officers' views coincided with those of councillors and Labour Group commitments.

However, the progress that was made in Sheffield, in this area, may not have been altogether negative. David Blunkett and Keith Jackson (1987, pp. 124-125) argue there had been real achievements in developing worker involvement in a constructive way in Sheffield Council. In the Cleansing Department the council lost a number of contracts, particularly between May 1983 and April 1984. In response, under the initiative of two shop stewards, council officers from a number of departments, councillors and trade unionists worked together to win back the contracts. Contracts were, indeed, won back and for Blunkett and Jackson (1987, pp. 124-125) 'By pooling experience a four-point strategy emerged based on capital investment in new equipment - bins, skips, miniskips, vehicles and adaptors; a low pricing policy; a cooperative approach to work organization; and lively promotion and publicity'. Moreover, they say 'Work-site meetings between councillors and the workforce threw up many suggestions about how improvements could be made and how work practices could be adapted to do a better job'.

Additionally, in the Joint Works Group, shop stewards in the Direct Labour Organization and committee members of the Federation of Tenants and Residents' Association 'consider city-wide policy based on direct personal experience of the service and its deliberations helped to prepare the ground for area-based management' (Blunkett and Jackson, 1987, p. 98). Although, as was shown in an earlier chapter, NALGO shop stewards had grave doubts about the success of the area management scheme in Housing.

Low pay supplement and single status

As the 1987 District Labour Party manifesto put it, the Labour Group would continue raising the wages of low paid council workers to reach the TUC minimum. This would be coupled with improvements in the nature and status of the work which was currently low paid, where that proved possible (Sheffield District Labour Party, 1987, p. 35). There was a commitment in the same manifesto to continue negotiations aimed at achieving single status of employment for all staff, both white collar and manual and craft. Moreover, a document produced by the city council in 1986, *Sheffield Putting You in the Picture* (Sheffield City Council, 1986, p. 6) said:

> And we are putting our own house in order, improving the pay
> and conditions of our own employees. Forty seven per cent of

Sheffield's workforce are manual workers, most of them in jobs which are low paid and traditionally have conditions of employment inferior to those of white collar staff. In 1984 we began to put this right. Holiday, sick pay and maternity entitlements have all been equalized. We set aside £1.5 m in 1985/1986 to increase the wages of our lower paid workers. And as part of our policy of moving towards genuinely single status employment we are consolidating bonuses and other payments in certain areas of work.

How did those interviewed, however, view the council's achievements in this area? The views of councillors will be considered first.

Councillors

Labour councillors are very pleased with the council's low pay policy and its moves to achieve single status between employees. David Blunkett said he was very proud of the Low Pay Supplement but felt it could have gone further. Another councillor said the Labour Group recognized it was only scratching the surface in its policies on low pay. For more to have been achieved the Labour Party would have needed to win the 1987 general election. He accepted that progress had not been made at the pace the Labour Group had hoped. At the time of the interview, the council was very much on the defensive, he said. 'In the past', he said, 'a large number of NALGO members were suspicious of single status seeing it as being introduced at their expense. It took a long time to convince NALGO members that that was not the case'. This councillor did not suggest that NALGO had, in a concerted way, tried to block the council's policy on single status. But his remarks did suggest that progress had been 'held up' by the attitude of some NALGO members. For the then chair of the Personnel Sub-Committee, the NALGO wariness abut single status was understandable. While the policy was aimed at bringing people up to the better standards, some councillors saw it as an averaging out exercise. Hence, for him, the NALGO attitude was quite explicable.

Trade Unionists

A number of trade union representatives in Sheffield also regarded the low pay supplement and the single status policy of the council as a sign of the council's good industrial relations practices and the council trying to act as a good employer. For a full-time NUPE officer, most of the initiatives aimed at improving the position of manual, low paid, low status workers were introduced as a result of proposals by councillors. He regarded the low pay supplement as a positive move by the council, as were the moves to promote single status among workers. A NUPE steward, however, was more circumspect in her attitudes towards single status. For her, the council applied the principle only when it suited them and not otherwise. Hence, single status was a 'mixed blessing', for that steward. A GMB full-time officer said the progress on single status varied from department to department. In some departments, he said, a great deal of progress had been made, while in others, such as Recreation, little progress had been achieved.

The views among NALGO shop stewards on this issue were mixed. A branch officer and a shop steward, for example, saw the scheme as worthy of support, and said it had been supported by the NALGO branch. The branch, however, had some suspicions of the scheme seeing it as a means of levelling down rather than up. On the low pay supplement, the branch officer said that David Blunkett, when he was Leader of the Council, genuinely wanted to improve the position of low paid workers. However, he, and the NALGO branch, felt that the way to tackle low pay was not to pay a supplement to those in low paid positions but to put such workers on higher grades. 'NALGO', he said, 'wants to negotiate people out of low pay, to eliminate low pay in the council' - a view endorsed by other NALGO representatives. This steward questioned the practical commitment of the council to ending low pay when it had insisted, against NALGO's opposition, that paternity, maternity and adoption money should come out of the money set aside for the Low Pay Supplement. The last point was strongly endorsed by another NALGO steward.

Another NALGO steward saw the Low Pay Supplement, single status and other initiatives, as showing the council had tried to be a good employer. 'Those initiatives show the council trying in a positive manner to put its "good employer" aims into practice', for this steward. But this view was opposed by another steward who saw the council making commitments to fight low pay and then refusing to re-grade low paid clerical workers. 'That made it very difficult to take seriously the council's commitment to end low pay', he said.

One can see, therefore, a high degree of unity among trade union representatives. Most accepted the aims of the council, in principle, to end low pay and promote single status but some questioned how strong the commitment was in practice. The attitude of NALGO representatives, who argued the council was tackling the problem of low pay in the wrong way, can be analyzed in at least two ways. On the one hand, the argument that the council should take workers out of low pay by placing them on a higher grade can be seen as a way for NALGO to get higher pay for its members. If those on the lowest grade were placed on higher grades then workers on higher grades would also have to be placed on higher grades. In that way NALGO could be seen as protecting the privileges of its professional members. However, on the other hand, the NALGO branch consistently supported flat rate increases for council workers, during the 1980s. There were, thus, good grounds for believing NALGO representatives' views on how to tackle low pay were genuine.

Equal opportunities

One of the prime policy commitments of new urban left Labour councils was the development of equal opportunities policies. That, as has been shown, was also an important commitment for Sheffield City Council, despite the comment of David Blunkett (1984) that he did not want to see a Women's Committee established as it might detract from the class struggle. Both the 1983 and 1984 District Labour Party council election manifestos contained commitments to improving the position of women and ethnic minorities in the council. The policies proposed, included positive action in respect of workers from those groups. The 1987 manifesto said the council would further develop the Race Equality Unit, establish a Women's Unit and develop similar initiatives for disabled people. The aim would be to prevent prejudices along lines of race, sex or disability affecting recruitment, career development, service delivery and working conditions (Sheffield District Labour Party, 1987, p. 35). Moreover, *Sheffield Putting You in the Picture* (Sheffield City Council, 1986, pp. 6-7) said:

> The council has recognised that it employs few black or disabled workers and that its women workers are concentrated in low paid, low status jobs. This has presented a major challenge. We have responded by developing policies to begin to change attitudes and structures. We have appointed a specialist equal opportunities officer with responsibility for people with disabilities. Our Race Equality Unit has been strengthened. We are reviewing the way we select and employ people and we are using positive action to make sure that, where appropriate, posts on ethnic minority projects are filled by black or Asian workers. These posts are being made more accountable to the communities they serve. In a parallel development a new Women's Unit is being set up to continue the process of eliminating discrimination against women workers.

Despite the commitments and proud recounting of achievements, how far did those interviewed believe the council's objectives on equal opportunities had been achieved? The views of councillors will be recounted first.

Councillors

When asked about the manifesto commitment to increase the number of black and women workers in the Recreation Department, the Chair of the Leisure Service Committee commented that there had been a big push to employ more women in the Sports Development and Community Recreation sections. He admitted the balance was wrong in the department but he said aiming to employ more women often meant good men were lost to the department. When total recruitment was at a low level it was very difficult to meet aims such as increasing the number of ethnic minorities and women employed, especially at the higher levels. That view was endorsed by other councillors. In an article in *The Sheffield Star* (25 January 1989, p. 3), the then Council Leader was reported as admitting the council's equal opportunities policy had failed. On employment in the Recreation Department, it is informative to examine figures supplied by the Director of Recreation for the period October 1988 to January 1989. They show that disabled people comprised 1.62 per cent of the department's workforce; black workers comprised 1.55 per cent of the workforce and women 21 per cent of the total departmental workforce - 31.3 per cent of non-manual workers and 19 per cent of manual workers (Sheffield City Council Report to Policy Committee. *Summary of Departmental Four-Monthly Monitoring Reports,* February 1989).

Trade Unionists

For a manual worker trade unionist in the Recreation Department, the employment of blacks and women in the department was not a live issue. He said nothing positive was being done to recruit black people and ethnic minorities in the department. The department did recruit girls from school but as soon as they reached maturity they tended to disappear, either taking jobs in the white collar section or leaving the council, he said. The unions, he commented, were not promoting the issue at all. Another manual worker shop steward in the same department said more women gardeners were being employed but they faced problems because of the sexist views of many male workers in the department. He said, 'There's no positive policy to get more black workers into the Recreation Department'.

A NALGO steward said the Women's Committee and the Race Relations Committee were given very little money to do their job. There was absolutely no positive action or discrimination to try to get women and black workers into high level positions. The council's equal opportunities policy was non-existent, in practice, for that steward. Another NALGO steward endorsed and underlined that view, arguing that there was no woman near the top of the F and C S hierarchy. 'The council simply plays lip service to equal opportunities', in that steward's opinion. An ex-NALGO shop steward said that the union branch had fought hard for a council nursery to be created. The council opposition, it was argued, was due to a belief that only 'middle class' women wanted the nursery. The council eventually acceded to the union's demand, the ex-steward said. 'The council agreed to provide the facility but at its full cost. In response, the NALGO branch rejected the offer because most staff couldn't have afforded to use it'.

Officers

The Director of Recreation said that despite the commitments in Labour Party manifestos, there had been little progress towards employing more black people and women in the Recreation Department. The problem was not a lack of will or trade union obstruction but simply a lack of finance. This view was endorsed by the PIRO in the Recreation Department who believed, however, that a number of the Sports Development and Community Recreation Officers were black and that the number of black people in the department was quite good. As already reported, the PIRO in the Housing Department believed the commitment to equal opportunities still existed among councillors but was now lower down the list of priorities.

The Chief Personnel Officer said low pay was an issue of gender. Most low paid workers in the council were women. He argued the unions in the council were giving the issue a lower priority than it deserved because of that. The best way of helping women workers in the council, for him, was to tackle the problem of low pay. He also commented that the council did a great deal to help young black people by recruiting them to the council. If the council lost contracts due to compulsory competitive tendering, he said, the position of black youngsters would be badly affected.

It seems, therefore, that despite the claims in *Sheffield Putting You in the Picture*, only limited progress had been made towards implementing an active equal opportunities policy in the council by the end of the 1980s. Councillors, trade union representatives and officers all agreed on the limited progress. However, there were different explanations for the slow progress, with councillors, officers and manual shop stewards generally seeing the slow progress in terms of the council lacking resources and the small number of appointments being made. NALGO stewards, however, questioned much more strongly the general commitment of the council in this area. The Chief Personnel Officer, however, criticized the unions for not giving a greater commitment to tackling the problem of low pay, as that was crucial to improving the position of women workers.

Up to date figures on the gender and ethnic composition of the council workforce at the end of the 1980s are scarce. Some departments provided a quarterly breakdown of the number of black and women workers employed in their departments along with the grades they occupied. Other departments produced no such figures. There were no up to date overall figures showing the ethnic and gender composition of the total council workforce for the end of the 1980s. Figures on the gender composition of the workforce, both overall and departmentally, were collected as part of the *Positive Action for Women Project* completed in 1984. Figures showing the ethnic and gender composition of the workforce were provided quarterly by the Housing Department. Without wishing to suggest that the position in Housing is any better or worse than in other departments, as figures for that department were available, it is possible to examine the position on the equal opportunities front there in a way that is not the case with most other departments. However, while the figures collected for the *Positive Action Project* will be set out first, as they relate simply to salaried workers in the Housing Department, it will not be possible to compare them with the current figures supplied by the Housing Department which relate to all departmental employees.

The figures for the Housing Department, show that in 1984 of salaried staff eight black people were employed in the department, representing 1.5 per cent of the total workforce; 26 per cent of all women in the department, but only 7 per cent of men, were on or below clerical scale 2; 84 per cent of women were on scale 4 or below; only 29 women were above the scale 4 level compared to 113 men representing 42 per cent of male workers in Housing; only ten women out of 65 Senior or Principal Officers in the department were female and all were white; 20 per cent of men in Housing were in Senior or Principal Officer grades but only 5 per cent of women ('Case study summary Housing Department: "Career" grades', *Positive Action for Women Final Report 1984*). Figures for the period from August 1988 - November 1988, covering all the workforce, show that there were 26 registered disabled workers in the Housing Department, representing 2.35 per cent of the total; 37 black people representing 3.34 per cent of the total workforce were employed, only one of whom was on grade

SO1 or above; women comprised 49.28 per cent of the workforce but only 4.4 per cent were on grade SO1 or above, while 11.74 per cent of men were on scale SO1 or above. There were 244 manual workers and 864 APT and C staff in the department (Sheffield City Council Report to Policy Committee. *Summary of Departmental Four-Monthly Monitoring Reports*, February 1989).

Hence, one can see that even in 1988 a considerably larger proportion of male workers were in the highest grades in Housing than women. The figures supplied by the Housing Department do not, however, show the proportion of male and female workers employed in the various lower grades. It is impossible, therefore, to determine what progress, if any, had been made overall in reducing gender inequality.

As the report represented the most detailed survey of the composition of the Sheffield Council workforce in the 1980s, it is probably useful to set out the findings of *The Positive Action for Women Project* which recorded considerable differences in the employment position of men and women in the council. All percentages in the report have been rounded either up or down to the nearest full figure. *The Positive Action for Women Project Final Report* showed that in 1984, 88 per cent of all salaried workers on scale 1 or 2 were women, whereas 83 per cent of all workers in grade SO1 or above were men. As the grade and pay scales increase the proportion of male workers also increased, while as the grade and pay scales decrease the proportion of female workers increased. The figures also showed that out of every 100 salaried female workers, 56 were on scale 1 or 2; 24 were on scale 3 or 4; 11 on scale 5 or 6; 5 on Senior Officer scales and 3 on Principal Officer scales. For men, 10 out of every 100 workers were on scale 1 or 2; 26 were on scale 3 or 4; 25 were on scale 5 or 6; 14 were on Senior Officer scales and 25 were on Principal Officer scales (*Sheffield City Council Positive Action for Women Project Statistical Profile 1984*, p. 3).

For hourly paid workers, the report showed that 90 per cent of workers in the hourly pay range of £1.80 to £1.99 were women, whereas 97 per cent of workers in the pay range of £2.80 to £2.99 were men. As with salaried workers, as the pay rate increased so the proportion of men increased, while as the pay rate fell the proportion of women increased. Of every 100 female weekly paid workers, 87 were on basic hourly rates of between £1.80 and £1.99. No women received hourly pay of more than £2.59. For every 100 men employed on hourly rates, however, 15 were paid between £1.80 and £1.99 an hour; 33 were paid between £2.00 and £2.19 an hour; 5 were paid between £2.20 and £2.39 an hour; 25 were paid between £2.40 and £2.59 an hour; 9 were paid between £2.60 and £2.79 an hour and 1 was paid between £2.80 and £2.99 an hour (*Sheffield City Council Positive Action for Women Project Statistical Profile 1984*, p. 12).

Job satisfaction survey

The Job Satisfaction Survey in the Recreation Department was carried out by Services to Community Action and Trade Unions (SCAT, 1985) with trade union involvement. The findings of, and the recommendations arising from, the survey, as well as calling for workers to be involved in the selection of their supervisors, raised a number of other points. The survey recommended that all supervisors be given full training in industrial relations and motivation. This would enable supervisors to give advice, share information and discuss the work of individuals and their place in wider council plans. There was also a demand for 'shopfloor involvement in decision making and to have an input into financial decisions taken within the quadrant because they will ultimately affect all workers' (SCAT, 1985, p. 11). The survey found that 73 per cent of manual workers and 80 per cent of clerical workers 'want more control over how they carry out their work' (SCAT 1985, p. 5). Workers also wanted better training and improved training was one of the recommendations coming out of the survey (SCAT 1985, p. 11).

The interviews attempted to find out how councillors, trade unionists and officers connected with the Recreation Department reacted to the points in the survey and believed the council had responded to them.

Councillors

The then Leader of the Council said the survey was put into committees for consideration. The council did not take a considered line on the issues involved. On the issue of training, the Chair of the Leisure Committee said that training in the outdoor section in the Department was good. However, he admitted, there was not much training for workers in the indoor section. On industrial relations training for managers, he admitted little had been achieved in the past. Money, however, in a contracting budget, had been set aside for management training, a decision with which he did not necessarily agree. On the broader points of the survey, the Chair of the Leisure Committee said some effort was being made to implement the recommendations. Those changes which had occurred originated principally from the council side, he said. However, he said, enlarging jobs was a slow process, partly because many older workers were hesitant about change.

Trade Unionists

A NUPE steward, who had been involved in running the survey, said that little had been done to implement the recommendations of, or to tackle the 'problems' unearthed by, the survey. This was due, he said, to management opposition, rather than a lack of will on the side of politicians. He commented 'Whenever we ask for anything positive to be done on job satisfaction they're [management] not keen'. Issues, he said, had only been taken up informally with politicians, there had been no formal approach to them. The trade unions had asked for groups of workers to have control over their work. The management response, however, he said, was negative. As he commented 'I don't think management's interested'. On training, for this steward, the department was good on job training but there was not much being done to improve training on the horticultural side. As he commented, 'I'm afraid that's not been taken up'. Moreover, 'Under the new pay structure training's been struck out altogether'.

The view that management was hostile to the whole SCAT project was endorsed by another shop steward from a manual worker trade union. For him 'The whole SCAT Programme met again the resistance of management in the department and the Shop Stewards Committee didn't take it up enough'. The council, for this steward, had little commitment to the project. He commented, 'The SCAT report never really took off because it was produced outside the council and it was never really taken up by the Sheffield City Council'. The report was also seen, he argued, as threatening management's position, although he felt 'A good management would have taken up the recommendations' to achieve a more committed workforce. For this steward, the Recreation Department was at the forefront of training its workforce nationally. The criticism he had was that workers' skills were not used fully.

A NALGO steward also believed that there was little commitment in the council in support of the *Job Satisfaction Survey* project. For this steward, neither management nor councillors reacted positively to the report's suggestions. The report was quietly buried.

The views of the trade unionists, then, strongly suggest that management was hostile to the survey report and worked to block its recommendations being implemented. There was also a view that the politicians were lukewarm in their attitude, as well. However, for whatever reasons, it does seem that councillors have done little to press for the changes suggested in the report to be put into effect. This finding must lead one to question the strength of the Labour Group's commitment to at least some of its stated objectives on the industrial relations front. The failure of the trade unions to push actively for the implementation of the report's recommendations, which was mentioned by some union representatives, gives support to the view that unions are generally reactive organizations. It also suggests that significant improvements in the position of workers will only be secured if the trade unions push for them in a concerted, determined, and perhaps militant way.

On the question of training in the council generally, the views of other trade union representatives were mixed. For a NUPE steward, training was quite good in the council. Facilities for training existed but there was often no cover when people went on training courses. A NUPE steward said that the *Take Ten* education initiative was good but the problem was to get people to go on the course. Everyone that he knew who had been on the course had really enjoyed it and gained a great deal from it. For a NUPE full-time officer, the *Take Ten* initiative had been one of the council's biggest success. The only problem was that it reached so few people. This view was broadly endorsed by a GMB full-time officer and by a GMB shop steward, both of whom believed the scheme had worked well.

For a NALGO Branch Officer, the commitment of departments to introduce industrial relations training for managers was weak. When the council put money aside for management training at first no department made a bid for any of the funds. The budget then became two times over subscribed after pressure was put on departments. The money was being used, he said, to help to train managers to implement cuts and not to improve industrial relations. Other stewards felt that enough was not done to train either workers or managers. A GMB shop steward said that courses existed for workers to attend but afterwards those who had been on courses still receive the same rate of pay. There was, thus, little incentive for workers to attend courses.

Officers

On training, the Director of Recreation said there had been a big improvement in recent years. He felt, however, that the council was still scratching the surface. The problem management faced was getting the job done. Encouraging workers to go on training courses could conflict with that aim. For him, the council was not 'geared up' for training. Despite the recommendations in the *Job Satisfaction Survey Report*, the trade unions were not pushing for improvements in training.

It can be seen, therefore, that there was a fairly widespread agreement among people from all three groups, that the council's record on training was mixed. Nearly everyone believed there was room for improvement in this area. There were differences in the emphasis that it was felt the council should give to training. Some NALGO stewards believed it should be given a much higher priority and all trade unionists thought managers should receive training in industrial relations. It was particularly interesting that the Director of Recreation saw a commitment to improve training as probably clashing with his main concern which was to see that the 'job was done'. Once again, it can be argued, from the evidence, that progress is only likely to be secured if the trade unions push hard for improvements and changes.

On the impact of the *Take Ten* education initiative, it is interesting to note that, in an evaluation of the programme, a number of workers who had been on the course said there were sometimes problems in gaining the support of managers to go on the course. Among those workers there was some feeling that managers undervalued the course because it was not directly related to improving work skills. The council Planned Educational Leave managers interviewed as part of the evaluation of the *Take Ten* scheme, also said that it was not always easy for workers to gain time off to go on the course. It was strongly argued that managers' approach to the initiative needed to change and that more workers, to replace those going on the course, should be provided (Sheffield City Council Education Department, n.d., pp. 13-14 and Hampton and Davies, 1987).

Passport to Leisure and EPSUs

As it has been argued strongly in much published literature that NALGO blocks radical initiatives in left Labour councils, it was decided to look at two 'radical initiatives' introduced by Sheffield City Council. The Passport to Leisure scheme was a programme whereby people in the 1980s could gain free or cheap access to council leisure facilities after acquiring a 'Passport to Leisure Card'. The scheme was aimed at improving access to leisure facilities among the population of Sheffield and especially those who found the cost of participation inhibitive. The aim of Elderly Persons' Support Units (EPSUs) was to improve the care that is given to old people and to integrate the caring services that old people received. David Blunkett has argued that 'Innovatory schemes like Sheffield's elderly persons' units ensure that key workers like home helps and wardens, can contribute their ideas about the needs of different groups' (Blunkett and Jackson 1987, p. 100). As a result of the operation of the EPSU idea 'The concept of home helps has broadened into one of community support workers' (Blunkett and Jackson 1987, p. 100). Hence, for David Blunkett, the EPSU idea involved improving the jobs of those providing care services for the elderly. The research enabled an examination of the views of others involved in that initiative to be considered to see if they agreed with Blunkett's position and to gauge how much progress had been made in this area. An examination of whether NALGO had taken an unequally negative attitude in respect of the initiatives would also be made possible by the research. The views of councillors will be laid out first.

Councillors

The Chair of the Leisure Committee said that the trade unions were worried the Passport to Leisure scheme would create more work for workers without their receiving extra payment. The union reaction to the scheme was not particularly enthusiastic, as a result. From his remarks, it seemed that the manual unions were more worried about the consequences of the scheme than NALGO. This was understandable and resulted from the scheme having more impact on manual than white collar workers. This in turn suggests that it was when workers fear they would be losing out if proposals were introduced that they took a negative stance.

For the Chair of the Family and Community Services Committee, the EPSU established at Ecclesfield was a first step, not a cure all. However, he would have liked to see EPSUs introduced across the city. He said the council had no intention of relinquishing its commitment to developing EPSUs. He felt angry that union regrading and other disputes with the unions, both manual and white collar, had held back the introduction of further units. One of the problems concerned the opposition of the manual unions to workers on the next unit being regraded as white collar workers. Their opposition revolved around their fear of losing members. Disputes with the unions were not the only obstacles, however, preventing progress on the setting up of support units. Financial constraints were also a major difficulty preventing the development of the support units. For him, the units were set up to help improve the services provided for elderly people. However, he believed the units should enable manual workers to have more responsibility and rewards.

An ex-Chair of the F and C S Committee felt that there had not been enough consultation with the community before the first unit was introduced. Some of the trade unions, he said, opposed the introduction of the first scheme, at Ecclesfield. There had been, and still was, he said, an uncertainty among the manual worker trade unions about workers receiving the correct rate for the job. While the scheme, which was imported from Scandinavia, was introduced to improve the service, a subsidiary aim was to enlarge the jobs of wardens and home helps by turning them into Support Workers.

Trade Unionists

A full-time NUPE officer said support workers in the Ecclesfield EPSU were not happy about the staffing levels in the unit which, they believed, prevented them from working properly. They were also, he said, not entirely happy with their pay rates. However, despite these problems, the jobs of home helps had been broadened in the unit, in his view.

For a NUPE steward in the Ecclesfield unit, the unit was linked to keeping old people at home and with care in the community. The unit had made the jobs of home helps more interesting. 'Now', it was said, 'one key worker deals with each person in the EPSU. This has cut red tape and improved things', this steward said. The EPSU avoided the problem of one worker not knowing what other workers were doing. In her unit, people were being encouraged to become more informed about developments. She said that in Children's Homes, non-professional workers were still not allowed to speak to the children. The work of the unit was based on good will, she said. 'Jobs have been made better in the unit and old people are getting a better service'. She argued the council now was 'not putting enough money into the unit and the service was bound to fall if that didn't change'.

Another manual worker steward was adamant, however, that the EPSUs did not work. The units, she said, did not give a 24 hour service. The home help service was now being prioritized by the council, she said. 'Care comes first with cleaning not being important any more'. This means, she said, that some people are now receiving only three hours help a month rather than the three hours a week they used to get. The introduction of EPSUs, she said, has made the position worse.

On the issue of the Passport to Leisure scheme, the views of trade unionists were very similar. Those asked, regarded the scheme as failing to bring in money when that was one of the main aims of the department. For those interviewed, the Passport to Leisure scheme seemed the wrong policy at the wrong time. That view was common across unions. The unions, it seems, opposed the scheme from the beginning.

Officers

For the Director of Social Services, the Elderly Persons Support Unit at Ecclesfield had been a partial success. He played a part in setting up the unit. For him, there had been major problems with the trade unions regarding the establishment of the second unit. He accepted that management had had the wrong negotiating strategy, especially in the early days. He said, 'the costs of the unit were staggering. The Ecclesfield unit was established as a pioneer which was intended to lead to other units springing up right across the city. Now', he admitted, 'financial constraints are limiting what is possible'.

For the Director of Recreation, the Passport to Leisure scheme was proving too costly. The scheme, for him, had not worked well. Today, the scheme was losing direction, in his opinion. He believed the introduction of charges on passports was inevitable. The council now has to decide, he thought, whether certain disadvantaged groups should have free access to facilities. He accepted that in a period of growth, leisure facilities should be free for everyone but that was not the position in which the council found itself.

It seems, then, that the views about EPSUs differed considerably. Councillors asked, regarded the units as a very good idea, in principle. There was some quite strong feeling, expressed by the Director of Social Services as well, that the trade unions had prevented further progress being made on the development of the units. However, it seems the opposition to the units was greater among manual worker unions than among NALGO. There seemed little support for the view that NALGO by trying to protect professional privileges, was blocking the development of the units. As already suggested, the reaction of manual worker union representatives to the proposals tends to support the view that if unions feel threatened they will react negatively. The need for councillors to convince workers that change is in their interests is once again exposed. The strongly contrasting views of the NUPE steward and the GMB steward are worth noting. Their differences seem to show conflicting ideas about what represents an improvement in service. Such differences suggest there is a need to find the views of those receiving or using a service if clear improvements in that service are to be achieved. The views of service users is the central piece missing in the discussion of the Elderly Persons' Support Units set out above.

As far as the Passport to Leisure scheme is concerned, there was agreement among trade unionists and the Director of Recreation that the scheme could not be supported at a time of financial cut backs. It seems that all the unions opposed the scheme from the beginning. There is no evidence of NALGO alone trying to block the scheme's development. The unions were worried about the scheme bankrupting the department and preventing people who were willing to pay using facilities and hence bringing revenue into the department. The opposition of the trade union representatives and the Director of

Recreation was due much more to worries about the financial implications for the department than to a principled objection to the underlying aims of the scheme.

Having considered the themes associated with the field work, in the next and concluding chapter I will draw some broader and more developed conclusions from the field work material and the other elements of the research set out in the book.

9 Conclusions

In this concluding chapter, arising out of the case study findings, it will be argued that Sheffield City Council largely failed to achieve its aim of increasing the involvement of the providers and users of council services and the local community in the provision and development of council services and activities. The council also largely failed to create a socialist industrial relations and management practice in the council, it will be argued. Two broad reasons for the lack of progress will be advanced - the failure of the Sheffield City Council Labour Group to work out clearly what a socialist management and industrial relations practice would be like, and structural constraints. The structural factors which constrained the actions of Sheffield City Council are various. They include the power of chief officers and the relationship between chief officers and councillors; the actions and practices of the council trade unions; the unwillingness of leading councillors to relinquish or share power with others; and the general inertia and conservatism induced by the traditional workings of local government. The failure to effectively change the internal structures and the supporting mechanisms of the council was a result of a lack of strategic thinking on the part of the Labour councillors, which was paralleled among sections of the new urban left and the left more generally. Hence, the two factors inhibiting progress were closely connected.

The chapter will be structured around a number of interlinked themes and areas where Sheffield City Council had radical commitments on the industrial relations front. The commitments included: tackling low pay among the council's workforce; promoting equal opportunities in council employment; promoting industrial democracy; decentralization; working towards 'single status' in employment conditions for all council staff. The argument of the chapter will be that in all those areas progress towards the council's aims was limited due to the twin failures to produce a distinctive socialist management and industrial relations practice and to tackle the structural constraints to radical change. I will begin the detailed examination by first considering the issue of low pay.

Low pay

Low pay was a major problem in local government as a whole in the 1980s and not just in Sheffield or Doncaster Councils. Rahman (1986, pp. 9-10), taking the definition of low pay established by the Low Pay Unit as two-thirds of median male earnings, shows that 45 per cent of all full-time manual local government workers in England and Wales were low paid in 1985. In addition, 80 per cent of full-time and 92 per cent of part-time women manual workers were low paid, along with 38 per cent of full-time and 68 per cent of part-time women non-manual workers. As shown in an earlier chapter, some new urban left councils, Camden, Greenwich, Lambeth, Hackney and Sheffield, have all had policies to tackle low pay among their council workforces.

As Sheffield councillors admitted, the Low Pay Supplement run by the council had only a marginal effect on the position of those in low paid jobs in the council. Even though many councillors were proud of the scheme, there was a recognition that it had not eliminated low pay. Councillors claimed the council would have done more if it had had the resources. I have no reason to dispute that claim. But NALGO representatives in the council to whom I spoke strongly criticized the council's strategy on the whole low pay issue. For them, the way to tackle low pay was to place low paid workers on higher grades.

Two broad objections to that idea can be made. First, placing workers on low grades on higher ones would have a 'knock on' effect. While the lowest paid workers would receive higher pay, those on high grades would also demand higher pay in order to protect their differentials. As a result the relative poverty of low paid workers would not improve although their absolute position would. Second, in the climate prevailing in local government in the 1980s, councils like Sheffield did not have the resources to finance such a scheme.

On the first point, there are good grounds for believing that the best paid council staff would fight very hard to protect their privileged position. The experience of the GLC on this issue is of particular relevance. Between 1981-1986 the GLC aimed to reduce the number of job grades in the council. While the large scale changes aimed for were nor achieved, the council did make some progress in this area. As Paul Soto (1987, pp. 94-95) shows, the GLC did change the grading system for white collar workers despite the opposition of the main white collar union, the GLC Staff Association. Access to jobs was broadened but the number of grades was not significantly reduced. Pay increases for white collar workers were either flat rate or helped the low paid most and differentials between the main white collar grades were reduced. In addition, meals allowances were equalized for manual workers with white collar workers and the £10 weekly difference in the London Weighting Allowance for manual workers as compared with white collar workers was reduced by £6. However, as Livingstone (1987, pp. 235-238) argues, progress on those and other issues was restricted by the attitude of the GLC Staff Association protecting the privileges of its better paid members.

The GLC experience suggests progress can be made on improving the absolute and relative position of low paid workers but that progress is limited by opposition from those representing higher paid staff. However, in Sheffield Council, there was some evidence to suggest the council, unlike the GLC, would not have faced the strong opposition of the main white collar union branch in the council, NALGO, if it had made a firmer push to help the relative position of the low paid. For while NALGO's call for low paid workers to be placed on higher grades could be seen as a ploy to win higher pay for better paid workers, it must be borne in mind that, in the 1980s, the branch supported flat rate increases for council workers. It is likely senior council staff would not react favourably to a reduction in their pay differentials and the council leadership may not be prepared to provoke discontent among such a powerful group of workers within the council. The council leadership might also feel that the quality of senior staff would fall if they reduced pay differentials. Hence there might have been structural constraints on what a council like Sheffield could do to fight low pay. However, the council would almost certainly have gained the support of the manual worker unions if it tried to improve the relative position of low paid workers, if the case study material is any guide.

As Sheffield councillors whom I interviewed argued, in the financial climate that existed, substantial increases for low paid workers on top of existing commitments, could not be afforded by a council like Sheffield. Unless, that is, a redistribution of income among council staff took place. Bearing in mind the points made above, it would seem that the council leadership would have had to overcome opposition from senior staff if its low pay policies were to be taken further. Whether the council would be prepared to risk such opposition is open to debate.

Equal opportunities

While Sheffield City Council did not give equal opportunities policies the priority they were given by some other new urban left councils, as argued earlier, the council recognized the importance of trying to improve the position of women council workers, council workers from the ethnic minorities and disabled workers. Equal opportunities policies had far greater prominence in Sheffield Council than Doncaster Council, as the case studies show. During the 1980s, Sheffield Council introduced maternity and paternity leave programmes, allowed certain workers up to two years' leave from their jobs, engaged in equal opportunities training for its staff, pursued a limited form of job sharing and established a Race Equality Unit and a Women's Unit (the latter, however, only after much internal resistance). However, the response of those interviewed strongly suggested that progress in the area of equal opportunities was limited. Moreover, what figures are available suggest that policies to tackle racial discrimination in the council had little success. In 1988 Sheffield Council employed just 520 'black' people (1.5 per cent of the total workforce), most in low paid jobs or jobs with poor promotion prospects (Sheffield City Council, 1988a, p. 9). The proportion of 'black' people in the Sheffield population was 3.2 per cent in 1981 and estimated at 4.2 per cent in 1986 (Sheffield City Council, 1988a, fig. 1). The number of 'black' people joining the council's Youth Training Scheme fell in the 1980s. In 1984, 23 out of 164 trainees on the scheme were 'black', by 1987 out of 144 trainees only 10 were 'black' (*Women in Sheffield Number 6*). Moreover, the figures from *The Positive Action for Women Project Statistical Profile 1984*, set out in chapter 9, show that women were disproportionately found in lower grade, lower paid jobs. Why, then, was so little progress made on the equal opportunities front?

One explanation rests in the priority given to the issue by the Labour Group who probably always regarded other issues as more important, as the case study suggests. One small example of the low priority of councillors to fighting discrimination in the council was the lack of training for councillors on avoiding racist and sexist attitudes in job interviews. Moreover, it was strange that in a council with a declared commitment to equal opportunities there was no systematic ethnic or gender monitoring of the council workforce and council job applications in Sheffield Council in the 1980s. *The Positive Action for Women Final Report* 'Checklist for positive action' (Sheffield City Council, 1984b, p. 6) called for gender monitoring of the council's workforce. Towards the end of 1988 the council attempted to take a census of its workforce with the aim of furthering its equal opportunities policy. The census was based on a questionnaire survey of the workforce and the results, in terms of those responding, were very disappointing. Efforts were being made to update all departmental personnel records and to incorporate the findings into the new Computerised Personal Information System being phased in throughout the council in April 1989 (cf. *Working for Sheffield*, April 1989). The failure to pursue a coherent system of ethnic and gender monitoring suggests that the equal opportunities policy was not given a particularly high priority by councillors or by senior staff.

That senior officers did not generally give equal opportunities a high priority was further suggested by the paucity of information contained in the reports which had to be compiled by departmental management on the composition of departmental workforces and developments in departments on overtime working and other matters. Many of the reports which I studied did not even show the number and percentage of black people employed, although departmental managers were officially required to produce such information.

Another reason for the lack of progress in this area was the attitude of the council trade unions. As shown in the fieldwork chapters, the trade union representatives in the Recreation Department, and others, when asked about the union attitudes to the council's commitment to employ more women and black workers in that department, said the issue was not being pressed by the trade unions. While the NALGO branch set up an equal opportunities sub-committee and engaged in equal opportunities training for its activists in the 1980s, united, concerted efforts by the council unions to improve the position of black, women and disabled workers, seems to have been lacking in the council.

Inertia

The internal structures of local government create inertia and conservatism with a small 'c'. That comes out strongly from the case study material. There is a great tendency, particularly for councillors and senior officers, to simply keep the operations of their council going. That is the source of much of the criticism of Doncaster councillors by the council NALGO representatives and, to a lesser extent, of Sheffield councillors by NALGO shop stewards, as well as the criticism of senior officers in both councils by trade union representatives and some Sheffield councillors. But the inertia possibly goes further than that and affects everyone, even in a left council like Sheffield. That may be one of the explanations, along with the traditional reactive stance adopted by unions, why many council union representatives were loath to support radical initiatives such as the Passport to Leisure Scheme in Sheffield or worker representation on council committees. However, those specific subjects will be considered in more detail later. The inertia produced by council structures may make it hard for novel policies, such as those relating to equal opportunities, to make headway. If there is any truth in that suggestion, then a council, like Sheffield after 1980, wanting to introduce radical changes, such as pursuing equal opportunities policies, will need to think clearly about how the council structures can be changed and 'opened up' to allow new ideas and ways of working to make progress.

Senior officer power

The inertia and conservatism created by internal council structures served to cement and underpin the power and privileges of senior, and particularly chief, officers in the council. In Wright's term, the officers concerned exercised control over organization assets (Wright, 1985) While most of the senior officers I interviewed argued that it was councillors who took the final policy decisions, I have already questioned the extent to which that was in any meaningful sense the case. For by setting the policy agenda, determining what was feasible, setting out policy recommendations within narrow parameters and couching their advice in highly technical terms, senior officers could so constrain the options facing councillors that effectively it was only in name that councillors took policy decisions. Moreover, the way in which policy is implemented is often as important as the actual policy decisions. In many cases it is impossible to divorce policy-making and policy implementation. Many new urban left leaders and councils recognized that point. In Sheffield, David Blunkett's pronouncements in the early and mid 1980s frequently stressed the point (cf., for example, Blunkett and Green, 1983) and he referred to it when I interviewed him. It is interesting and informative to note, therefore, that the Leader of Sheffield council at the time of my research argued that the new council leadership after 1980 was unaware of the power of the chief officer machine when they took over.

The case study findings on the power and influence of senior, and particularly chief, council officers suggests that the exercise of that power was generally not as nakedly overt as Livingstone and Murray have argued was the case in the GLC between 1981 and 1986 (cf. chapters 2 and 7 for an outline of their positions). In that sense, the argument of the officer in the Sheffield City Council Central Policy Unit, who argued that officers in Sheffield did not try to overtly prevent or obstruct the council implementing its radical policies, was borne out. There seemed little evidence from the case study to support the view that senior officers opposed council policy, in either council, in an openly hostile way. However, there was a real sense in which the priorities and commitments of senior officers and councillors in Sheffield appeared to diverge, as argued in earlier chapters.

The comments of some officers who clearly believed Sheffield Council gave too much emphasis to the development of radical industrial relations policies often at the expense of service delivery was a prime example of the divergence of priorities. The differences in the priorities of Labour councillors and senior officers over decentralization in the F and C S Department in Sheffield Council was another example of the phenomenon under consideration. (Incidentally, the lessons of the decentralization experience in the F and C S Department will be considered in detail later.) In broad terms, the evidence from the Sheffield part of the case study suggests that without a very strong direction from councillors, policies which do not have the support of senior officers can get buried and stifled in the complexities of the internal local government departmental machine. That would certainly seem to be the case in respect of gender and ethnic council employment monitoring. There are ample opportunities for senior staff in local government to stifle policies and commitments with which they disagree, for the internal structures of local government make innovation very difficult.

The new leadership in Sheffield Council after 1980 appeared to have no real strategy or plan to overcome, what might be termed, the structural or institutional power of chief, and senior, council officers. The council did appoint two strategy advisers. But, as one of them made clear when interviewed, they were not appointed to interfere in the running of departments. Moreover, as shown in the fieldwork chapters, many representatives in Sheffield were highly critical of middle managers in the council, whom they saw as taking up very reactionary positions. The comments of the PIRO in the Housing Department, who was disappointed that he could not spend more time on helping to develop equal opportunities policies, as most of his time was taken up with more mundane and immediate concerns, added to the evidence suggesting that internal local government structures create institutional inertia.

The important point, which was not really taken up by Sheffield councillors or by many others on the local government left, is that senior staff used the structures and procedures of local government in a covert and 'constitutional' way to impose their view and conceptions of what should be done and in that way cemented their power. In Wright's terms, chief officers made use of their 'organization assets' (Wright, 1985). Moreover, and allied to the last point, the structures of local government encouraged and promoted conservatism throughout the organization. The structures of local government are so entrenched and so strong that they encourage almost everyone from the bottom to the top to feel threatened by, and to be suspicious of, change. Hence, it is possible for groups within local government to be highly suspicious of changes which, at the very least, might bring some improvements in their positions. That would seem to be part of the explanation for the failure of the trade unions in Sheffield Council, and particularly the

NALGO branch, to take a more 'positive' approach on the issue of industrial democracy.

Industrial democracy

As was shown in the last chapter, Sheffield City Council had firm, if unspecified, commitments to introduce industrial democracy in the council, in the 1980s. However, as the findings of the case study showed, the progress made in this area was limited, although at least one councillor doubted if much greater progress could be made. Doncaster Council had no commitments to increasing worker involvement in policy development. Therefore, the 'failure' of the Doncaster councillors to make progress in that area is hardly surprising. The lack of progress in Sheffield was more surprising, at least on the face of it.

One possible reason for the lack of progress in Sheffield was that the proposals on industrial democracy were promoted in very much a top down manner. The new industrial relations procedures in Sheffield were given an impetus by the 1984 NALGO strike in the council. They were also very much the 'brainchild' of the Chief Personnel Officer. The proposals were not the result of considered and detailed negotiations with the unions and did not represent an agreed strategy for progress. Moreover, David Blunkett's comment that the council offered workers seats on policy-making committees again strongly suggests a top down approach was being pursued. Perhaps the aftermath of a major industrial dispute was not the time to try to make a radical move on industrial democracy, as NALGO was likely to be suspicious of the council's motives. Additionally, as a senior council officer and others commented, among many Labour councillors and other influential people in the council, support for greater worker involvement in policy development and related issues declined in the aftermath of the strike.

The comments of many of the union representatives whom I interviewed, in Doncaster as well as Sheffield Council, suggest that neither set of councillors were really that committed to involving the council unions, and their members, in the development of council policy. That view was, of course, most strongly expressed by NALGO stewards but some Sheffield council manual worker representatives also saw councillors in Sheffield making decisions and then the council presenting them to the unions in completed form.

The low priority given to increasing worker involvement in council affairs in Sheffield in practice may be due, in part, to the unwillingness of councillors to relinquish what little power they have. As the removal of corporal punishment and the wearing of school uniform in Sheffield and the arguments of some Sheffield NALGO shop stewards suggest, councillors in Sheffield were very loath in reality to share power with others, however illusory was the actual power councillors wielded. However, beyond councillors wanting to maintain the trappings of personal power, is a deeper issue, concerning the relationship between traditional political representative democracy and direct or social democracy. There can be a real conflict between the two types of democracy and it may well be that not only in Sheffield but in other new urban left councils the existence of the conflict was not properly and fully explored and dealt with (Gyford, 1985, pp. 81-94 considers this issue in some detail).

The conflict facing new urban left councils in this area can be expressed in the following terms. If a council is elected with a clear commitment to do A and another clear commitment to involve the providers and users of council services in council policy development, where does the council stand if, after involving council service providers and service users, the result is outright opposition for policy A and support for policy B? In that case does, or should, the council push ahead and simply implement policy A as it was elected with a clear commitment to do exactly that? Or does, and should, the council accept the views of the service users and providers and implement policy B, in the process abandoning policy A on which it fought the election? Of course, the position is even more complex if service users support policy B and council workers support policy C. The dilemmas facing new urban left councils in trying to graft some form of direct or participatory democracy onto the existing representative system are acute. Of course, on issues where the council does not have a considered view or the ruling group does not have a clear manifesto commitment the problem is less serious. In those cases the council can genuinely use the views of council service users and the providers of services in the policy-making process. But in Sheffield at least, it appears that the dilemmas which occur when service providers and service users want to do things which go against the council's policies were not really overcome. In the end, the council largely abandoned its commitments to greater worker and user involvement, in practice.

None of the above discussion is meant to suggest that the problems or dilemmas highlighted are intractable or insoluble. But if the dilemmas are to be avoided or overcome hard thinking is needed about the implications of the council's commitments. That is something to which Sheffield City Council Labour Group never really came to terms.

The lack of progress on industrial democracy in Sheffield was not only due to the council adopting a top down approach, the inertia of council structures, the unwillingness of councillors to relinquish 'power' and the conflict between representative and direct democracy, it was also due to the attitude of the council unions. The case study shows that while some union representatives in both councils supported workers having seats on council policy-making committees, there was also a certain ambivalence and outright hostility to the idea from others. While many union representatives wanted greater worker involvement in council policy making, there was still a strong underlying feeling, especially among NALGO shop stewards in Sheffield, that the unions should respond to council proposals. Support for the argument that it was the job of councillors and officers to manage and of the unions to respond to their proposals, was implicit in the statements of many union representatives. That basic defensiveness among council unions seems to have been common in many councils including those wanting to involve workers in the development of their policies to decentralize council structures (cf., for example, Heery, 1987, and Hoggett, Lawrence and Fudge, 1984).

In one sense the ambivalence and defensiveness of council union branches on the issue of industrial democracy is understandable and rational. Union representatives were wary of agreeing to become more involved in council policy-making at a time when councils were cutting back on spending and staff. There were also real dangers, as some NALGO shop stewards in Sheffield remarked, that unions would become responsible for decisions over which they had no real control. That could be a real problem if worker representatives were 'given' only a small number of seats on committees or were 'given' seats without voting rights, as was argued in chapter 4. But there was no reason why the unions themselves should not have come forward with the policies and structures to promote the type of industrial democracy that they believed would meet their members' interests. For trade unionists, in the end, the issue boils down to whether workers' interests can best be furthered by the trade unions reacting to management and state proposals and decisions or by democratically elected worker representatives being involved in the active formation of policy.

Another explanation of the slow progress on industrial democracy in Sheffield Council, may have been the lack of trust between the different council trade unions. Most forms of industrial democracy require workers in different unions and doing different jobs to co-operate to the extent, at least, that they agree on how representation will be allocated between different sections, be they unions or workers. In Sheffield, as shown in the field work chapters, relations between the manual unions and between the manual unions and NALGO were at best 'patchy'. In Doncaster, relations between NUPE and NALGO appeared to be poor and relations between all the manual worker unions may not have been totally harmonious either. However, the manual unions in Doncaster appeared to have worked well together on the issue of competitive tendering. At council level, the council unions in Sheffield worked together quite fruitfully, it seems, on preparation for the competitive tendering of council services. Without worker unity, systems of industrial democracy are unlikely to succeed in increasing the control of council workers. However much the interests of most council workers may be in unison, and I argued in chapter 5 they have much more in common than divides them, the evidence of the field work shows that divisions between the unions and different types of worker were strong in Sheffield Council. Unless, or until, those divisions are closed progress towards industrial democracy is likely to be very slow.

Industrial democracy can, of course, take a variety of forms and is not just concerned with workers having representation or control at the highest policy-making level. Industrial democracy can also involve workers having greater control over their day to day work. Policies like job rotation, worker control over their immediate work, job enlargement and job enrichment can all be part of a strategy to increase industrial democracy. Such policies can also form part of an equal opportunities policy in the council and help to improve the position of women and ethnic minority council workers who are often found in the most boring and repetitive jobs, over which they have little or no control (cf. Sheffield City Council, 1984b). The unions in Sheffield City Council did not make a great push to try to ensure the promotion of policies like those mentioned, not even in the Recreation Department where many similar proposals were contained in the *Job Satisfaction Survey*.

The unions may have been worried that job rotation, job enlargement and job enrichment schemes could be used by the council management to increase the productivity of workers and to undermine union bargaining strength without any increased pay for the workers concerned. However, Sheffield Council, it appeared from my research, was not promoting or calling for such policies either. That may, in part, be due to a fear that such policies would be used by the unions to win extra pay for their members.

Potential opposition from departmental management could be another factor blocking progress, as the evidence concerning the implementation of the *Job Satisfaction Survey* recommendations in the Recreation Department suggests. The failure to push for such policies by workers and their unions could also be due to the general inertia in local government and the lack of creative thinking produced as a result. It seems, however, that through the development of job rotation, job enlargement, worker control over their immediate work and the allocation of work in their department, the twin aims of promoting industrial democracy and equal opportunities could be furthered. That is an area which Sheffield Council could have profitably investigated, if its commitments to industrial democracy and equal opportunities were to be given substance. Industrial democracy, however, was unlikely to be extended without strong pressure from the council union branches. Whether developments in that area would have benefited council workers would ultimately have depended upon the control workers were able to achieve.

Decentralization

Decentralization, as shown in chapter 3, was one of the main ways in which many new urban left Labour councils intended to increase the involvement of council users and the local community and, in some cases, council workers in the development and provision of council services. It was a policy given some prominence by Sheffield City Council, though none at all by Doncaster Council. In Sheffield, as shown in earlier chapters, the council reorganized the Housing Department on an area basis and set up a limited number of Neighbourhood Forums covering deprived areas of the city. The field work strongly suggests that the decentralization of housing in Sheffield did not produce increased worker and user involvement in the running of housing services. The council also had a commitment to decentralizing the Family and Community Services Department. Progress on the latter issue was limited. The case study material suggests some reasons why.

    As with workers in other new urban left councils committed to decentralization, the unions in Sheffield, particularly NALGO the main union which would be affected, were wary of decentralization because they saw it being introduced without the council making sufficient resources available for the scheme to work. Those NALGO stewards to whom I spoke were not opposed to decentralization in principle. Indeed, the general position was that NALGO members were more committed to decentralization than management. The union did, however, demand that sufficient 'back up' staff, receptionists, clerical workers, typists, were made available and that, as they were taking on greater responsibilities, the jobs of many workers should be regraded. Another concern of NALGO members in Sheffield, which was also expressed by NALGO branches in other councils (cf., for example, Heery, 1987; Beavis, 1985), was that the union's members would end up being accountable to two different bosses - the council, and service users or the local community. NALGO shop stewards were worried that they would face different managerial demands and that the pay and conditions of their members would be adversely affected if service users gained control of those matters.

The worries of NALGO members about service users and the local community gaining control of their pay and working conditions and the whole decentralization issue raise questions about the relationship between the interests of council workers on the one hand and service users and the local community on the other. As has been shown, the case study material reported a number of the people I interviewed, including some trade union representatives, arguing that there was a conflict between good service delivery and the interests of council workers. For council workers wanted good pay and working conditions and, especially at a time of financial constraint, a council may not be able to provide the pay and working conditions council workers demand while maintaining or improving council services. However, as others whom I interviewed stressed, it may be that good service delivery and meeting the needs and interests of service users is dependent upon a committed and enthusiastic workforce.

At a deeper level, there is a dispute about whether extending the involvement of both service providers and service users in council policy-making is possible. On the one hand, it can be argued workers would want to control how they did their work, at what speed and intensity and so on, and that probably would not coincide with the demands of service users for prompt, effective and cheap solutions to their problems. On the other hand, it can be argued the skill, knowledge and enthusiasm of workers need to be released if good quality services are to be provided and the demands of service users met. For workers know what is possible and what needs to be done to produce desired results. Those I interviewed took differing views on the whole issue. While the issue will only finally be resolved in practice, it seems that a council committed to increasing the involvement of service users and service providers, as Sheffield council has been, would need to consider fully and carefully whether the twin aims are in fact always mutually compatible and if not how any possible conflicts can be overcome. Once again the failure of Sheffield Labour Group to resolve that question feeds into a bigger and more general failure among the left in Britain, and elsewhere.

On the specific issue of decentralization in Sheffield Council, for some councillors, the attitude of NALGO locally was unreasonable and had blocked progress on decentralization. The union had been unwilling to reach a sensible agreement with the council. However, for many councillors, the main obstacle to decentralization in social services was the attitude of departmental managers. Many councillors saw managers in F and C S as opposed to decentralization because it threatened their power and privileges. It certainly seems, both from the comments of councillors and those of NALGO shop stewards, that many managers in F and C S did not give decentralization a very high priority. The Director of Social Services, for example, while expressing support for physical decentralization was much more ambivalent on the question of the devolution of power. It is also instructive that he put great emphasis on the need to find appropriate management structures in the decentralized scheme. Whether that concern for management structures can be seen as a commitment to the maintenance or extension of management control is an open question which is nonetheless raised by his comments. Indeed, his comments may lend some support to Hoggett's argument that decentralization can be used by managers and others to increase management power and managerial control in the public as in the private sector (Hoggett, 1987b).

There is also evidence from the case study that Labour councillors were not all in favour of the devolution of power. It seems that at least some Labour councillors were worried that decentralization would reduce their power. Indeed, the Chair of the F and C S Committee believed that physical decentralization should precede the devolution of power. Whether that shows, in reality, a weak commitment to devolution of power is, at least, open to question. Once again, the whole issue of the relationship between representative and direct democracy is raised by the councillors' attitudes to decentralization.

From the evidence of the field work, there would seem to be little support for the view that NALGO in Sheffield blocked the development of decentralization in the F and C S Department because it was trying to protect the privileges of its professional, social worker in this case, members. No one I interviewed specifically suggested NALGO had tried to stop decentralization for that reason and the Director of Social Services, as well as NALGO shop stewards, specifically rejected that argument.

The lessons from the experience of decentralization in Sheffield Council's F and C S Department would seem to be that councillors need to be clear about what they are trying to achieve through decentralization, committed to the project, prepared to overcome probable managerial opposition to the project and to put in the resources to make the scheme work. There is also a need, as the experience of other councils suggests (cf. the articles in Hoggett and Hambleton, 1987), to convince unions, and particularly NALGO, that decentralization is not being introduced on the cheap and that their pay and working conditions will not be adversely affected by the devolution of power.

Convincing workers on the last point should be possible as the council could ensure it retained control of negotiations on workers' pay and conditions. Convincing workers that sufficient resources were being devoted to the decentralization project to make the scheme work successfully would be more difficult. For at a time of financial constraints, a council, like Sheffield, is unlikely to have much spare money to spend on decentralization schemes. Indeed, as already reported, the Director of Social Services in Sheffield believed the main problem preventing progress to decentralization was the lack of resources. In a difficult financial situation, it is probably wise for a council like Sheffield to ask itself whether decentralizing council services is the best way forward, the best way, that is, to increase the control council service users, the local community and council workers have over council activities and to improve the quality of services. Whatever the answer to that question, local councils are likely to make little progress towards 'empowering the powerless' unless they seriously resolve the conflicts between representative and direct democracy and really clarify what it is they are trying to achieve. There is also a need for councils to look seriously at the question of whether the interests of council workers and service users are always compatible and, if not, to find ways of resolving any conflicts which retain the commitments of the council in this area. The field work suggests that Sheffield Council Labour Group did not do enough work in any of those areas.

If the needs of service users and council workers are to be furthered, the development of forms of discursive or deliberative democracy may well be needed. As Jurgen Habermas (1984, 1987) has argued, the best solutions to public issues are likely to be found when democracy is extended and all points of view can be articulated. In that way, provided people are trying to find the best solutions, and provided no group or class is able to impose its solution on others because of power inequalities, the best argument is likely to be supported. The implication for local government is that policy-making should be 'opened up' and workers and service users, along with councillors, as representatives of the local community, allowed to discuss issues and problems in a free, egalitarian way. However, for discursive democracy to be extended, councillors would have to be prepared to give up the trappings of power and the organizational control (cf. Wright, 1985) and instrumental rationality (cf. Habermas, 1984) of chief officers would have to be eliminated in order to reduce the obstacles to the implementation of decisions in the way intended. Whether any council would be likely to promote such a strategy is open to question. Indeed, it may be that progress in this area will only occur if workers, service users and community groups are prepared to fight vigorously for it. That seems unlikely to happen in the foreseeable future.

Trade union practice

The discussion of NALGO's attitude to decentralization in the F and C S Department in Sheffield Council feeds into the broader issue of trade union activity and practice in the two councils studied. The case study found some evidence that NALGO shop stewards did have a different approach from the manual unions and that NALGO locally approached issues differently from the manual unions, as already shown. NALGO did seem to be more sceptical of council initiatives in Sheffield than the main manual worker unions. As has been shown, the NALGO shop stewards I interviewed put that greater scepticism down to a greater realism on their part as, in their view, many of Sheffield Council's ostensibly more radical policies were, on inspection, either not so radical or lacking in coherence.

There was little sign in the case study that NALGO opposed radical initiatives by Sheffield Council for basically reactionary reasons. The union branch did not have a hostile attitude to the council's proposals because it lacked socialist commitment, on the whole. In that respect, however, the views of the PIRO in the Housing Department, who saw the local NALGO branch as a strange mixture of conservative traditional council officers who were very wary of radical change and much more radical elements who wanted change at a faster pace, is very relevant. There was evidence to suggest that some councillors, in Doncaster as well as Sheffield Council, regarded NALGO as a union with some suspicion because the union was not affiliated to the Labour Party. There was also some evidence that NALGO, unlike the manual worker unions, was unable to use affiliation to the Labour Party locally to create a better working relationship between itself and the council. However, there was no evidence that NALGO took a different approach to issues because it was not affiliated to the Labour Party. While some NALGO shop stewards were members of the Socialist Workers Party and hostile towards the council because of that, the impression I gained from NALGO representatives was that the majority of NALGO activists were either members of the Labour Party or socialists of one sort or another who were not in principle hostile to the council.

While it does seem that NALGO in both councils was on the whole more critical of the council than the manual worker unions, there was also evidence that the manual worker unions did not always support radical initiatives by Sheffield Council with open arms. The manual worker unions were not entirely happy with the way Elderly Persons' Support Units in Sheffield were developing and their opposition was one of the reasons for delays in the extension of the scheme. Moreover, the manual worker unions were not happy about the introduction of the Passport to Leisure scheme in the Recreation Department in Sheffield Council. Hence, on two major radical initiatives in Sheffield, the manual worker unions were not more 'supportive' of the council's efforts than was NALGO.

The research tends to support the argument that unions are basically reactive organizations. For the research suggests that the unions in the two councils did generally adopt a reactive approach and stance. Except on compulsory competitive tendering, where there was evidence that the unions, or some of them, had taken the lead in pressing for the development of a council strategy, or strongly supported the need for such a strategy, council unions appeared to have been prepared to respond to council initiatives or outside pressures and measures. The reactive stance of the unions appeared to have been fairly uniform with little difference between the manual unions and NALGO.

The case study also suggests that if a council, like Sheffield, is to successfully introduce radical change, especially if it affects the position of workers, it will need to expend much energy trying to win over the unions to the desirability of change. It may also be that the sooner the unions are involved in discussions about major changes the greater will be the chances of change being introduced successfully. However, as the experience in Hackney Council (cf. Kendall, 1984) and Islington Council (cf. Heery, 1987), and my interview with a national NALGO official strongly suggest, any discussion should be with the recognized union negotiators and integrated into formal, recognized structures. Evidence suggests that councils trying to undertake informal discussions with workers outside union structures will create union suspicion, however innocent and well-meaning the action of the council may be.

A council needs to convince the unions, and the members they represent, that they are not threatened by proposed changes, if the council is to stand any chance of winning union co-operation. One of the reasons for the negative reaction of the Sheffield NALGO branch to council initiatives, as shown in earlier chapters, may have been a feeling among the members of the union that the proposed changes represented an attack on their interests. It would seem, from the field work findings, that Sheffield councillors did not give enough time or a high enough priority to convincing NALGO members and their representatives that they would gain, and their interests certainly were not threatened by, the council's proposed changes.

Differences between Sheffield and Doncaster Councils

During the 1980s, there were big differences between the position in Sheffield City Council and that in Doncaster Borough Council on the industrial relations front. While I have shown, in some cases, and strongly suggested in others, that it made only limited progress towards its aims, Sheffield City Council in the 1980s was very different from Doncaster Borough Council in the issues it raised and the style of its operation. Sheffield Council did make commitments to tackle low pay among its workforce and to promote single status employment in the council and the council made some, though limited, progress in that direction. Sheffield Council was aware that something needed to be done to help the position of women and ethnic minorities in the council. The Sheffield Council did make commitments to change the way in which the council operated, so that the users and providers of council services could have more control over council activities. Sheffield City Council tried to provide an alternative to the policies and politics of the Conservative central governments.

Doncaster Borough Council, on the other hand, made few commitments, and hence little or no progress, in any of the above areas. Doncaster Council made no special effort to improve the position of its low paid workers. Doncaster Council did not give a high priority to the development of equal opportunities. Doncaster Council made no commitment to trying to change the workings of the council so that council service users and council workers could gain more control over council activities and hence their lives. Doncaster Council accepted central government constraints and financial controls on local government after 1980, believing that to challenge the government was futile and would end in defeat.

For Doncaster councillors and officers, Sheffield City Council shouted a lot, took up poses but achieved and did very little. Many Doncaster councillors and officers were only too willing to criticize the record of Sheffield Council and to decry its aims and its style. But there was little critical analysis of Doncaster Council's own record. Councillors in Sheffield seemed more willing to examine critically the record of the council. I gained the impression that many Doncaster councillors and officers were happy to see the council 'tick over' and avoid major problems. Sheffield City Council made an effort to do more than that and, while it may not have been all that successful, at least it offered, if only for a while, some hope that social change was possible.

However, the views of Doncaster councillors and officers that trying to challenge the central government was bound to fail raises very important questions. For if a hostile central government with the backing of the whole central state machine would necessarily be able to block the efforts of new urban left councils to introduce radical social change, the whole new urban left project in local government is brought into question. As suggested elsewhere in the work, there are good grounds to believe that the new urban left project could only have succeeded if the Conservative central government had been forced to change its attitude to, and policies in respect of, local government. For that to have succeeded, the new urban left would have needed to win mass positive support for the defence or development of its policies and programmes or some other pressure, such as industrial militancy, would have needed to force a complete change of course from the central government. As argued elsewhere, the new urban left councils failed to mobilize the necessary popular pressure and support to defeat the actions and programme of the central government. Once again, there are grounds for believing that new urban left councils, including Sheffield City Council, did not think sufficiently clearly about the problems it would face or the ways in which the problems could be overcome. New urban left councils, including Sheffield City Council, recognized in principle the need to win active, mass, popular support but in practice did not really work out how such support could be mobilized. It is in that sense that the arguments of councillors and officers in Doncaster Borough Council have force.

Obituary on the new urban left experience in local government

The new urban left in local government no longer exists as a recognizable force (cf. Lansley, Goss and Wolmar, 1989). All the councils included in the list in chapter 2 either made big spending cuts and dropped many of their more ambitious schemes and proposals in the late 1980s or moved out of Labour control. In general, the experience of new urban left councils was similar to that of Sheffield on the industrial relations front. The councils did try to do something new and exciting and they achieved some temporary successes, such as the GLC on cultural issues. The policies and programmes they supported, had they succeeded in the long term, would have helped to improve the position of very many working-class and oppressed and disadvantaged groups. The councils did try to give Labour government a new, more democratic and socialist dimension and content. They failed in their bigger aims for reasons suggested in this work. Not least of the reasons for their failure was a lack of a clear idea of how local government could be run in practice on more democratic and egalitarian lines. The problem of finding a socialist way of running public institutions generally and not just local government remains as unanswered as ever. That problem may be the prime one facing socialists in Britain in the last few years of the twentieth century. For a number of writers have argued that support for the whole socialist cause has been dissipated by the failure to find a democratic way of running public organizations (cf. Williams, 1981; Held and Keane, 1984; Hall, 1984; Panitch, 1986).

My research suggests strongly that socialists need to think clearly about the power structure in public institutions and the internal, as well as external, obstacles to change in public organizations. For unless the internal obstacles are overcome it is unlikely that the external ones will be. The relationship between trade union praxis and socialist change is another area where further work needs to be done by socialists. There is also scope, and a need for, more research on the relationship between the different elements and apparatuses of the state. Work on the relationship between 'traditional' political representative democracy and direct or 'social' democracy to clarify potential problems between the two forms of democracy is also required.

While the new urban left did not succeed in achieving its major aims, its legacy is not totally negative. For the experience of the new urban left has had an important impact in certain areas. In many cases, new urban left councils gave the promotion of equal opportunities a high priority, as argued earlier. Equal opportunities is given a much higher priority in Labour local government, if sometimes only in formal terms, than was the case fifteen years ago. The new urban left councils played an important part in changing the agenda and thinking on equal opportunities, and not just in Labour councils, even if the actions of some new urban left councils in this area produced criticisms and even contempt, both from inside and outside the Labour Party. Most local authorities and public bodies, as well as many private organizations, now regard themselves as equal opportunities employers. The formal emphasis on equal opportunities over the last decade is due to developments such as the passing of the Equal Pay Act and the Sex Discrimination Act in the mid 1970s and the activities of the women's movement. However, the new urban left councils, some of whom were strongly influenced by feminism, also helped to push the issue up the political agenda and to give the subject a greater importance.

In addition, new urban left councils helped to produce a new agenda for local government. The concern with industrial, employment and cultural issues and the prominence given to those subjects, for example, was a new departure for local government. Some of the new urban left councils attempted to produce a more proactive role for local government in areas such as employment where councils have traditionally reacted to market led imperatives. The new urban left councils may not have achieved their substantial goals in the areas where they tried to be proactive rather than reactive but they helped to put new issues onto the local government agenda.

Over the abolition of the GLC and the Metropolitan County Councils in the mid 1980s, the government faced strong opposition, not just from the Labour Party, certain academics and others, but from within its own parliamentary supporters, nearly losing a crucial vote in the House of Lords over its abolition proposals as a result (cf. Livingstone, 1987, pp. 278-279). The Conservative government on this issue was seen as undermining democracy and acting in a dictatorial manner. The campaign launched by the threatened councils, and particularly by the new urban left led GLC, helped to produce the 'democratic' opposition to the government's proposals and actions (cf. Gyford, Leach and Game, 1989, pp. 304-307 and Forrester, Lansley and Pauley, 1985). Moreover, many of the measures which the governments introduced since 1979, often with one aim, if not the sole aim, of reducing the ability of new urban left councils to pursue their objectives, have proved unpopular. That is especially true of the poll tax or community charge, which was partly introduced to control the spending, and consequently the activities, of new urban left Labour local authorities, as is implied in remarks made by Nicholas Ridley in a speech in Liverpool in August 1987 (cf. Child Poverty Action Group, 1987, pp. 5-9).

The new urban left councils during the 1980s played an important part in pushing issues of democracy to the forefront of the political agenda. In fighting for the independence of local government and by highlighting the central government's attacks on local authority autonomy, the actions of new urban left councils fed into the rise of interest in constitutional issues and issues of democracy. The whole interest in democracy and what it means, expressed by organizations such as Charter 88 can be seen as informed by the campaigns of the new urban left councils.

In the end, the new urban left in local government probably raised more questions than they provided answers. But the problems with which they were concerned, and which the experience of the new urban left in local government raises, remain crucial for socialists and are likely to recur the next time an effort is made to develop an empowering and liberating form of socialism.

Bibliography

Alcock, P., Cochrane, A. and Lee, P. (1984) Interview with J. Bennington 'A parable of how things might be done differently', *Critical Social Policy*, no. 9, pp. 69-97.

Alcock, P. and Lee, P. (1981) 'Struggles in the welfare state. The socialist republic of South Yorkshire', *Critical Social Policy*, vol. 1, no. 2, pp. 72-93.

Alexander, A. (1986) *Managing Local Socialism*, Fabian Society Tract no. 511, Fabian Society, London.

Anderson, P. (1965) 'Problems of socialist strategy', in P. Anderson and R. Blackburn (eds.), *Towards Socialism*, Fontana, London, pp. 21-290.

Anderson, P. (1967) 'The limits of trade union action' in A. Cockburn and R. Blackburn (eds.) *The Incompatibles*, Penguin, Harmondsworth, pp. 263-280.

Anderson, P. (1980) *Arguments Within English Marxism*, Verso, London.

Bain, G. S., Coates, D. and Ellis, V. (1973) *Social Stratification and Trade Unionism*, Heinemann, London.

Bainbridge, C. (1987) 'Lewisham: NALGO awaits council's reaction', *Going Local*, no. 7, March, p. 5.

Baker, C., Hambleton, R., Hoggett, P. (1987) 'Decentralisation in Birmingham: a case study', in P. Hoggett and R. Hambleton (eds.), *Decentralisation and Democracy*, Bristol, SAUS Occasional Paper 28, pp. 84-119.

Baker, J. (1987) *Arguing for Equality*, Verso, London.

Banks, J. A. (1970) *Marxist Sociology in Action*, Faber and Faber, London.

Barnes, D. and Reid, E. (1980) *Governments and Trade Unions*, Heinemann, London.

Barnett, A. (1987) 'Socialism from below', *Marxism Today*, October, pp. 49-50.

Barratt Brown, M. (1972) *From Labourism to Socialism*, Spokesman, Nottingham.

Beavis, I. (1985) 'Sacrificing the unions - who shot NALGO?', *Going Local?*, April.

Beechey, V. (1982) 'The sexual division of labour and the labour process: A critical assessment of Braverman' in S. Wood (ed.) *The Degradation of Work?*, Hutchinson, London, pp. 54- 73.

Beetham, D. (1981) 'Beyond Liberal democracy', in R. Miliband and J. Saville (eds.), *The Socialist Register 1981*, Merlin Press, London, pp. 190-206.

Benn, T. (1982) *Parliament, People and Power Agenda for a Free Society. Interviews with New Left Review*, New Left Books, London.

Beresford, P. and Croft, S. (1983) 'Making our own plans', *Chartist*, no. 94, pp. 26-27.

Beresford, P. and Croft, S. (1984) 'Welfare pluralism: the new face of Fabianism', *Critical Social Policy*, issue 9, pp. 19-39.

Beresford, P. and Croft, S. (1986) *Whose Welfare Private Care or Public Service*, Brighton, Lewis Cohen Urban Studies.

Beuret, K. and Stoker, J. (1986) 'The Labour Party and neighbourhood decentralisation: flirtation or commitment?', *Critical Social Policy*, issue 17, pp. 4-22.

Bevan, A. (1961) *In Place of Fear*, MacGibbon and Kee, London.

Beynon, H. (1973) *Working for Ford*, Harmondsworth, Penguin.

Beynon, H. and Wainwright, H. (1979) *The Vickers Report*, London, Pluto.

Blackburn, R. M. (1967) *Union Character and Social Class*, Batsford, London.

Blackburn, R. M. and Prandy, K. (1966) 'White-collar unionisation: a conceptual framework', *British Journal of Sociology*, vol. 16, pp. 111-122.

Blatchford, R. (1894) *Merrie England*, Clarion, London.

Blunkett, D. (1981) 'Towards a socialist social policy', *Local Government Policy Making*, vol. 8, no. 1, pp. 95-103.

Blunkett, D. (1982) 'Sheffield Steel', *New Socialist*, November/December, pp. 56-57.

Blunkett, D. (1984) 'Interviewed by M. Boddy and C. Fudge', in M. Boddy and C. Fudge (eds.), *Local Socialism?*, Macmillan, London, pp. 242-260.

Blunkett, D. (1985) 'Interview', *Marxism Today*, March, pp. 7-11.

Blunkett, D. and Green, G. (1983) *Building from the Bottom,* Fabian Tract no. 491, Fabian Society, London.

Blunkett, D. and Jackson, K. (1987) *Democracy In Crisis,* Hogarth, London.

Boddy, M. (1984) 'Local economic and employment initiatives', in M. Boddy and C. Fudge (eds.), *Local Socialism?* Macmillan, London, pp. 160-191.

Boddy, M. and Fudge, C. (1984) 'Left councils and new left alternatives', in M. Boddy and C. Fudge (eds.), *Local Socialism?*, Macmillan, London, pp. 1-21.

Bolger, S., Corrigan, P., Docking, J. and Frost, N. (1981) *Towards Socialist Welfare Work,* Macmillan, London.

Boynton, J. (1986) *Job at the Top*, Longman, London.

Branson, N. (1979) *Poplarism 1919-1925*, Lawrence and Wishart, London.

Braverman, H. (1974) *Labor and Monopoly Capital*, Monthly Review Press, London.

Bye, B. and Beatie, J. (1982) *Local Economic Planning and the Unions*, Workers Educational Association, London.

Carter, R. (1985) *Capitalism, Class Conflict and the New Middle Class*, Routledge and Kegan Paul, London.

Carvel, J. (1984) *Citizen Ken*, Chatto and Windus, London.

Chamberlain, N. W. and Kuhn, J. W. (1951) *Collective Bargaining*, McGraw-Hill, New York.

Chandler, J. (1988) *Public Policy-Making for Local Government*, Croom Helm, London.

Child, D. and Paddon, M. (1984) 'Sheffield: steelyard blues', *Marxism Today*, July, pp. 18-22.

Child Poverty Action Group, (1987) *A Tax on All the People-The Poll Tax*, CPAG London.

Clapham, D. (1985) 'Management of the local state: the example of corporate planning', *Critical Social Policy*, issue 14, pp. 27-42.

Clarke, A. and Cochrane, A. (1989) 'Inside the machine: the left and finance professionals in local government', *Capital and Class*, no. 37, Spring, pp. 35-61.

Clarke, S. (1988) 'Why do we have a capitalist state?' *Interlink*, no. 9, October-November, pp. 22-23.

Clegg, H. A. (1975) 'Pluralism in Industrial Relations', *British Journal of Industrial Relations*, vol. 13, pp. 309-316.

Clegg, H. A. (1979) *The Changing System of Industrial Relations in Great Britain*, Blackwell, Oxford.

Cliff, T. and Gluckstein, D. (1986) *Marxism and Trade Union Struggle: The General Strike of 1926*, Bookmarks, London.

Coates, D. (1975) *The Labour Party and the Struggle for Socialism*, Cambridge University Press, Cambridge.

Coates, D. (1980) *Labour in Power?*, Longman, London.

Coates, D. (1983) 'The question of trade union power', in D. Coates and G. Johnson (eds.) *Socialist Arguments*, Martin Robertson, Oxford, pp. 55-82.

Coates, D. (1989) *The Crisis of Labour*, Philip Allan, Oxford.

Coates, K. (1967) 'Wage slaves', in R. Blackburn and A. Cockburn (eds.), *The Incompatibles*, Penguin, Harmondsworth, pp. 56-92.

Coates, K. (1973) 'Socialists and the Labour Party', in R. Miliband and J. Saville (eds.) *Socialist Register 1973*, Merlin, London, pp. 155-178.

Coates, K. (ed.), (1979a) *What Went Wrong*, Spokesman, Nottingham.

Coates, K. (1979b) 'Whatever happened to industrial democracy?', in K. Coates (ed.), *What Went Wrong*, Spokesman, Nottingham, pp. 124-136.

Coates, K. (1981) *Work-ins, Sit-ins and Industrial Democracy*, Spokesman, Nottingham.

Coates, K. and Topham, T. (1988) *Trade Unions in Britain*, 3rd edn, Fontana Press, London.

Cochrane, A. (1993) *Whatever Happened to Local Government*, Open University Press, Buckingham.

Cockburn, C. (1977) *The Local State*, Pluto, London.

Cockburn, C. (1987) *Women, Trade Unions and Political Parties*, Fabian Research Series No. 349, Fabian Society, London.

Cole, G. D. H. (1918) *Self Government in Industry*, G. Bell and Sons, London.

Community Care (1985) 'Decentralisation, who's doing what?', April 18, p. 19.

Conference of Socialist Economists State Apparatus and Expenditure Group, (1979) *Struggle Over the State*, CSE Books, London.

Cook, C. and Taylor, I. (1980) *The Labour Party*, Longman, London.

Cook, F. G., Clark, S. C., Roberts, K. and Semeonoff, E. (1975/1976) '"White and blue collar workers" attitudes to trade unionism and social class', *Industrial Relations Journal*, Vol. 6, no. 4, Winter, pp. 47-58.

Corrigan, P. (1979) 'The local state: the struggle for democracy', *Marxism Today*, July, pp. 203-209.

Corrigan, P., Jones, T., Lloyd, J. and Young, J. (1988), 'Citizen gains', *Marxism Today*, August, pp. 18-21.

Coventry, Liverpool, Newcastle and North Tyneside Trades Councils (1980) *State Intervention in Industry*, Spokesman, Nottingham.

Coyle, A. (1989) 'The limits of change: local government and equal opportunities for women', *Public Administration*, vol. 67, no. 1, Spring, pp. 39-50.

Cox, A. (1983) 'On the role of the state in urban policy-making: the case of inner-city and dispersal policies in Britain', in V. Pons and R. Francis (eds.), *Urban Social Research Problems and Prospects, Sociological Review Monograph 30*, Routledge and Kegan Paul, London, pp. 31-65.

Cripps, F. and Morrell, F. (1979) 'The abandonment of full employment', in K. Coates (ed.), *What Went Wrong*, Spokesman, Nottingham, pp. 95-102.

Crompton, R. and Jones, G. (1984) *White-Collar Proletariat*, Macmillan, London.

Crouch, C. (1982) *Trade Unions   the Logic of Collective Action*, Fontana, Glasgow.

Crouch, C. (1982) 'The peculiar relationship: the party and the unions', in D. Kavanagh (ed.), *The Politics of the Labour Party*, George Allen and Unwin, London, pp. 171-190.

Currie, R. (1979) *Industrial Politics*, Clarendon Press, Oxford.

Darke, J. and Goulay, K. (1985) 'United we stand', *New Socialist*, no. 24, February, p. 48.

David, J. (1983) 'Walsall and decentralisation', *Critical Social Policy,* Issue 7, pp. 75-79.

Davis, M., Misrahi, B., Shield, R., McDonnell, K., Hoggett, P., Tyrall, R. (1984) *Go Local to Survive,* Labour Co-ordinating Committee, London.

Day, P. and Klein, R. (1987) *Accountabilities*, Tavistock Publications, London.

Deakin, N. (1984a) 'Decentralisation panacea or blind alley', *Local Government Policy Making*, vol. 11, no. 1, July, pp. 17-24.

Deakin, N. (1984b) 'Two cheers for decentralisation' , in A. Wright, J. Stewart and N. Deakin, *Socialism and Decentralisation,* Fabian Society Tract no. 496, Fabian Society, London, pp. 8-17.

Dearlove, J. (1973) *The Politics of Policy in Local Government*, Cambridge University Press, Cambridge.

Dearlove, J. (1985) *Restructuring for Capital versus Restructuring For Labour: Central Control, Local Democracy and Local Economic Policies,* Urban and Regional Studies, University of Sussex, Working Paper 45.

Dennis, N., Henriques, F. and Slaughter, C. (1969) *Coal is Our Life,* 2nd edn, Tavistock, London.

Dickens, P. (1988) *One Nation*, Pluto Press, London.

Doncaster District Labour Party (1987) *1987 Council Election Manifesto,* Doncaster District Labour Party.

Doncaster District Labour Party (1988) *1988 Council Election Manifesto, Doncaster* District Labour Party.

Doncaster Metropolitan Borough Council (1980) *Constitution of Manual Employees' Joint Committee,* Doncaster Borough Council.

Doncaster Metropolitan Borough Council (1980) *Constitution of Departmental Employees' Joint Committee,* Doncaster Borough Council.

Doncaster Metropolitan Borough Council (n. d.) *Constitution of the Doncaster Council Joint Staff Consultative Committee*, Doncaster Borough Council.

Drucker, H. M. (1979) *Doctrine and Ethos in the Labour Party,* Allen and Unwin, London.

Duncan, G. (1983) 'Human nature and radical democratic theory', in G. Duncan (ed.), *Democratic Theory and Practice*, Cambridge University Press, Cambridge, pp. 187-203.

Duncan, S. and Goodwin, M. (1980) *The Local State and Restructuring Local Relations: Theory and Practice*, Urban and Regional Studies, University of Sussex, Working Paper 24.

Duncan, S. and Goodwin, M. (1982) 'The local state and restructuring in social relations', *International Journal of Urban and Regional Research*, pp. 157-185.

Duncan, S. and Goodwin, M. (1988) *The Local State and Underdevelopment,* Polity Press, Cambridge.

Dunleavy, P. (1979) *The Policy Implications of Professionalism in the Advanced Industrial State,* Paper presented to PSA Policy Group, Birmingham.

Dunleavy, P. (1980) *Urban Political Analysis,* Macmillan, London.

Dunleavy, P. (1981) 'Professions and policy change: notes towards a model of ideological corporatism', *Public Administration Bulletin,* no. 36, August, pp. 3-16.

Eaton, J. and Gill, C. (1983) *The Trade Union Directory,* 2nd edn, Pluto, London.

Edge, G. (1981) *The Guardian,* 6 October.

Engels, F. (1881) 'Trade Unions', in *K. Marx and F. Engels, Articles on Britain,* Progress Publishers, Moscow, 1975, pp. 371-377.

Enrenreich, B. and Enrenreich J. (1979) 'The professional-managerial class', in P. Walker (ed.), *Between Labour and Capital,* Harvester Press, Brighton, pp. 5-45.

Esland, G. (1980) 'Professions and Professionalism', in G. Esland and G. Salaman (eds.), *The Politics of Work and Occupations,* Open University Press, Milton Keynes, pp. 213-250.

Fairbrother, P. (1982) *Working for the State,* London, Workers' Educational Association, Studies for Trade Unionists, vol. 8, no. 29.

Fairbrother, P. (1984) *All Those In Favour,* London, Pluto Press.

Fatchett, D. (1987) *Trade Unions and Politics in the 1980s,* Croom Helm, London.

Flanders, A. (1968) *Trade Unions,* 7th edn, Hutchinson, London.

Flanders, A. (1970) *Management and Unions: The Theory and Reform of Industrial Relations,* Faber and Faber, London.

Foote, G. (1986) *The Labour Party's Political Thought, A History,* 2nd edn, Croom Helm, London.

Forrester, A., Lansley, S. and Pauley, R. (1985) *Beyond Our Ken: A Guide to the Battle for London,* 4th Estate, London.

Forester, T. (1978) *The Labour Party and the Working Class,* Heinemann, London.

Forester, T. (1979) 'Neutralising the industrial strategy', in K. Coates (ed.), *What Went Wrong,* Nottingham, Spokesman, pp. 74-94.

Fowler, A. (1980) *Personnel Management in Local Government,* 2nd edn, Institute of Personnel Management, London.

Fox, A. (1971) *A Sociology of Work and Industry,* L, Macmillan, London.

Fox, A. (1974) *Beyond Contract: Power, Work and Trust Relations,* Faber and Faber, London.

Fox, A. (1985) *History and Heritage: the Social Origins of the British Industrial Relations System,* Allen and Unwin, London.

Fretwell, L. (1987) 'Good management is also socialism', *Local Government Chronicle,* 20 November.

Fryer, R. (1979) 'British trade unions and the cuts', *Capital and Class,* Summer, pp. 94-112.

Fryer, R. (1989) 'Public service trade unionism in the twentieth century', in Mailly, R., Dimmock, S. J. and Seth, A. S. (eds.), *Industrial Relations in Public Services,* Routledge, London, pp. 17-67.

Fudge, C. (1984) 'Decentralisation: socialism goes local', in M. Boddy and C. Fudge (eds.), *Local Socialism?,* Macmillan, London, pp. 192-214.

Geddes, M. (1988) 'The capitalist state and the local economy: "Restructuring for labour" and after', *Capital and Class*, no. 35, Summer, pp. 85-120.

General, Municipal, Boilermakers and Allied Trade Union (1986) *General, Municipal, Boilermakers and Allied Trade Union, Its History, Benefits and Services*, Esher, GMB.

Goodrich, C. L. (1975) *The Frontier of Control*, Pluto Press, London.

Goodwin, M. (1985) *Locality and Local State: Sheffield's Economic Policy*, Urban and Regional Studies, University of Sussex, Working Paper 52.

Gordon, I. and Whiteley, P. (1979) 'Social class and political attitudes: the case of Labour councillors', *Political Studies*, vol. xxvii, no. 1, pp. 99-113.

Goss, S. (1984) 'Women's initiatives in local government', in M. Boddy and C. Fudge (eds.), *Local Socialism?*, Macmillan, London, pp. 109-132.

Goss, S., Hillier, J. and Rule, J. (eds.), (1988) *Labour Councils in the Cold, A Blueprint for Survival*, Labour Co-ordinating Committee, London.

Gough, I. (1983) 'Thatcherism and the welfare state', in S. Hall and M. Jacques (eds.), *The Politics of Thatcherism*, Lawrence and Wishart, London, pp. 148-168.

Graham, K. (1986) *The Battle for Democracy*, Wheatsheaf, Brighton.

Gramsci, A. (1971) *Selections From the Prison Notebooks*, Lawrence and Wishart, London.

Green, D. G. (1981) *Power and Party in an English City*, George Allen and Unwin, London.

Green, G. (1987) 'The new municipal socialism', in M. Loney (ed.), *The State or the Market*, Sage, London, pp. 203-221.

Greenwood, R. and Hinnings, C. R. (1973) 'Local Government Organisation: 1972-6', *Policy and Politics*, March, pp. 213- 221.

Griffith, J. (1985) *The Politics of the Judiciary*, 3rd edn, Fontana, London.

Gyford, J. (1983a) 'The new urban left: a local road to socialism?', *New Society*, 21 April, pp. 91-93.

Gyford, J. (1983b) *The New Urban Left Origins, Style and Strategy*, Town Planning Discussion Paper No. 38, University College London.

Gyford, J. (1985) *The Politics of Local Socialism*, Allen and Unwin, London.

Gyford, J., Leach, B. and Game, C. (1989) *The Changing Politics of Local Government*, Unwin Hyman, London.

Habermas, J. (1984) *The Theory of Communicative Action*, Vol. 1, Heinemann, London.

Habermas, J. (1987) *The Theory of Communicative Action*, Vol. 2, Polity, Cambridge.

Habermas, J. (1991) *Communication and the Evolution of Society*, Polity, Cambridge.

Hackney Labour Parties (1982) *Hackney 1982 Manifesto Decentralisation - why we want it, how it will work, proposals for discussion*, Hackney Local Government Committee.

Hain, P. (1986) *Political Strikes: the State and Trade Unionism in Britain*, Penguin, Harmondsworth.

Hall, S. (1983) 'The great moving right show', in S. Hall and M. Jacques (eds.), *The Politics of Thatcherism*, London, Lawrence and Wishart, pp. 19-39.

Hall, S. (1984) 'The state - socialism's old caretaker', *Marxism Today*, November, pp. 24-29.

Hall, S. (1987) Interview by T. Fisher 'Old left, new left and the third road', *Chartist*, no.113, January/February , pp. 12-15.

Hall, S. (n. d.) *The Battle for Socialist Ideas in the 1980s*, Merlin Press, London.

Hambleton, R. and Hoggett, P. (1987) 'The democratisation of public services', in P. Hoggett and R. Hambleton (eds.), *Decentralisation and Democracy*, Bristol, SAUS Occasional Paper 28, pp. 53-83.

Hampton, W. (1970) *Democracy and Community*, Oxford University Press, Oxford.

Hampton, W. (1978) 'Sir Ronald Ironmonger: leader through consensus', in G. W. Jones and A. Norton (eds.), *Political Leadership in Local Authorities*, Institute of Local Government Studies, University of Birmingham, pp. 153-166.

Hampton, W. (1987) *Local Government and Urban Politics*, Longman, London.

Hampton, W. and Davies, R. E. (1987) *Take Ten: Evaluation. Analysis of Interviews and Questionnaires*, Sheffield City Council, Sheffield.

Hancox, A., Worrell, L. and Pay, J. (1989) 'Developing a customer orientated approach to service delivery: the Wrekin approach', *Local Government Studies*, vol. 15, no. 1, January/February, pp. 16-25.

Harrison, M. (1960) *Trade Unions and the Labour Party*, Macmillan, London.

Hatton, D. (1988) *Inside Left*, Bloomsbury, London.

Hedley, R. (1989) 'New bill offers little surprises on detail', *Local Government Chronicle*, 17 February.

Heery, E. (1987) 'A common labour movement? Left Labour councils and the trade unions', in P. Hoggett and R. Hambleton (eds.), *Decentralisation and Democracy*, Bristol, SAUS Occasional Paper 28, pp. 194-214.

Held, D. (1987) *Models of Democracy*, Polity Press, Cambridge.

Held, D. and Keane, J. (1984) 'Socialism and the limits of state action', in J. Curren (ed.), *The future of the Left*, Polity Press, Cambridge, pp. 170-181.

Hewitt, M. (1992) *Welfare Ideology and Need*, Harvester Wheatsheaf, Hemel Hempstead.

Hill, M. (1981) 'The policy-implementation distinction: a quest for rational control', in S. Barrett and C. Fudge (eds.), *Policy and Action*, Methuen, London, pp. 207-223.

Hindess, B. (1983) *Parliamentary Democracy and Socialist Politics*, Routledge and Kegan Paul, London.

Hinton, J. (1973) *The First Shop Stewards' Movement*, Allen and Unwin, London.

Hodge, M. (1987) 'Central/local conflicts: the view from Islington', in P. Hoggett and R. Hambleton (eds.), *Decentralisation and Democracy*, Bristol, SAUS Occasional Paper 28, pp. 29-36.

Hodgson, G. (1984) *The Democratic Economy*, Penguin, Harmondsworth.

Hoggett, P. (1984) 'Decentralisation, labourism and the professionalised welfare state apparatus', in R. Hambleton and P. Hoggett (eds.), *The Politics of Decentralisation: Theory and Practice of a Radical Local Government Initiative*, Bristol, SAUS Working Paper 46, pp. 16-34.

Hoggett, P. (1987a) 'Waste disposal', *New Socialist*, no. 47, March, pp. 30-35.

Hoggett, P. (1987b) 'A farewell to mass production? Decentralisation as an emergent private and public sector paradigm', in P. Hoggett and R. Hambleton (eds.), *Decentralisation and Democracy*, Bristol, SAUS Occasional Paper 28, pp. 215-232.

Hoggett, P. and Hambleton, R. (1984) 'Decentralisation strategies for achieving change', in R. Hambleton and P. Hoggett (eds.), *The Politics of Decentralisation: Theory and Practice of a Radical Local Government Initiative,* Bristol, SAUS Working Paper 46, pp. 96-113.

Hoggett, P., Lawrence, S. and Fudge, C. (1984) 'The Politics of Decentralisation in Hackney', in R. Hambleton and P. Hoggett (eds.), *The Politics of Decentralisation: Theory and Practice of a Radical Local Government Initiative,* Bristol, SAUS Working Paper 46, pp. 62-79.

Howell, D. (1980) *British Social Democracy,* 2nd edn, Croom Helm, London.

Hyman, R. (1971) *Marxism and the Sociology of Trade Unionism,* Pluto Press, London.

Hyman, R. (1979) 'The politics of workplace trade unionism: recent tendencies and some problems for theory', *Capital and Class,* Summer, pp. 54-63.

Hyman, R. (1980) 'Trade unions, control and resistance', in G. Esland and G. Salaman (eds.), *The Politics of Work and Occupation,* Open University Press, Milton Keynes, pp. 303-334.

Hyman, R. and Bough, I. (1975) *Social Values and Industrial Relations,* Blackwell, Oxford.

Hyman, R. (1989) *The Political Economy of Industrial Relations,* Macmillan, London.

Ingham, M. (1985) 'Industrial relations in British local government', *Industrial Relations Journal,* vol. 6, no. 1, pp. 6-15.

Islington Borough Council (1987) *Service Provision and Living Standards,* London Borough of Islington, Islington.

Islington Labour Parties Local Government Committee (1981) *A Socialist Programme for Islington 1982,* Islington Labour Parties.

Islington Labour Parties Local Government Committee (1986) *Council Manifesto 1986,* Islington Labour Parties.

Islington NALGO Branch (1986a) *Decentralisation,* 20 February.

Islington NALGO Branch (1986b) *Decentralisation,* 13 March.

Islington NALGO Branch (1986c) *Clause 11 dispute Greater London Whitley Council, Decentralisation Problems in Operation of Neighbourhood Offices,* 21 May.

Jenkins, P. (1970) *The Battle of Downing Street,* Charles Knight, London.

Jensen, F. (1989) 'Manchester decides not to fight the Tories', *Labour Briefing,* April 19-3 May.

Jessop, B. (1982) *The Capitalist State,* Martin Robertson, Oxford.

Jessop, B. (1985) *Nicos Poulantzas Marxist Thought and Political Strategy,* Macmillan, London.

Johnson, T. (1972) *Professions and Power,* Macmillan, London.

Johhnson, T. (1980) 'Work and power', in G. Esland and G. Salaman (eds.), *The Politics of Work and Occupations,* Open University Press, Milton Keynes, pp. 335-373.

Jones, C. (1983) *State Social Work and the Working Class,* Macmillan, London.

Jones, G. and Stewart J. (1983) *The Case for Local Government,* George Allen and Unwin, London.

Joyce, P., Corrigan, P. and Hayes, M. (1988) *Striking Out,* Macmillan, London.

Kelly, J. (1987) *Labour and the Unions,* Verso, London.

Kelly, J. (1988) *Trade Unions and Socialist Politics*, Verso, London.

Kendall, A. (1984) 'Decentralisation: promise or delusion?', *Going Local?*, no. 1, December, p. 6.

Kogan, M. and Kogan, D. (1983) *The Battle for the Labour Party*, 2nd edn, Fontana, London.

Korpi, W. (1983) *The Democratic Class Struggle*, Routledge and Kegan Paul, London.

Labour Briefing 1988-1989.

Labour Research Department/SCAT/Birmingham TURC (1985) *Putting the Rates to Work*, LRD Publications, London.

Laffin, M. (1986) *Professionalism and Policy: The Role of the Professions in the Central-Local Government Relationship*, Gower, Aldershot.

Laffin, M. (1989) *Managing Under Pressure*, Macmillan, London.

Laffin, M. and Newton, K. (1985) 'The changing roles and responsibilities of local authority chief officers', *Public Administration*, Spring, vol. 63, no. 1, pp. 41-59.

Lansley, S. (1985) 'The Phoney War', *New Socialist*, no. 29, July/August, pp. 29-31.

Lansley, S., Goss, S. and Wolmar, C. (1989) *Councils in Conflict: The Rise and Fall of the Municipal Left*, Macmillan, London.

Larson, M. S. (1977) *The Rise of Professionalism*, University of California Press, California.

Lenin, V. I. (1899) 'On strikes', in *V. I. Lenin Collected Works* vol. 4, Foreign Languages Publishing House, Moscow, 1960, pp. 310-319.

Lenin, V. I. (1902) *What is to be Done?*, Moscow, Foreign Languages Publishing House, Moscow, 1947.

Lenin, V. I. (1905) 'The reorganisation of the party', in *V. I. Lenin Collected Works*, vol. 10, Foreign Languages Publishing House, Moscow, 1964, pp. 29-39.

Lenin, V. I. (1917) 'Lecture on 1905 revolution', in *V. I. Lenin Collected Works*, vol. 23, Progress Publishers, Moscow, 1964, pp. 236-253.

Lipsey, P. (1982) 'Labour's new (non-manual) breed of councillor', *Sunday Times*, 19 September.

Littler, C. (1983) 'Deskilling and changing structures of control', in S. Wood (ed.), *The Degradation of Work?*, Hutchinson, London, pp. 122-145.

Livingstone, K. (1981) 'Interview', in *Marxism Today*, November, pp. 16-20.

Livingstone, K. (1984) 'Interviewed by M. Boddy and C. Fudge', in M. Boddy and C. Fudge (eds.), *Local Socialism?*, Macmillan, London, pp. 260-283.

Livingstone, K. (1987) *If Voting Changed Anything, They'd Abolish It*, Collins, London.

London Edinburgh Weekend Return Group (1980), *In and Against the State*, Pluto, London.

London Evening Standard, (1982) 7 May.

Mackintosh, M. and Wainwright, H. (eds.), (1987) *A Taste of Power*, Verso, London.

Mackintosh, M. and Wainwright, H. (1987a) 'Introduction', in M. Mackintosh and H. Wainwright (eds.), *A Taste of Power*, Verso, London, pp. 1-19.

Mackintosh, M. and Wainwright, H. (1987b) 'Conclusion', in M. Mackintosh and H. Wainwright (eds.), *A Taste of Power*, Verso, London, pp. 398-433.

Marchington, M. and Armstrong, R. (1982) 'A comparison between shop steward activity in local government and the private sector', *Local Government Studies*, vol. 8, no. 6, November/December pp. 33-48.

Markovic, M. (1974) *The Contemporary Marx*, Spokesman, Nottingham.

Marphet, J. (1987) 'Local authority decentralisation - Tower Hamlets goes all the way', *Policy and Politics*, vol. 15, no. 2, pp. 119-126.

McDonnell, J. (1984) 'Decentralisation and new social relations', *Going Local?*, no. 1, December.

McDonnell, J. (1987) cited in *The Guardian*, October 21.

Meacher, M. (1979) 'Whitehall's short way with democracy', in K. Coates (ed.), *What Went Wrong*, Spokesman, Nottingham, pp. 170-186.

Miliband, R. (1961) *Parliamentary Socialism*, George Allen and Unwin, London.

Miliband, R. (1969) *The State in Capitalist Society*, Weidenfeld and Nicolson, London.

Miliband, R. and Liebman, M. (1986) 'Beyond social democracy', in R. Miliband and J. Saville (eds.), *Socialist Register 1985/86*, Merlin Press, London, pp. 50-97.

Minkin, L. (1974) 'The British Labour Party and the trade unions: crisis and compact', *Industrial and Labor Relations Review*, vol. 28, no. 1, October, pp. 7-37.

Minkin, L. (1977) 'The Labour Party has not been hi-jacked', *New Society*, 6 October, pp. 6-8.

Minkin, L. (1978) 'The Labour Party connection: divergence and convergence in the British Labour movement', *Government and Opposition*, vol. 13, no. 4, pp. 458-483.

Morris, W. (1885) 'Useful work versus useless toil', in A. Briggs (ed.), *William Morris Selected Writings and Designs*, Penguin, Harmondsworth, 1970, pp. 117-135.

Municipal Year Book 1989 (1989) Municipal Journal, London.

Murray, R. (1984) 'New directions in municipal socialism', in B. Pimlott (ed.), *Fabian Essays in Socialist Thought*, Heinemann, London, pp. 206-229.

Murray, R. (1987) *Breaking with Bureaucracy*, CLES, Manchester.

Nairn, T. (1965) 'The nature of the Labour Party', in P. Anderson and R. Blackburn (eds.), *Towards Socialism*, Fontana, London, pp. 159-217.

National and Local Government Officers Association (1977a) *Industrial Democracy*, NALGO, London.

National and Local Government Officers Association (1977b) *Circular to Branches, District Local Government Committees, District Councils and Sectional and Professional Societies, Industrial Democracy*.

National and Local Government Officers Association (1978) *Circular to Branches, District Councils and Sectional and Professional Societies, Industrial Democracy: Trade Union Representation on Management Boards*, 3 October.

National and Local Government Officers Association (1979) *Circular to District Councils, Branches and Sectional and Professional Societies, Industrial Democracy*, 10 January.

National and Local Government Officers Association (1988) *NALGO Annual Conference 13-17 June 1988, Preliminary Agenda*, Local Government Officers Association, London.

National Union of Public Employees Doncaster and District (1988) *News Flash*, NUPE, Doncaster.

National Union of Public Employees (1987) *Local Government Privatisation Broadsheet 3*, NUPE, London.

National Union of Public Employees (n. d.) *Local Services, The Case Against Privatisation*, NUPE, London.

Neill, E. (1979) 'NALGO and the development of occupational associations in local government', *Industrial Relations Journal*, vol. 10, no. 2, Summer, pp. 31-40.

Newman, G. (1982) *Path to Maturity NALGO 1965-1980*, Manchester, Co-operative Press.

Newton, K. (1976) *Second City Politics*, Clarendon Press, Oxford.

Nicholson, N., Ursell, G. and Blyton, P. (1981) *The Dynamics of White Collar Unionism*, London, Academic Press.

Offe, C. (1975) 'The capitalist state and policy formation', in L. Lindberg, R. Alford, C. Crouch, C. Offe (eds.), *Stress and Contradictions in Modern Capitalism*, Lexington Books, New York pp. 125-144.

Offe, C. (1984) 'Some contradictions of the modern welfare state', in J. Keene (ed.), *Contradictions of the Welfare State*, Hutchinson, London, pp. 147-161.

Ouseley, H. (1984) 'Local authority race initiatives', in M. Boddy and C. Fudge (eds.), *Local Socialism?*, Macmillan, London, pp. 133-159.

Outhwaite, W. (1994) *Habermas*, Polity Press, Cambridge.

Panitch, L. (1986) *Working Class Politics in Crisis*, Verso, London.

Parkinson, M. (1985) *Liverpool on the Brink*, Policy Journals, Hermitage.

Perlman, S. (1949) *A Theory of the Labor Movement*, Kelley, New York.

Phillips, A. (1983) *Hidden Hands*, Pluto Press, London.

Phillips, L. (1987) 'Docklands for the people', in M. Mackintosh and H. Wainwright (eds.), *A Taste of Power*, Verso, London, pp. 298-325.

Pilkington, E. (1985) 'Looking for new friends', *New Statesman*, 5 April, pp. 8-9.

Pimlott, B. (1977) *Labour and the Left in the 1930s*, Cambridge University Press, Cambridge.

Platt, S. (1988) 'Skeleton service', *New Statesman*, 17 June, pp. 20-22.

Pollard, S. (1959) *A History of Labour in Sheffield*, Liverpool University Press, Liverpool.

Poulantzas, N. (1978) *State, Power, Socialism*, New Left Books, London.

Prashar, U. and Nicholas, S. (1986) *Routes or Roadblocks?*, Runnymede Trust, London.

Puddephatt, A. (1987) 'Local state and local community: the Hackney experience', in P. Hoggett and R. Hambleton (eds.), *Decentralisation and Democracy*, Bristol, SAUS Occasional Paper 28, pp. 187-193.

Rahman, N. (1986) *Council Non-Manual Workers and Low Pay*, Low Pay Pamphlet 38, London.

Salaman, G. (1979) *Work Organisation, Resistance and Control*, Longman, London.

Samuel, R. (1986) 'The cult of planning', *New Socialist*, no. 34, January, pp. 25-29.

Saunders, P. (1981) *Social Theory and the Urban Question*, Hutchinson, London.

Saunders, P. (1983) *Urban Politics, A Sociological Interpretation*, Hutchinson, London.

Seabrook, J. (1984) *The Idea of Neighbourhood*, Pluto Press, London.

Seex, A. (1997) 'Manchester's approach to decentralisation', *Local Government Policy Making*, vol. 14, no. 2, September, pp. 21-27.

Seyd, P. (1987) *The Rise and Fall of the Labour Left*, Macmillan, London.

Sharron, H. (1985) 'Overcoming trade union resistance to local change', *Public Money*, vol. 4, no. 4, March, pp. 17-23.

Services to Community Action and Trade Unions (1985) *Working Report on Job Satisfaction Survey of Manual and Clerical Workers in Parks and Recreation Department, Sheffield City Council*, SCAT, London.

Sheffield City Council (1984) *Positive Action for Women Project Final Report and Statistical Profile 1984*, Sheffield City Council.

Sheffield City Council (1986a) *Sheffield Putting You in the Picture*, Sheffield City Council.

Sheffield City Council (1986b) *Industrial Relations, A New Procedural Framework*, Sheffield City Council.

Sheffield City Council (1986c) *Responding to Change*, Sheffield City Council.

Sheffield City Council (1987) *A Guide to Improving Service Delivery*, Sheffield City Council.

Sheffield City Council (1988a) *Black Sheffielders*, Sheffield City Council.

Sheffield City Council (1988b) *Working Paper on Decentralisation (Policy)*, 7 October.

Sheffield City Council (1989) *Working for Sheffield*, April, Sheffield City Council.

Sheffield City Council (n. d.) *Race Equality Unit*, Sheffield City Council.

Sheffield City Council (n. d.) *Services in Sheffield, A Guide to Policy 1983/4*, Sheffield City Council, Central Policy Unit.

Sheffield City Council (n. d.) *Services in Sheffield, A Guide to Policy 1984/5*, Sheffield City Council, Central Policy Unit.

Sheffield City Council (1989) *Reports to Policy Committee, Summary of Departmental Four-Monthly Monitoring Reports*, Sheffield City Council.

Sheffield City Council Education Department (n. d.) *An Evaluation of 'Take Ten'*, Sheffield City Council.

Sheffield City Council Department of Employment and Economic Development (1987) *The Uncertain Future of Special Steels*, Sheffield City Council.

Sheffield City Council Department of Employment and Economic Development (1988) *Women in Sheffield*, no. 6, Sheffield City Council.

Sheffield City Libraries (1989) *Departmental Report 1988/1989 on Race Equality to Libraries and Information Sub-Committee*, 12 April.

Sheffield District Labour Party (1980) *Sheffield District Labour Party 1980 Manifesto*, Sheffield District Labour Party.

Sheffield District Labour Party (1982) *Sheffield District Labour Party 1982 Manifesto*, Sheffield District Labour Party.

Sheffield District Labour Party (1986) *Sheffield District Labour Party 1986 Manifesto*, Sheffield District Labour Party.

Sheffield District Labour Party (1987) *Sheffield District Labour Party 1987 Manifesto*, Sheffield District Labour Party.

Sheffield District Labour Party (1988) *Sheffield District Labour Party 1988 Manifesto,* Sheffield District Labour Party.

Sherman, B. (1986) *The State of the Unions,* John Wiley, London.

Simon, B. (1989) *Bending the Rules: The Baker Reform of Education,* 2nd edn, Lawrence and Wishart, London.

Smith, B. C. (1988) *Bureaucracy and Political Power,* Wheatsheaf, Brighton.

Soto, P. (1987) 'Setting an example? The GLC as an employer', in M. Mackintosh and H. Wainwright (eds.), *A Taste of Power,* Verso, London, pp. 80-104.

Stephens, J. D. (1979) *The Transition from Capitalism to Socialism,* Macmillan, London.

Stewart, J. (1983) *Local Government: The Conditions of Local Choice,* George Allen and Unwin, London.

Stewart, J. (1984) 'Decentralisation and local government', in A. Wright, J. Stewart and N. Deakin, *Socialism and Decentralisation,* Fabian Society Tract no. 496, London, pp. 8-17.

Stewart, J. (1986) *The New Management of Local Government,* Allen and Unwin, London.

Stewart, J. and Stoker, G. (1988) *From Local Administration to Community Government,* Fabian Research Series 351, London.

Stoker, G. (1988 and 1991) *The Politics of Local Government,* Macmillan, London.

Taaffe, P. and Mulhearn T. (1988) *Liverpool, A City That Dared to Fight,* Fortress Books, London.

Tariq Ali and Hore, Q. (1982) 'Socialists and the crisis of labourism', *New Left Review* 132, March/April, pp. 59-81.

Taylor, A. J. (1987) *The Trade Unions and the Labour Party,* Croom Helm, London.

Taylor, R. (1980) *The Fifth Estate,* Pan, London.

Terry, M. (1982) 'Organising a fragmented workforce: Shop stewards in local government', *British Journal of Industrial Relations,* vol. xx, pp. 1-19.

Thompson, D. F. (1983) 'Bureaucracy and Democracy', in G. Duncan (ed.), *Democratic Theory and Practice,* Cambridge University Press, Cambridge, pp. 235-250.

Thompson, E. P. (1979) 'The Poverty of Theory', in *The Poverty of Theory and Other Essays,* London, Merlin, pp. 1-210.

Thompson, P. (1983) *The Nature of Work,* Macmillan, London.

Thomson, A. (1982) 'Local government as an employer', in R. Rose and E. Page (eds.), *Fiscal Crisis in Cities,* Cambridge University Press, Cambridge, pp. 107-136.

Tomlinson, M. (1986a) 'A state of decentralisation', *Going Local?,* no. 5, July, pp. 16-17.

Tomlinson, M. (1986b) *Decentralisation Learning the Lessons?,* Polytechnic of Central London, London.

Townsend, P. and Bosanquet, N. (eds.), (1972) *Labour and Equality,* Fabian Society, London.

Undy, R., Ellis, V., McCarthy, W. E. J. and Halmos, A. M. (1981) *Change in Trade Unions,* Hutchinson, London.

Wainwright, H. (1984) 'The GLC: so what's new?', *Bulletin of the Socialist Society,* Autumn.

Wainwright, H. (1987) *Labour, A Tale of Two Parties*, Hogarth Press, London.

Wainwright, H. and Elliott, D. (1982) *The Lucas Plan*, Pluto Press, London.

Walsh, K. (1982) 'Local government militancy in Britain and the United States', *Local Government Studies*, vol. 8, no. 6, November/December pp. 1-18.

Weinstein, J. (1986) 'Angry arguments across the picket lines: Left Labour councils and white collar trade unionism', *Critical Social Policy,* issue 17, pp. 41-60.

White, S. (1988) *The Recent Work of Jurgen Habermas, Reason, Justice and Morality,* Cambridge University Press, Cambridge.

Whitely, P. (1983) *The Labour Party in Crisis*, Methuen, London.

Williams, R. (ed.), (1968) *May Day Manifesto 1968*, Penguin, Harmondsworth.

Williams, R. (1981) 'An alternative politics', in R. Miliband and J. Saville (eds.), *The Socialist Register 1981*, Merlin, London, pp. 1-10.

Wolmar, C. (1984) 'Divided we stand', *New Socialist,* December, pp. 13-15.

Wolmar, C. (1987) 'The fresh face of the capital's politics', *New Statesman,* 18 September, pp. 10-12.

Wood, S. (ed.), (1982) *The Degradation of Work?*, Hutchinson, London.

Wright, E. O. (1985) *Classes,* Verso, London.

Index